D0609087

796

ED

ED

Organizational cultures

Types and transformations

Diana C. Pheysey

London and New York

First published 1993
by Routledge
11 New Fetter Lane, London EC4P 4EE

Simultaneously published in the USA and Canada
by Routledge
29 West 35th Street, New York, NY 10001

© 1993 Diana C. Pheysey

Typeset in Garamond by
NWL Editorial Services, Langport, Somerset

Printed and bound in Great Britain by
Mackays of Chatham PLC, Chatham, Kent

British Library Cataloguing in Publication Data
A catalogue record for this book is available from the British
Library

ISBN 0–415–08291–9
        0–415–08292–7 (pbk)

Library of Congress Cataloging in Publication Data
has been applied for.

301
.4
PHE

To Derek S. Pugh, researcher, mentor and friend.

Contents

Case studies and exercises

Figures and tables

FIGURES

TABLES

Preface

THE SUBJECT OF THE BOOK

The aim of this book is to provide a text in Organizational Behaviour (OB) which provokes thinking about values. Shared values in an organization form its culture, hence the title.

OB is an academic discipline with broad scope. It covers the full range of human activity associated with any corporate enterprise. So a text must be selective. Cultures are stressed here because they affect many other things that go on. An *organizational culture* includes commonly held values, but also common beliefs and attitudes. It prescribes *'the way we do things here'*. However, it is possible to change the prescription. So, as the subtitle suggests, methods of cultural transformation are described as well as types of culture.

Human beings, to survive, have to get food and shelter, defend themselves against dangers, and hand on their knowledge and skills to the next generation. Hunting bands, nomadic herdsmen, settled agriculturalists and societies engaged in trade and commerce have their own economies, governance and culture. In the modern world, however, global trade and telecommunications are spreading the influence of large multinational forms of organization. The values of those who run such powerful organizations may be critical for the welfare of many people. For multinational corporations have their own cultures which can be in competition with the cultures of some of the societies where they operate.

A society's culture is expressed not only in art but also in how it solves its survival problems. It is argued here that cultural patterns in societies can be matched, to some extent, by cultural patterns in organizations. Similar patterns can even be found in small groups and in leadership styles. Finally, at the personal level, there are personality types which seem suited to the group and organizational cultures. So the realizing of a personal identity in a small group can be related to the cultural identity of an organization. For simplicity, just four examples are selected and followed through each level of correspondence. This is not the nesting of Chinese boxes, however. Differences exist among similarities, and many processes of transformation are at work. Some change stems from economic, political and social conditions at national or international level, some stems from the efforts of individuals and groups to realize their own goals, some occurs outside conscious awareness. Several theories of change are outlined. Some writers see change as cyclical, others as more like a pendulum, swinging from one extreme to its opposite. The position taken here is that there are chance elements and skill elements in change. None of the cultures described is invariant or inevitable. What is important is the values held by those in key positions and their readiness to test the social, economic and political constraints.

FEATURES OF THE BOOK

The theme of culture is used in an original way to bring the diverse topics together and to give them meaning. However, the book is no more than an introduction to the subject, illustrated by simple diagrams. Readers can assess their own progress using the chapter objectives and chapter summaries. There are extensive reading lists for those who want to take the subject further.

OB has tended to be somewhat insular in approach, drawing exclusively on Western academic knowledge and Western case material. In this book both public and private organizations are considered, with case material for analysis drawn from Europe, Asia and Africa.

OB has also suffered from a divorce between the contributions from psychology and from sociology, the former concentrating on behaviour and the latter on organization. This book closes the gap by drawing on both disciplines. The overall plan is given below. The topics are interrelated, and so most of the cases can be used for more than one chapter. Cases are therefore placed at the end, but fully cross-referenced.

THE PLAN OF THE BOOK

In Chapter 1, four examples of societal cultures and four of organizational cultures are described, and two theories of cyclical change *at societal level* are introduced. Culture affects change via preferences among economic, ideological and order goals, both nationally and in organizations.

Chapter 2 explains how organizations with different cultures attempt to control both internal problems and external turbulence, so as to hold a steady course between extremes. The concept of 'the golden mean' is related to such values as innovation, competition, collaboration, strong leadership and efficiency. Two theories are given which suggest cyclical changes *in organizations*. Culture affects control of these changes through preferences for regulation or 'appreciation' (judgement).

Different forms of organization are needed to realize the values discussed in Chapter 2. Choice of the 'right design' for an organization is the subject of Chapter 3, which gives examples of structures that fit the four organizational cultures. Other things being equal, culture affects organization design through a preference for hierarchical or non-hierarchical forms. The number of supra-national organizations is likely to increase. They can be managed well or badly, for the good of humanity, or to increase the power of some peoples at the expense of others.

In the different cultures, the purpose of design for jobs is perceived differently. This is the subject of Chapter 4, which contrasts the problems of standardizing work with those of enriching it. The sociotechnical systems approach is explained. Culture affects job design through preferences for work simplification or job enlargement.

Job design can affect people's motivation. Chapter 5 describes how attitudes can be coloured by the match, or mismatch, between personal preferences and the design of jobs. It also examines the views of managers in the four cultures on how to motivate people. It outlines some OB theories on motivation. Culture affects motivation through preferences for extrinsic or intrinsic motivators.

Chapter 6 shows how the nature of problems and the power of particular interests influence decisions. Culture also affects decision-making through a preference for the more analytical or the more intuitive styles, and through conflictive or co-operative approaches. But not all decisions are taken consciously. There are also hidden agenda, especially in committees, where group phenomena appear.

Chapter 7 describes how personality differences affect the development of groups, and how group dynamics can be seen as a cultural microcosm. Culture affects groups through preferences for working in isolation, competing with other individuals within groups or collaborating in groups.

Chapter 8 describes how leaders emerge, or are appointed, the sources of their authority and the styles they use in the four cultures. Culture affects the preferences of leaders for directive or participative styles.

Leadership is also necessary for organizational development (OD), which enhances the capacity of an organization to transform itself. This is the subject of Chapter 9. Organizational culture influences decisions on ends and means for OD.

The final chapter summarizes what has been said about culture and practice. Academic cultures tend to want OB either to copy, or to avoid, the methods of the natural sciences. The chapter links the ideas that have been presented to the academic schools of thought with which they are associated, and clearly shows that there is no simple prescription for organizing, but that the reader should examine his or her own beliefs and values.

Chapter 1

Cultures and change

CHAPTER OBJECTIVES

By the end of this chapter you will be able to:

1 name Hofstede's four measures of national cultures
2 explain the Skinner and Winckler model
3 show how change could be related to values
4 examine the argument that cyclical conflict occurs in British industrial relations
5 name Harrison's four organizational cultures
6 do the recommended exercise and study the case

1 INTRODUCTION

Organizational behaviour can be defined as 'how enterprises work and how the people associated with them act'. (The phrase 'associated with' is used to indicate that employees are not the sole focus of attention, though they do get major consideration.) 'Organizational behaviour' can refer both to the academic discipline which studies these things and to what is being studied. When the discipline is meant the abbreviation OB will be used.

OB combines the interests of psychologists, sociologists, political scientists and economists. OB theories differ in the emphasis they give to organizations as such compared, on the one hand, with the individuals and groups of which they are composed and, on the other hand, with the wider society of which they are a part (see Whitley, 1977).

The verb 'to organize' means to 'give orderly structure to', but it is sometimes difficult to say where one orderly structure ends and another begins. Empedocles, in the fifth century BC, defined God as 'a circle whose centre is everywhere and whose circumference is nowhere'. Organization is a bit like that. It is only possible to say what counts as an organization from a particular perspective. The perspective adopted here is the practical one, namely that the law recognizes orderly structures known as 'corporate bodies', which can be named and which are authorized to act. It is also possible to see an 'orderly structure' in, for example, a ship, with its captain, officers and crew, even though this ship may be part of a fleet which belongs to a company or to a navy. No organization exists in isolation. It is part of other structures, such as economies, societies and nation states. The subject is therefore complex, and so, in sections 2–4 of this chapter, and throughout the book, diagrams and tables are used to simplify. Sometimes the diagram is called a *model*. It would be well to pause for a moment to ask what can be achieved by putting ideas in squares or circles and calling the result a model. We are familiar with displays in the form of dials which tell us how much fuel is in a tank, or how fast a car is travelling. We know that some happening in the real world, fuel being used or brakes applied, is linked with what the dial shows. We know that when the fuel gauge registers 'empty' we had better fill up. We do not know that when our speed exceeds a speed limit we shall be stopped by police, or have an accident, or both. We can ignore the visual display, or we can interpret it in various ways. Some visual displays, such as satellite weather pictures, are of value for only a limited period ahead, since there may be chaotic changes that do not emit warning signals far in advance. People may react to a model of economic activity in ways that interfere with the functioning of the model itself. The kinds of diagrams which appear in this book are not intended to be interpreted as analogues of what is 'really' happening in a society or organization. Their purpose is to focus attention on *possible* ways in which things might be connected, and to suggest that you, the reader, examine your own experience to decide for yourself whether the presentation is a help or a hindrance to you in thinking about the matters depicted. The figures and tables may also be an aid to memory, since the ones in later chapters are linked to those in earlier chapters.

2 CULTURES

This chapter is about one aspect of a society, nation or continent which may also permeate its organizations, namely *culture*. The term culture is derived from the same stem as the verb 'to cultivate'. In biology, cells are grown in a culture; in anthropology, culture sometimes refers to the whole way of life in which people grow up. In OB the word is used in a more restricted sense as the values and beliefs which provide people with 'a programmed way of seeing' (Hofstede 1980a). A culture is thus *a way of seeing that is common to many people*. (Usually there are sub-cultures, or ways of seeing by minorities also.) Culture itself is subject to transformation. Managers may deliberately seek to change it. To reshape an organization's culture they may use a scheme of cultural types. Four types are described in Section 4 below. First, however, we survey the larger scene.

2.1 East–West cultural differences

We begin by drawing attention to some differences between West and East in ideas about knowledge. The West has tended to think, for example, that a cause precedes an effect, and that things happen one after another. In the Orient there is more appreciation of two-way causation. Something can both be caused by, and be the cause of, something else, and the future, the present and the past can affect each other (Redding 1980). The West tends to perceive things in categories, and the East in contexts. For example, the word for man in both Chinese and Japanese has a broader sense than in English in that it takes in the state of transactions with fellow human beings. Western culture tends to be oriented towards mastery over nature, and bases reality or ultimate truth on science and pragmatism. The East seeks harmony with nature and sees reality as based more on revealed truth than on empirical experimentation. The physicist Bohm has a concept that seems close to an oriental perspective. He speaks of reality as a 'holomovement', a totality of enfoldment and unfoldment, from which each theory will abstract some aspect that is relevant only in some limited context. 'To *relevate* a certain content (is) to lift it into attention so that it stands out in relief' (Bohm 1980, his emphasis). Much of what we 'know' is subconscious, and only surfaces in consciousness when conditions are ripe. Western scientists know this, but the East pays greater regard to intuition. OB is largely a creation of the West, and this book will reflect this, but an attempt will be made to draw the reader's attention to other cultural perspectives from time to time.

2.2 National cultures

Every culture has its values. Values are whatever is esteemed, prized or appreciated in that culture. In some nations a large proportion of the population accepts the values of the state religion. Loyalty and obedience are stressed in both Shintoism and Islam, for example. The value that comes nearest to being universally espoused is that of concern for others (love). It is found in the 'golden rule' common to Buddhism, Christianity, Classical Paganism, Confucianism, Hinduism, Jainism, Judaism, the Sikh religion and Zoroastrianism – 'Do to others as you would they should do to you'. The 'golden rule' may be widely espoused, but it is not widely practised. A question of interest to OB is the extent to which values are found the world over in a certain type of organization, for example a business firm, or the extent to which 'local' organizations adopt values commonly held in their society.

Hofstede (1980a) surveyed 16,000 employees of a large multinational company. The employees, who worked in forty countries, were asked to complete questionnaires.[1] The sample used by Hofstede was sufficiently large for him to analyse his data by age, sex and nationality. Table 1.1 shows, in italics, the names he gave to four patterns he found. Below the name is a country, or some countries, where the pattern is strong, and below that are some things which are prized by the national culture.

The *uncertainty avoidance* culture likes to be clear about what is allowed and what is not, so that there can be respect for order. West

Table 1.1 National cultures and associated values

Uncertainty avoidance	*Individualism (versus collectivism)*
West Germany	Great Britain
Legality Orderliness Clarity	Competition Independence
Power distance	*Femininity (versus masculinity)*
Indonesia Philippines Nigeria	Singapore Taiwan Kenya
Status Obedience Control	Sharing Involvement Friendship

Germany was a high scorer. British members of the sample placed a high value on *individualism*, competing with each other for position, and wanting independence. In Indonesia, the Philippines and Nigeria, persons of senior status were regarded with awe and were thought to have the right to exercise control over many aspects of their subordinates' work and lives. There was *power distance* between higher and lower members of the organization. In Singapore, Taiwan and Kenya there were low scores on what Westerners think of as masculinity. People valued friendship, sharing and involvement at work which Hofstede considers to be *feminine* values.

We must not conclude that the entire populations of the countries listed in the figure can be characterized in the ways shown. The Nigerian and Kenyan scores were obtained by Seddon (1985a) using Hofstede's methods. The important thing about these studies is that employees *of the same company* replied differently according to which country they worked in.

Hofstede's national cultures provide 'compass points' by which key people in organizations attempt to orient themselves and to pursue their goals. Change can come from the countless actions which national leaders take based on their own perceptions of whether or not they are deviating from their central course. We shall link these ideas to a couple of models of cycles of change drawn from experience in the People's Republic of China and in Great Britain.

2.3 Values, goals and behaviour

Skinner and Winckler (1980) build their model on the basis of three types of goals. It is possible, however, to reclassify Hofstede's values under Skinner and Winckler's headings, and this is done in Table 1.2.

Skinner and Winckler assert that each type of goal is best reached through the use of an appropriate type of power which encourages a certain type of behaviour. The goals with their corresponding forms of power and behaviour are listed below.

Goals	Economic	Ideological	Order
Power	Remunerative	Normative	Coercive
Behavioural Involvement	Indifference	Commitment	Alienation

Economic goals are concerned with the supply and demand for goods and services. China has national plans for agriculture, heavy

Table 1.2 Hofstede's cultural values listed as goals

	Economic goals Competition Independence
Order goals Legality Orderliness Clarity Status Obedience Control	*Ideological goals* Sharing Involvement Friendship

and light industries, and transport. Competition is to achieve the targets set. To prevent dependence, the government aims for self-sufficiency in some sectors, for favourable terms of trade in others. (Goals of competition and independence take different forms in capitalist economies where financial markets operate.)

'Remunerative' power is simply the ability to reward people (as producers, consumers, tax-payers, savers etc.). By 'indifferent' behaviour Skinner and Winckler imply that people are primarily self-interested, will seek personal benefits, but neither support nor oppose the sources of those benefits.

Ideological goals are linked to moral values. In China, 'sharing' as a goal implies Communist solidarity in 'serving the masses'. In Britain, the monarchy symbolizes shared national traditions. Politicians use normative power to obtain commitment from party members. Charismatic leaders rely on it (see Table 8.1).

The goals described as 'order' goals are associated with the roles of the police and the military, and of industrial relations managers. There has to be 'law and order' in any society. However, when 'coercive power' is used it tends to alienate those subjected to it, that is, it makes them angry or scared.

3 CYCLES OF CHANGE

3.1 Change and the mean

In pursuing economic, ideological or order goals, leaders may find themselves seeking to keep to a centre path, since to deviate from this would lead to deficiencies or excesses. This idea can be traced to Aristotle, who according to Kraemer (1975) laid the philosophical foundations of management. Aristotle lived in Greece from 384 to 322 BC where he was tutor to Alexander the Great. In his *Ethics* Aristotle says:

> Moral excellence is a mean ... between two forms of badness, one of excess and the other of defect, and is so described because it aims at hitting the mean point in feelings and in actions. This makes virtue hard of achievement because finding the middle point is never easy. It is not everybody, for instance, who can find the centre of a circle – that calls for a geometrician. Thus, too, it is easy to fly into a passion – anybody can do that – but to be angry with the right person and to the right extent and at the right time and with the right object in the right way – that is not easy, and it is not everybody who can do it.

Aristotle did not think all virtues are means but, for example, courage, self-control, friendliness and modesty all have their attendant excesses and deficiences. It is interesting that a similar idea is present in the writings of the Chinese philosopher Kung Fu Tse (556–479 BC) better known as Confucius, who is said to have had a profound influence on Japanese business. In his *Analects*, Book Twenty, we read:

> Sincerely hold fast the due Mean ... the person in authority is beneficent without great expenditure; ... he lays tasks on the people without their repining; ... he pursues what he desires without being covetous; ... he maintains a dignified ease without being proud; ... he is majestic without being fierce.

Figure 1.1 develops a framework to suggest how the values grouped by Hofstede, and the goals of Skinner and Winckler, can be linked to the idea of the 'golden mean'. The arrows are pointing to four possible desired states of society, each of them a mean: law-abiding (top left), economically competitive (top right), powerfully led (bottom left) and harmonious (bottom right). Hofstede's terms are shown in italics. The left side represents order goals and the right side economic and ideological goals. The broken lines represent deviations from the desired state towards a deficiency (marked minus) or an excess (marked plus). The figure can be interpreted in two ways. One might argue that one would like to pursue all four golden means simultaneously, and that *turbulence* is the oscillations that are occurring through under-shooting or over-shooting the mark. One might also argue for a cyclical progression. Let us start with economic individualism in the top right quarter. Movement to excess might lead to cut-throat competition which harmed the weaker members of the society. Political pressures against such an uncaring state of affairs might then lead to more stress on welfare and co-operation. However, a state of harmony around these values might be short-lived as there would be complaints that people were becoming irresponsible in their enjoyment of the more permissive state of affairs. Stronger leadership would be called for to tighten up on the lax conditions. However, leaders who assume too much power are liable to be corrupted by it, and to attempt to repress opposition. This leads to people 'taking the law into their own hands', and so to demands for more constitutional methods of control and less personal power for leaders. In the early stages new constitutional measures might be approved and the populace law-abiding, but there is a danger of bureaucratic legalism setting in, so that the difficulties that people experience with 'red tape' result in apathy and poor economic performance. This might be countered by simplifying the

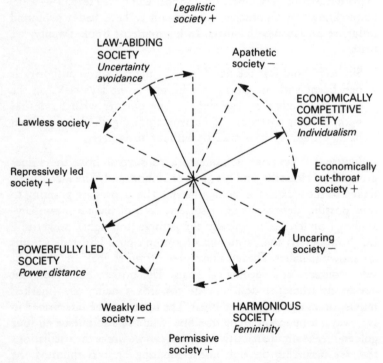

Figure 1.1 Societal context of change and the golden mean

law and stimulating demand and production. Can something like this be seen in the People's Republic of China? Skinner and Winckler thought so.

3.2 Change in the People's Republic of China

Skinner and Winckler studied the history of the People's Republic of China (PRC) from 1949, when the Communists proclaimed the Republic, until 1965. During the period, the political pendulum there swung back and forth between radicalism and moderation. Skinner and Winckler's model is an attempt to account for this phenomenon. They argue that there is a sequence in which the three types of goal (economic, order and ideological) assume priority for people, superiors exert power and subordinates behave characteristically. Although leaders want to attain all three goals together it is not possible for the three types of power to be used together on the same people, since they cannot be simultaneously committed, indifferent and antagonistic. One solution is to apply the different types of power to different parts of the population. The slaves of ancient Athens were coerced, the artisans and merchants were remunerated and the nobles were normatively committed to their civic pursuits. If goals cannot be compartmentalized in this way, then they have to be achieved in succession. In the PRC the majority of the population are peasants. Skinner and Winckler argue that the close-knit rural areas make it impossible to compartmentalize goals, and so sequencing is necessary. However, the three components in the power mix are never optimally blended, and there are separate cycles of goals, power and behaviour which are never perfectly synchronized. They argue that when the regime

> achieved a satisfactory level of order it tried to maximise economic and ideological goals, favouring the latter whenever minimal attainment of the former permitted. . . . This tendency to sacrifice economics to ideology has led repeatedly to a crisis in the order and economic sectors.
>
> (Skinner and Winckler 1980: 404)

Around the perimeter of Figure 1.2 are six phases of the PRC control cycle (in capital letters) and six policies (in small letters). The Chinese themselves describe their progress as 'Two steps forward, one step back'. Skinner and Winckler use the PRC case to make the more general point that movement around a control cycle 'appears to

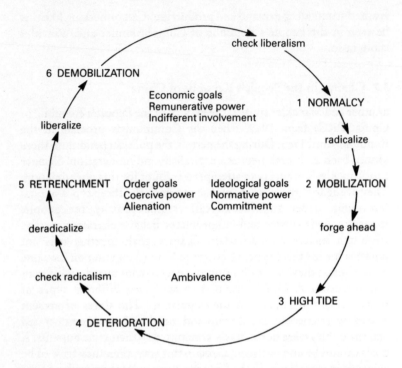

Figure 1.2 Six phases in the control cycle of the People's Republic
           of China
Source: Adapted from Skinner and Winkler 1980

be generated by the alternation in power of leaders representing
alternative philosophies', the Marxist radicals and the Marxist
moderates, with the former 'being basically in the stronger position,
but forced to accede to [the moderates] at those phases of the cycle in
which economic performance and social order are dangerously
impaired'.

An explanation of one round of the cycle goes like this. Goals,
power, and behavioural involvement are in balance during
NORMALCY, but the condition does not persist. The reason is the
impatience of certain radical members of the Communist party to
inaugurate further reforms. (From 1949 to 1951 it was post-war
reconstruction and land reform; from 1952 to 1955 it was mutual aid
teams, water conservancy and co-operatives; from 1957 to 1960 it was
'The Great Leap Forward' in economic growth; from 1961 to 1965 it
was rural party reorganization and a socialist educational campaign;

from 1966 to 1970 it was 'the Cultural Revolution'. In 1978 Deng Xiaoping used the grass roots democracy movement but ended it with mass arrests. This happened twice more, culminating in the tragedy of Tiananmen in June 1989.)

At the beginning of each cycle there is therefore a decision to radicalize. This leads to MOBILIZATION, a phase when technical and social objectives are envisaged, mass meetings are held and an aura of charisma surrounds the party chain of command. More and more people are enrolled in collective activity. The policy is to forge ahead. In the absence of remunerative incentives, commitment to ideology is all important at the HIGH TIDE phase which follows. The solidarity of the people as citizens is stressed, with no distinctions between workers, soldiers and peasants. Performance is judged by its 'socialist correctness' rather than by economic results. For a time the ideological goals are in balance with normative power and committed involvement.

It is only as the feasibility of attaining some of the goals becomes doubtful that DETERIORATION sets in. Traitors in the midst are suspected and dissensus and ambivalence grow. The first response is to increase discipline, drawing on coercive power. (Examples of this are refusal to assign people jobs, arbitrary deduction of wage points, increases in tax assessments, denial of access to irrigation facilities, freezing of bank deposits, arbitrary increase in delivery quotas, even shooting and mass arrests.) Such coercive measures only serve to alienate people. The more radical goals have to be curtailed or abandoned. The period of RETRENCHMENT now sets in with waves of superiors descending on the basic level cadre (officials) to see what is going on. The lower cadre gets blamed for failures, while the state, concerned over the poor return on investment, cuts back.

There is no formal announcement of DEMOBILIZATION, but it takes place quietly, as economically rational performance criteria are reintroduced and a greater variety of viewpoints is tolerated (as in the period when Mau Zedong invited free expression through the wall posters under the slogan 'Let one hundred flowers bloom'). This liberalism is checked (sometimes ruthlessly) when too much criticism is expressed, and the country reverts to NORMALCY, an agrarian society going about its normal peasant business.

The duration of each national control cycle is roughly two to four years. Goal cycles at lower levels may recur on the basis of the 'marketing week', or of the 'seasonal and annual schedules whereby work and leisure in agricultural China are arranged'. With the growth of science and technology in the PRC and the reopening of the country to foreign influence, there has been a growth in the numbers of urban intellectuals. China's ethnic minorities (for example, Tibetans) have also become more vocal in demands for cultural distinctiveness. Peasants still account for the largest part of the population, but Skinner and Winckler's premise, that it is only possible to vary the types of power used over time, may not hold for much longer. It may be possible to use different power strategies for different sections of the population at the same time (for example, reward the peasants, coerce the intellectuals and use normative power with the majority ethnic group).

We turn now to the cycle which Hill and Thurley (1974) think they can discern in British industrial relations.

3.3 Change in industrial relations

Hill and Thurley point out that in cyclical phenomena there are long-term and short-term processes simultaneously at work. The basic causes of conflict 'are in fact rooted in the types of social structure and the nature of the long-term changes which take place'. Some of these are country specific. They describe the different class structures in the UK and Japan. They also suggest that four apparently incompatible sociological explanations of industrial conflict can all be relevant to a conflict cycle 'because each is typified as being critical at a different point in the process'. To illustrate the short-term cycles they consider the UK. Table 1.3 is based on their analysis. In each quarter there are differences in economic conditions, in government policy and in collective bargaining strategies. These sets of conditions are associated with different ways of expressing conflict. Explanations are given which they consider have limited application, since none of them will account in a satisfactory way for all disputes.

Stage I

The common, or *universalistic*, value of material prosperity informs behaviour. Since the economy is growing, the unions change their strategy from one of relative inactivity to one of actively pressing for their members to have a share in that growth. The phenomenon of 'leap-frogging' occurs, in which the pay round of one industry sets off demands from others that match or exceed it. The society can be

Table 1.3 Model of industrial conflict cycle in the UK

	STAGE IV		STAGE I
(a)	Stagnant economy and high unemployment	(a)	Ecomonic growth
(b)	Easing of restrictions on investment	(b)	Policy of high credit expansion and high government spending
(c)	*Weak bargaining power; managements and workers 'withdraw' to personal life*	(c)	*Trade unions use strikes for higher pay; bargaining is based on relativities (comparisons)*
(d)	Apathy		
(e)	Economics becomes salient	(d)	Economically competitive Society
	STAGE III		**STAGE II**
(a)	Decline in output; unemployment	(a)	Boom; balance of payments crisis; labour shortages
(b)	Wages freeze	(b)	Credit restriction and government spending cuts
(c)	*'Political' strikes against incomes policy class interest more perceptible*	(c)	*Strikes moderated; collapse of accepted differentials; anomie*
(d)	Power distance		
(e)	Order becomes salient	(d)	Uncaring society
		(e)	Ideology becomes salient

Source: Adapted from Hill and Thurley 1974
Notes: (a), economic fluctuations; (b), government policy; (c), trade union strategies and forms of industrial conflict; (d), terms added to indicate links with Figure 1.1; (e), terms added to indicate links with Table 1.2 and Figure 1.2.

said to be *economically competitive* in the sense that different sectors are competing against each other for a share in the benefits of growth.

Stage II

Problems arise from the 'over-heating' of the economy. Because of labour shortages employers tend to pay higher wages in those occupations where scarcity exists. This plays havoc with the traditional 'differentials' that have governed the wage bargaining in Stage I. A condition of *anomie* now obtains. By this word is meant a condition in which the general goal (of increased material prosperity in this case) cannot be achieved through *legitimate* means, (namely wage rises in the customary 'pecking order'). When there is anomy there is ideological (or moral) conflict. It appears that the society is *uncaring* towards its weaker members.

Stage III

As output declines, and unemployment rises, the government attempts to improve the competitiveness of business by a tough incomes policy to keep costs down. This intervention heightens the *power distance* in industrial relations. *Oppositional* ideals of improving the status of the poorer members of society come to the fore, and political strikes occur.

Stage IV

In this stage conditions have worsened and there is high unemployment. The bargaining power of unions is weakened. The unemployed cannot share the sectional, or *particularist*, value of keeping one's job, held by those still employed. People do not express their frustration in strikes but rather in seeking alternative private satisfactions. Here the popular notions of the meaninglessness and helplessness of the individual against the bureaucracy may explain the form of conflict behaviour which may be called *apathetic*.

Hill and Thurley stress that their model is one intended to apply to the UK. They argue:

> By and large, bargaining has been restricted to wage and salary structures, relativities and questions of collective security of employment, so there has been little challenge to the authority of managers and even less to the claims of shareholders. There have been occasions, however, when the pursuit of bargaining has been perceived as a potential threat to the interests of capital and the relative power of the upper class in industry and society. In these instances bargaining has led to national crises and major government intervention, either directly on a case-by-case basis or indirectly, by means of economic management. . . . In Japan unionism and collective bargaining in the private sector have neither been competitive nor have they threatened the élite. . . . Enterprise unions are firmly locked into their respective firms. . . . Managers at all levels . . . have been union members themselves at some time. . . . Workers have and desire little control over job regulation, and are not concerned with managerial prerogative. . . . In the public

sector, however..., the survival of traditional elements of authoritarian relationships has led to peculiarly bitter disputes.

(Hill and Thurley 1974: 164, 166)

These differences, and others, are attributable to a different history of industrialization. In Hill and Thurley's view, historical and comparative study can clarify the forces which shape the different systems of industrial relations. The broader society is indissolubly linked to the groupings within it. The ways in which such linkages occur, however, are problematic. Some OB theorists assert that there has to be adaptation by organizations to the society, especially to the level of economic and technical development. Other OB theorists assert that it is the behaviour of people in organizations which shapes the society, not the other way round. One could take the view that there is adaptation in *both* directions, which is the position adopted in this book. Figures 1.1 and 1.2 and Table 1.3 suggest similarities and differences across countries in types of cyclical cultural change. China's prime concern is with ideology and Britain's is with economics, but both societies have to pay attention to other types of goal as well. Extremes lead to pressure to revert to the moderation of Aristotle's golden mean, but, failing this, a shift occurs to another stage in the cycle.

4 ORGANIZATIONAL CULTURES

We have shown (in Table 1.2) that some of Hofstede's terms for national cultures can be used to suggest economic, ideological (moral) and order goals, with possible connections to societal changes. Now, in Table 1.4, we suggest, from the perspective of each of Hofstede's cultures, how the organizations which exist within every society may be perceived. Examples are given of four actual organizations which, in terms of their cultures, approximately fit the definitions given. Below each example is the term for its *organizational culture* that is used by Harrison (1987a). (Earlier works by Harrison (1972a) and Handy (1978 and 1985) spoke of task and person cultures instead of achievement and support cultures.)

4.1 A role culture

In the top left corner of Table 1.4 a large firm is given as an example. This firm has 'articles of association' which set out the purposes of the business and the authority which the general meeting of the

Table 1.4 Ways of seeing organizations

	An organization is seen
In *uncertainty avoidance* terms as:	In *individualism* terms as:
a bounded rational instrument for the achievement of specified goals of where people respond to role	the outcome of the interaction of motivated people attempting to resolve their own problems, and satisfy their own needs and expectations
e.g. a large firm or government agency with a role culture	e.g. a small local shop with an achievement culture
In *power distance* terms as:	In *femininity* terms as:
a relatively bounded and stable occurence of social order based on habits of deference to authority	the mobilization of bias through personal relationships
e.g. a traditional Indian 'joint family' enterprise with a power culture	e.g. a Chinese factory during the 'Cultural Revolution' with a support culture

shareholders has conferred on the directors. Below the directors are several layers of managers and below them are the staff and workers engaged in clerical and manual operations. The whole organization forms a pyramid shape. The higher the layer, the fewer people there are. Hierarchical divisions are not the only ones; there are also departmental distinctions. The work of making the product is done by manufacturing; the work of selling it by sales; the work of obtaining materials by purchasing; the work of monitoring income and expenditure by accounting, and so on. The word 'role', which is used of the culture in such a business, refers to the way in which the occupant of each position in the firm is expected to act. There are usually job descriptions, rules and procedures to govern behaviour, and principles for fixing remuneration. A role culture is one which emphasises conformity to expectations. It is common in government departments as well as large businesses. Such organizations can be said to be 'bounded rational instruments for the achievement of specified goals', Harrison says.[2]

The Role orientation assumes that people work most effectively and efficiently when they have relatively simple, clearly defined, circumscribed and measurable tasks. Clarity and precision of roles and procedures are striven for in order to fit the parts of the organization together like a machine.

4.2 An achievement culture

The second example is the traditional local shop which is more likely to focus on the work to be done than on conforming to rules. The owner and his family will serve the public themselves. If other assistants are employed they will know as much about the stock as the owner does. In an achievement culture people are interested in the work itself, and have a personal stake in seeing that it is done. Small consulting firms and research institutes have also often been cited as exemplars of the achievement culture. They can be said to be 'the outcome of the interaction of motivated people attempting to solve their own problems.' Harrison says,

> the Achievement-oriented organization makes high demands on its people's energy and time, assuming that people actually enjoy working at tasks which are intrinsically satisfying.

4.3 A power culture

The Mafia is a Western example of a traditional power culture. It is a criminal organization which relies on thuggery to maintain allegiance. Of course, power cultures do not necessarily rely on brute force or engage in criminal activities. Brimmer (1955) described traditional Indian family-owned businesses in a way which suggests they had a recognized power culture. The traditional joint family enterprise combined the different enterprises of various family members under the superintendence of the family head who was responsible for the social status and financial well-being of the family. In a power culture certain persons are dominant and others subservient. There is 'a relatively bounded and stable occurrence of social order based on habits of deference to authority'. Harrison says,

> In the Power organization at its best, leadership is based on strength, justice and paternalistic benevolence. . . . The leaders are expected to be all-knowing as well as all-powerful. Subordinates are expected to be compliant and willing. . . . At its worst, the Power organization tends towards a rule by fear.

4.4 A support culture

Finally, a Chinese factory during the Cultural Revolution (1967–70) has been selected as an example of a Support Culture, on the basis of a description by King (1977). Chairman Mao was against hierarchy, against specialization and against routine. The revolutionaries temporarily ousted the old cadres and vigorously pursued the Maoist line. The revolutionary committees ran factories and strove to combat the evils of bureaucracy as they saw them. They shifted managers into manual work and created a decision-making system which involved workers' participation in administration. The committees themselves were a 'three-in-one' combination of representatives of 'the masses' (such as peasants, workers and students) and technicians and managers. Faith was placed in the political activism of the members – 'the mobilization of bias through personal relationships'. Harrison says,

> the Support-oriented organization offers its members satisfactions which come from relationships; mutuality, belonging, and connection. . . . The assumption is that people will contribute out of a sense of commitment to a group or organization of which they feel themselves truly to be members, and in which they believe they have a personal stake.

Handy (1985: 196) says, 'The kibbutz, the commune, the co-operative, are all striving after the [support] culture in organizational form.'

5 COMMENTS

We have introduced terms for four types of societal culture and four types of organizational culture. As stated in the preface, however, organizational cultures do not fit inside societal cultures like Chinese boxes or Russian dolls. At both levels cultures vary not only in content but also in strength. The greater the number of persons who agree about what the culture is, the greater its strength. Cultures also vary in intensity, the extent to which they include fundamental beliefs as well as attitudes, values and behaviour. A religious order has a more intense culture than a supermarket. A nation whose governing principles are Islamic fundamentalism has a more intense culture than a nation whose laws are not grounded in religious beliefs (see Figure 10.1 for core religious values). Because cultures vary in strength, intensity and content, the idea of four societal and four organizational cultures is a gross simplification. It does, however, serve as a useful method for considering organizational behaviour.

6 SUMMARY

In this chapter OB was introduced as the academic discipline which studies how enterprises work and how the people associated with them act. An important influence on organizational behaviour is *culture*, which is *a programmed way of seeing* derived from beliefs and values. It is possible to say that Western and Eastern ways of seeing differ, as do the cultures of different nations.

A study by Hofstede was used as the basis for selecting terms that suggest that culture affects economic, ideological and order goals. His individualism relates to economic goals, his femininity to ideological goals, his power distance and uncertainty avoidance to order goals. Nations (and organizations) follow goals in all three areas.

There is a *golden mean* of goal attainment between under-achievement or over-achievement. If the golden mean cannot be held, there is a shift leading to other goals and a cycle of change. This was illustrated in two very different countries, the People's Republic of China and the UK. In China, the leadership tends to give priority to ideological goals, but is forced to concentrate on order when disaffection shows itself and on economic goals when order has been restored, for only when the economy is growing is there a base from which to push further ideology. In the UK, governments tend to give priority to economic goals, but have to respond to political pressures of an ideological kind when social divisions grow. When strike activity is high, order becomes a problem, but there are few strikes in times of high unemployment, because people in work are concerned to keep their jobs.

The societal cultures at different stages of the cycle of change in both countries can be described in Hofstede's terms. It is also possible to link these terms with those used by other writers for organizational cultures. The pairs of terms are as follows: individualism and achievement culture, femininity and support culture, power distance and power culture and uncertainty avoidance and role culture. Examples were given of organizations which fitted the descriptions of these cultures. The relationship between national cultures and organizational cultures, however, is uncertain. Many different circumstances may affect the degree of similarity found. Further chapters will explore possible interactions in greater detail. It is plausible, however, that **culture affects change via preferences among economic, ideological, and order goals**.

NOTES

1 There are statistical techniques for grading the answers to questionnaires so that *scales* are created. Weighted scores on these scales can be combined into *factor* scores. A factor represents a pattern that has revealed itself during the analysis, and factor scores are a convenient summary. If factor scores themselves are associated in non-random ways with something else, the researcher can make a prediction that in a new sample this association, or *co-variation*, will also be found. Such a prediction may have to be qualified if other things also vary with the factor. Fortunately there are other techniques to enable the researcher to determine how much of the *variance* is attributable to one thing and how much to another, and to calculate the effect on the total variance of ignoring any of the *predictors*.

2 This and subsequent quotations from Harrison in this chapter are taken from *Diagnosing Organization Culture*, a questionnaire instrument designed by Roger Harrison and Herb Stokes, which is available from Harrison Associates Inc., 2719 Woolsey Street, Berkeley, CA 94705, USA; also available from Roffey Park Management College, Forest Road, Horsham, West Sussex RH12 4TD.

FURTHER READING

Each item in the list below has been selected for one of three reasons: it has been cited during Chapter 1; it deals with topics related to those discussed; it deals with a non-Western culture.

Handy, C.B. (1978) *The Gods of Management*, London: Penguin. Handy describes the four organizational cultures using four Greek gods as patrons. (As explained, Handy uses 'task' and 'person' where Harrison later uses 'achievement' and 'support'.)
—— (1985) *Understanding Organizations*, 3rd edn, London: Penguin. This is an introductory text in organizational behaviour, and covers much the same ground as the present book.
Harrison, R. (1972a) 'Understanding your organization's character', *Harvard Business Review* 50 (23): 119–28. Uses his earlier terms, but still useful in suggesting how to measure culture.
—— (1987a)'Harnessing personal energy: how companies can inspire employees', *Organizational Dynamics* 16 (2): 5–20. Written for (American) managers.
Hill, S. and Thurley, K. (1974) 'Sociology and industrial relations', *British Journal of Industrial Relations* 12: 147–170. Interesting, though perhaps not for beginners.

Hofstede, G. (1980) *Culture's Consequences*, Beverly Hills, CA: Sage. This is a large book, with many tables. Beginners will prefer the following article.

Hofstede, G. and Bond, M.H. (1988) 'The Confucius connection: from cultural roots to economic growth', *Organizational Dynamics* 16 (Spring) 5–21.

Morgan, G. (1986) *Images of Organization*, Beverly Hills, CA: Sage. Highly recommended. He takes a number of metaphors for organizations and develops each in a lucid and interesting way.

Pugh, D.S., Hickson, D.J. and Hinings, R. (1971) *Writers on Organizations*, 2nd edn, London: Penguin. This gives short notes on a few key OB writers from the present century.

Skinner, G.W. and Winckler, E.A. (1980) 'Compliance succession in rural communist China: a cyclical theory', in Etzioni, A. and Lehman, E.W. (eds) *A Sociological Reader on Complex Organizations*, 3rd edn, New York: Holt, Rinehart & Winston. This has been summarized in the present text.

Williams, A., Dobson, P. and Walters, M. (1989) *Changing Culture: New Organizational Approaches*, London: Institute of Personnel Management. The writers believe that personnel departments can play a key role in changing cultures.

Wright, P. (1981) 'Organizational behaviour in Islamic firms', *Management International Review* 21 (2): 86–94. An interesting account of how Islam influences business.

'Cross cultural management' is the theme of a whole issue of *International Studies of Management and Organizations* 13 (1–2), Spring/Summer, 1983.

'Indian studies on organizational effectiveness' is the theme of a whole issue of *International Studies of Management and Organizations* 14 (2–3), Summer/Fall, 1984.

'Management and organization in Africa' is the theme of a whole issue of *International Studies of Management and Organizations* 16, (2), 1986.

RECOMMENDED EXERCISE FOR CHAPTER 1

'Culture sort': This puts you in the position of having to decide what statements in a questionnaire will be characteristic of each of the four organizational cultures described in Section 4 of the chapter.

RECOMMENDED CASE STUDY

'Rivers State': A country with a power distance culture suppresses opposition.

Chapter 2

Cultures and control

CHAPTER OBJECTIVES

By the end of this chapter you will be able to:

1 explain why both deviance reduction and deviance generation may be necessary for control
2 explain how organizations with different cultures differ in the types of control they use
3 list five characteristics of control by regulation and five of control by appreciation
4 compare and contrast the Greiner and Touraine models, and state some ways in which changes occur
5 analyse the recommended cases.

1 INTRODUCTION

Chapter 1 introduced the idea that organizations and nation states have cultures which affect the priority they give to different goals. They may even have a cycle of priorities that is related to changing circumstances. We now consider some of the means whereby organizations attempt to control internal and external obstacles to reaching their goals. One meaning of the verb to control is 'purposefully to direct or restrain the action of a force or thing'. One thinks of the steersman at the helm of a ship. A non-human example is the thermostat which maintains temperature within a given range. It does so by regulating heat input in accordance with the feedback it receives from the thermometer on the effect of its own actions. In both these examples control is concerned with reducing current deviation or the adverse consequences of past deviation, rather as Figure 1.1 showed in relation to the golden mean. However, one can also think of control in an anticipatory sense as preparation for contingencies before they arise. The word 'contingency' refers to any 'force or thing' that is to be directed or restrained. Forward control involves having an understanding of what is likely to happen. In a one-person business, if the proprietor is to realize his or her ideals, self-control is needed. The inner contingencies are the person's own hopes and fears, knowledge, skills and experience, physical stamina and so on. There are also outer contingencies over which one-sided control is usually impossible. Many relationships with other people are involved in obtaining credit, finding customers or clients, obtaining space, equipment or materials, and selling any product or service. They involve reciprocity, but they can still be prepared for in advance. All of these can be viewed as contingencies. The present chapter describes how organizations with different cultures differ in the methods of control they prefer. If circumstances are not suited to the preferred method, those responsible may have to adopt other means. Systems theory and exchange theory suggest some criteria for choosing a control strategy. A switch of strategy may mean a shift in culture also, as the models of cyclical change in Chapter 1 suggested. Two further models of cyclical change processes are presented in the present chapter.

2   TYPES OF CONTROL ASSOCIATED WITH DIFFERENT ORGANIZATIONAL CULTURES

Table 2.1 shows the methods of control associated with the different organizational cultures. The centre column refers to control by *regulation* and the right-hand one to control by *appreciation*. Regulation is an attempt to reduce deviation. We discuss first its use to control internal contingencies, that is, things inside the organization which can go wrong. Then we look at attempts to use it to deal with problems created by people outside the organization. We shall do the same for appreciation.

2.1   Control by regulation

There are four aspects to regulation.

1 There is some *purpose* to be attained, some preferred state of affairs to be realized or maintained – a goal to be reached.
2 Some means for attaining the purpose are envisaged, that is, a *plan*.

3 There must be some way of knowing whether the means employed are having the desired effect (*monitoring*).
4 *Corrective* action can be taken if the desired effect is not being produced.

Examples of formal controls that are characteristic of role cultures are shown in Table 2.2. When 'everything is under control' we understand that 'everything is going according to plan'. The plan provides the direction for the 'force or thing', while the monitoring and correction provide the restraint. However, the cultures differ in the extent to which they separate planning from execution, in terms of both timing and personnel. In the hierarchical organizations of the role and power cultures the plans tend to be made by senior managers with advice from the professional staff. Execution of the plans is the function of the operating personnel (classed as 'office holders' in

Table 2.1 Preferred methods of control In different organizational cultures

Contingencies	Methods of control	
	ROLE CULTURE	ACHIEVEMENT CULTURE
Internal Contingencies	Hierarchical control via impersonal regulations	Self-control (personal accountability for delegated achievements)
External contingencies	Closure Separation	Problem-solving compromise
	POWER CULTURE	SUPPORT CULTURE
Internal contingencies	Hierarchical control via direction and supervision	Collaborative control with mutual accountability
External contingencies	Conquest Confrontation	Dynamic connectedness, transformation
	Control by regulation	*Control by appreciation*

Table 2.2 Four formal control systems often found in organizations with role cultures

System name and office holder responsible	Purpose in future to have	Plan	Monitoring	Correction
Cash control *Accountant*	A particular cash balance	Strategy to achieve desired funds	Cash forecasting	Action to invest surplus funds/ obtain overdraft etc.
Quality control *Inspector*	Raw materials of specified quality	'Action Sheet' with what to do, e.g. return to supplier	Testing procedure	E.g. goods returned and fresh supply obtained
Inventory control *Storekeeper*	An economic level of stocking	Reorder levels and reorder quantities are laid down	Computer calculates receipts, issues and stocks	Program executed and stock is topped up.
Labour control *Personnel officer*	Establishment figure modified as needs change	Strategy to correct mismatch between establishment and strength	Lists of present strength, shortages/ surpluses of staff	Recruitment, natural wastage, redundancy notices etc.

Table 2.2) whose work is monitored by their superiors. The lower levels alert the higher levels to anticipated, current or past difficulties. In role cultures provision for meeting such difficulties has been largely routinized so that there are procedures, as illustrated, for monitoring (spotting early signs that things are going wrong) and procedures for corrective action. In power cultures there is greater reliance on supervision as a means of ensuring implementation of plans. The four elements of Table 2.2 will still be present but, as plans

may not be written down, subordinates may have to appeal to a superior for a 'decision' before initiating corrective action. In both role and power cultures the planning precedes the execution, and the people doing the work are expected to comply with the instructions of others. There are limits that must be adhered to. We turn now to control of external contingencies by regulation.

The words 'closure' and 'separation' are used in Table 2.1 to indicate how role cultures regulate their environment. *Closure* refers to the principle of putting a limit or boundary between things for which you will take responsibility and things which you regard as outside your concern. This can be done by the 'small print' on travel tickets or theatre tickets, by such documents as insurance policies and generally by 'guarantees' which limit the extent to which other organizations or persons can make claims. *Separation* refers to the extent to which one can 'pass the buck' by claiming that a difficulty has been caused by some other person or organization so that the consequences must be dealt with elsewhere. A manufacturing firm, for example, may excuse itself from failure to deliver an order on time because its workers had been called out on strike by a trade union.

The power culture attempts to regulate its environment by conquest and confrontation. Conquest is illustrated by the strategy of 'buying out' the competition, either by price cutting or by taking over a competitor. Confrontation can be seen in the use of law suits, and in such tactics as wearing down the opposition by denying it access to resources, as in a lockout of workers, for example.

Regulation, whether directed at reducing internal or external obstacles to success, tends to be dealing with past or present deviations. Appreciation, to which we now turn, tends to be used in *anticipation of* contingencies, and is less formal than regulation.

2.2 Control by appreciation

This is the preferred method in achievement and support cultures. In practice, all organizations need to use both types of control, but the distinction is nevertheless important. Appreciation refers to 'the selection of what shall be noticed, how it shall be classified, and the way it shall be valued'. It is part of what Vickers (1965) calls 'the Art of Judgement'. Internal and external contingencies tend to be dealt with in similar fashion. The main difference is that the people involved in dealing with external contingencies are from more than one organization. They may be representatives, or even plenipotentiaries, that is, persons given full powers to act as they see fit according to how a situation develops. Planning and execution tend to be concurrent and to be carried out by the same people. The discretion given to 'autonomous work groups' (see Chapters 4, 6 and 7) means that these workers use their own judgement about the 'direction and restraint' that it is necessary to apply to their work. Often people have been specially trained through craft apprenticeships, or the qualifying examinations of professional bodies, to exercise appreciation. The responsibility for the quality of work rests with the person doing the job, not with somebody else. This is what is meant by the 'self-control' shown in Table 2.1 as associated with an Achievement culture. Finally, under the support culture, we have a consensual form of appreciative control. Here it is the collective judgement rather than the individual judgement that is exercised. Within the enterprise, persons are responsible to each other for the realization of their collective ideals. Outside the enterprise there is *dynamic connectedness*, as, for example between dealers and clients in stock exchange transactions, where changes in market prices are known simultaneously to persons in different parts of the world. The word 'transformation' refers to the ability, for example, to turn problems into challenges, and to surmount challenges through redefining them. Argyris and Schon (1976) call this transformation 'double-loop learning' because the person not only monitors the environment and decides what corrections are needed, but also decides whether the goals or policies themselves ought to be changed.

Table 2.3 summarizes the differences between regulative and appreciative control. It is extracted from Gadalla and Cooper (1978). Regulative control is closely linked to Western concepts of rationality, and appreciation is linked with the Eastern ways of thinking described in Chapter 1. So what, apart from cultural preferences, are the criteria for choosing regulation or appreciation? We turn to some ideas from systems theory for guidance.

3 A SYSTEMS THEORY FRAMEWORK FOR CHOOSING METHODS OF CONTROL

According to systems theory, an environment is 'an ensemble of more or less distinguishable elements, states, or events' (Buckley, 1921). *Variety* is evident in the distinguishable differences. *Constraint* is any connection within the ensemble. The connection may be fixed or variable. Chaos is a condition of variety without constraint.

Table 2.3 Regulative and appreciative forms of control

Regulative	Appreciative
Situations are confronted with a predetermined plan Management seeks to impose this plan	Situations are met as they are, and are responded to as such; the management is mutual adjustment between organization and situation
Management is seen to be focused on goal attainment	Management is seen to be a process focused on maintaining balance in a field of relationships
Narrow, specialized purpose is emphasized	General values or norms inform behaviour
Management relies on the application of techniques, and *extrinsic motivation*	The source of control is seen to be *within* people, i.e. in *intrinsic motivation*
Development is seen to require more sophisticated techniques and greater rationality	Development is seen to be a process of increasing understanding of the extent and depth of the context

Note: For a discussion of extrinsic and intrinsic motivation see Chapter 5, Section 3.1.

Turbulence, mentioned in Chapter 1, is a condition of high variability. The connections change.

Members of organizations have to deal with both variety and variability. Ashby (1981) formulated 'the law of requisite variety' which states that the variety within a system (for example in a person's brain or in a business organization) must be at least as great as the environmental variety against which it is attempting to regulate itself. Animals may meet contingencies on the basis of innate reflexes or 'releasers'. The hedgehog can protect itself against many predators by curling into a ball. This act, however, is ineffective against the motor car. Higher animals may learn, through a process of conditioning, to change their behaviour when variety increases. Individual humans can consciously formulate purposes which override past conditioning. Human societies can engage in ethical debate and reflection about changing norms and values. The resultant policies can override individual purposes. The human society faces greater external variety and variability than does the individual. It can also process information in more varied ways than the individual can.

The technical term for the correspondence between external variety and internal variety is *isomorphism*. There is isomorphism between the physical landscape and a good map. The system which produces the map has enough symbols to be able to indicate contours of the terrain, areas of water or vegetation or desert, man-made features such as roads and buildings, etc. The process of *mapping* deals with both the variety (number of different features) and the constraint (how the features are spatially related). However, there must also be persons capable of reading the maps, otherwise there is no 'meeting of minds', no 'common ground' and thus no meaning or information exchange, only uncertainty. Metaphorically speaking, appreciation refers to the process of mapping new territory – understanding or representing what is happening. Regulation, on the other hand, refers to the use of already established knowledge. A compass enables one to control one's movements so as to arrive at the desired destination if a good map already exists and if there have been no physical changes in the area covered by the map. If landmarks are subject to alteration, the constraints are no longer fixed but variable, and so regulation by the compass may not suffice. A change of direction may be needed to avert disaster. To determine what new direction to take, appreciation is needed.

These ideas from systems theory have been translated by Nelson and Machin (1976) into a matrix of control strategies based on the amount of variety present and on the stability or variability of constraints. This is shown in Table 2.4. Regulation can be used where the variety in the environment is constrained in fixed ways, and/or where the unit concerned can be relatively buffered from the outer variety. (This variety gets absorbed elsewhere. For example, a production section can be protected from fluctuations in the supply of materials if buffer stocks are held in store.) Appreciation is better where constraints are variable and where there is some, or a lot of, variety.

Nelson and Machin suggest that the objective of control for row 1 is to assure efficient operations; for row 2 it is to assure co-ordinated functioning; while for row 3 it is to assure effective interaction. In column (a) the type of constraint with which one is dealing is resource utilization, in column (b) it is commitments, and in column (c) it is relationships. In each of the cells there is an indication of what to do. The planning, monitoring, and correction in the four formal control systems of Table 2.2 can all be accommodated down column (a) Table 2.4. Where regulation is possible, interaction with other parties is not

Table 2.4 Control strategies within and across boundaries

Amount of variety to which system is subjected	Constraints		
	Mainly fixed Regulation is possible (a)	Appreciative area (b)	Mainly variable (c)
1 A little variety	Prescribe activities	Estimate outputs from given resources	Delegate and distribute authority to manage resources
2 Some variety	Programme resource utilization	Establish agreements among parties with common interests	Establish issues on which managers assume responsibility to co-operate
3 A lot of variety	Make plans in advance	Determine what other interested parties expect or can influence	Determine where supportive relations among units are critical

a problem. In the four cells in the bottom right of Table 2.4, however, relations with people are critical. We turn now to a different perspective which focuses directly on the issue of the motivation of the parties directly concerned, namely exchange theory.

4   AN EXCHANGE THEORY FRAMEWORK FOR CHOOSING METHODS OF CONTROL

Exchange theory is concerned with the inducements which are offered by those with *remunerative power* (see Chapter 1, Section 2.3) to obtain something that is desired from others. The question of choosing between regulation and appreciation on this view reduces to the question of what people will accept. Cammann and Nadler

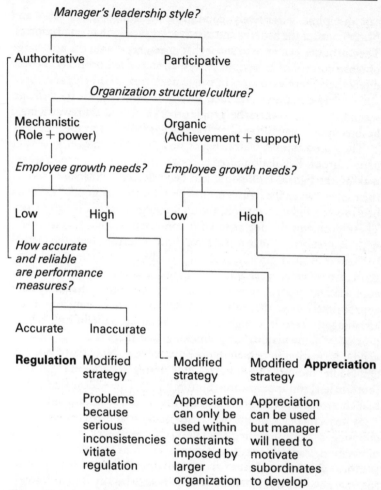

Manager's leadership style?

Authoritative   Participative

                       Organization structure/culture?

Mechanistic   Organic
(Role + power)   (Achievement + support)

Employee growth needs?   *Employee growth needs?*

Low   High   Low   High

*How accurate
and reliable
are performance
measures?*

Accurate   Inaccurate

Regulation Modified   Modified   Modified **Appreciation**
                strategy   strategy   strategy

                Problems   Appreciation Appreciation
                because   can only be   can be used
                serious   used within   but manager
                inconsistencies constraints   will need to
                vitiate   imposed by   motivate
                regulation   larger   subordinates
                                organization to develop

Figure 2.1 A decision tree for choosing a control strategy
Source: Cammann and Nadler 1976: 71

(1976) have produced a decision tree to help managers to choose
which type of control to apply. The outline of this tree is given in
Figure 2.1, though the terms are those employed in the present book,
not those of Camman and Nadler. More details of leadership styles
can be found in Chapter 8, while organization structure is discussed
in Chapter 3 and employee growth in Chapter 5. There will be greater
reliance on appreciative control where people have high growth
needs, and more reliance upon regulative control where supervisors

can discipline a relatively compliant workforce. Cammann and Nadler outline the benefits and disadvantages of each form of control. They produce evidence to show that managers obtain the advantage of close control of behaviour if regulation is used properly. People direct their energies to areas in which performance is being measured when three conditions are met. First, the targets must be *difficult*; second, the measures must be 'people proof'; and third, the rewards must be directly and openly tied to performance as indicated by the measures.

There are a number of drawbacks, however. Most measures are not people proof. Regulation often encourages people to concentrate on making the figures look good, and on collecting evidence to 'cover themselves' when the figures cannot be made to look good. There can be a loss of valid information, and an unwillingness to take any risks. These problems do not arise with appreciative control. However, with appreciation, managers have little control over the actual behaviour of subordinates, goals may be difficult to assess, and low-growth-need employees will not respond to the responsibility which appreciative control gives them. On the other hand, where appropriately used, appreciative control has the following important advantages: there is a high sense of 'total accountability', which precludes 'game playing' or politicking, and there is a large flow of valid information to help with problem solving. Note that Camman and Nadler indicate three intermediate strategies between regulation (bottom left) and appreciation (bottom right). These allow for the fact that control is more difficult than the discussion so far has indicated.

Systems theory suggests that variety and variability are criteria for choosing a control strategy, while exchange theory suggests that motivation, leadership style and employee needs are relevant. Other theories treat the choice as a provisional one, arguing that contingencies are not indefinitely controllable by any initial strategy or mix of strategies. We therefore turn to theories that regulation and appreciation appear to alternate (like retrenchment and mobilization did in Figure 1.2).

5   CONTROL CYCLES

5.1   Greiner's model of contingencies over time

Greiner called his model 'evolution and revolution as organizations grow'. He outlined two axes, time and size. His model shows a linear relationship between the two, with organizations starting life very

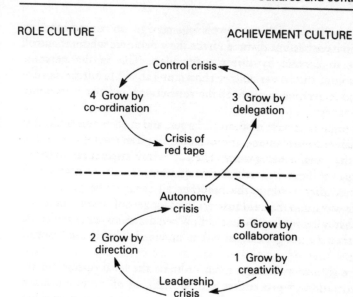

ROLE CULTURE

ACHIEVEMENT CULTURE

Control crisis

4 Grow by
co-ordination

3 Grow by
delegation

Crisis of
red tape

Autonomy
crisis

2 Grow by
direction

5 Grow by
collaboration

1 Grow by
creativity

Leadership
crisis

POWER CULTURE

SUPPORT CULTURE

Figure 2.2 Evolution and revolution in organizations
Source: Adapted from Greiner 1972

small and growing bigger and bigger as they get older. The control
that is exercised, in each of five periods of evolutionary growth, sows
the seeds of a 'revolutionary' crisis before the next growth period (if
the business survives). In Greiner's model, the relationship between
time and size is drawn as a straight diagonal line ascending from lower
left to top right where he puts a question mark after his fifth period
of growth. For our purposes, in Figure 2.2, the sequence is shown as
cyclical, starting in the support culture area, moving through power,
achievement and role cultures and back to support cultures. We now
summarize Greiner's argument, giving an explanation of the
categories in Figure 2.2. A business starts from the ideas of one or two
people working creatively together and exercising the kind of mutual
accountability and appreciative control described above (in Section
2). However, as numbers increase, some specialization of tasks
becomes necessary, and the founder member begins to dictate to the
other members. This is accepted for as long as the original leader
retains his charisma. The leadership crisis occurs when there is too
much work for one leader, or when it is necessary to find a successor.

The next leader gathers a top management group around him, but they will have become divorced from the workforce whom they still attempt to control by direct supervision. This is the personal regulation of the power culture shown in Table 2.1, but those subjected to it eventually chafe at the restrictions and the 'autonomy crisis' ensues.

The organization is now much larger, and it seems sensible that appreciative control of operations should be given to those nearest to where the work is being done. The autonomy crisis is resolved by delegation to branches, where an achievement culture is fostered. However, after a while, the branches all seem to be going their separate ways, and the headquarters is no longer sufficiently in touch with what is happening 'in the field'. When decisions are taken at the centre they do not get carried out as intended. This is the 'control crisis'.

There is now an attempt to co-ordinate the local operations by standardization of procedures and formalizing of communication lines up and down the hierarchy. The organization is now moving into a role culture, where regulation once more prevails. This, too, eventually breaks down as it proves insufficiently flexible to adjust rapidly to external changes. People operate within their job descriptions, and so if a task is on nobody's list it does not get done. This is the 'crisis of red tape'.

It is decided, once more, to get people to take personal responsibility for what they do, by moving to a more appreciative mode of control. It is likely that the organization will by now have reorganized to emphasize lateral communication, and units whose work is interdependent will be expected to initiate contacts with each other as often as is necessary for furthering common purposes. Greiner does not commit himself beyond this point. There may be scaling down into small creative units.

The internal contingencies which organizations must resolve as they grow are the four crises shown down the centre of Figure 2.2. Will the old crises recur, or will there be new crises to face? It may be that the limits to growth have been reached, and that there will be attempts to retain the flexibility of the appreciative mode of control by experimentation with alternatives to hierarchy (see Chapter 3, Section 1.5). It may be that the next crisis will be followed by a move back into a more regulatory mode. The model developed by Touraine suggests that the second possibility is more likely.

5.2 Touraine's model of cyclical contradictions

A rough version of Touraine's theory is that there is a constant contradiction between, on the one hand, the direction and restraint that is necessary if organizations are to achieve manufacturing or service goals and, on the other hand, the desire of employees to act autonomously.

In the early years of an organization the people involved may feel that their views are adequately represented, since they all know each other well. Opposition is considered irrational for the business is their own. They have a common stake in it. Nevertheless, even with a small group, differences can emerge about the direction to be followed. These differences may lead to informal alliances among some members to assert their autonomy.

The leader may prevent this from gaining strength by a policy of 'divide and rule'. Alternatively, the majority may tend to back the leader in his attempt to restore unity by coercion. This, in turn, becomes oppressive. The minority feel they have no stake in the organization.

Some people quit, but others become involved in 'treachery' which eventually ends the coercive regime and inaugurates an 'instrumental' one in which the stakes are strictly private self-interest. After a while informal opposition (for example the occasional 'wildcat' strike) again appears.

The leaders respond by recognizing the opposition and containing it within formal contractual arrangements which admit sectional interests. Breach of such arrangements is considered highly 'irregular'. This form of integrative control again becomes onerous, and dissent eventually leads to the beginnings of a new representation and the cycle repeats itself.

Figure 2.3 shows the organizational cultures below Touraine's terms. Comparison of Figures 2.3 and 2.2. suggests similarities with Greiner's ideas. Both models depict a series of internal crises, though they differ as to causation. Greiner asserts that past solutions contain the potential for future crises. Touraine asserts that the basic contradiction is between restraint and autonomy. In their different ways these writers are both illustrating the problems of managing variety and variability, and so both models suggest swings between regulative and appreciative control (shown, respectively, on the left and right sides of the figures).

Whether we see change as linear (as Greiner actually did) or as

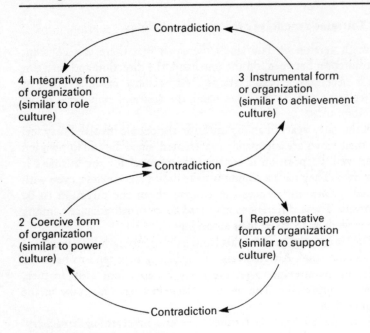

Figure 2.3 The cycle of control
Source: Adapted from Touraine 1965

cyclical, it is still necessary to consider *how* it occurs. In the next section we consider several methods for introducing change. (Chapter 9 deals with major transformations brought about by organizational development.)

5.3 Methods for introducing change

The four cultures are associated with four preferred methods of introducing change, but all of them involve people doing their normal tasks. Mant (1976), points out that 'no one can see an organization, all anyone can see is people behaving, each according to his own views of reality'. The cultures shape those views through the daily encounters of people at work.

The daily encounters help people to define their roles, and it is through acting out these roles that changes are made. 'Role' is a metaphor taken from the theatre, indicating the part an actor is expected to play. But no two actors play the same part in identical ways. Enactment of a role in an organization is also subject to personal interpretations and improvizations. In role cultures, more of the role is 'scripted' than in other cultures. The job duties and responsibilities are written down, but they can still be renegotiated and the script rewritten. Some terms from role theory are needed to describe how this happens.

Kahn *et al.* (1964) give the name *role episode* to the way in which a role comes to be 'an interactive performance that is negotiated'. Their model is shown below. 'Focal role' means the one which is the centre of attention. The 'role senders' are those persons who have dealings with the focal role. Together they form a 'role set'.

Role senders	*Focal role*
experience and evaluate the behaviour of the person in the focal role, and respond by further compatible or incompatible pressures.	feels or perceives that some demands are being made which are compatible or incompatible, and responds by coping, compliance, or symptom formation.

Role perceptions include:

- how one thinks one should behave (one's *espoused* role)
- how one thinks *others* think one should behave (one's *received* role).

How others *actually* think one should behave (the *sent* role) may differ from what one receives or espouses, and so there is a strong possibility of *role conflict*. Coping or complying with what others want is one way of dealing with such conflict. 'Symptom formation' refers to the signs of stress that persons may show if the received and sent roles conflict, or if it is impossible either to change or to meet the sent expectations. However, since each focal role is also a 'sender' for others, it is often possible to modify their expectations through striking a bargain. Remunerative power (mentioned in Section 4 above) is useful here. Role negotiation is a technique which can be learned (it is described in Chapter 9, Section 4.3, 'Mentor and understudy').

'Boundary roles' are particularly stressful because the role set includes people from other levels, from other departments or from outside. However, stressful roles have great change potential. Many managers have found, through thinking about their own roles, that 'it is possible to bridge organizational chasms, cross boundaries, and run all manner of risks'. Cumulatively the modifications they negotiate can change the organization.

Table 2.5 Methods of making changes

4 By constitutional authority (e.g. of electorate over elected in a role culture)	3 By lateral authority (e.g. as used by experts in an achievement culture)
2 By hierarchical authority (e.g. that of a superior over subordinates in a power culture)	1 By mutual authority (e.g. of ideas exchanged in a support culture)

Note: 'Authority' is the legitimate power. Compare the power bases of leaders in Table 8.1.

Table 2.5 shows four ways of risking change through 'role enactment', one suited to each of the four cultures. We look at them, in turn, in the order corresponding to the discussion of the models of Greiner and Touraine.

Mutual authority among colleagues

Chapter 6 (section 4.2) describes collaborative decision-making. Problem-solving through the exchange of ideas by persons who respect and like each other, enables changes to be brought about by mutual consent.

Hierarchical authority, for example that of 'the boss'

Here a manager gets his or her subordinates to do new things, or to do things in new ways. Chapter 8 sets out the type of authority that may be used and the styles that may be employed. Peters (1978) speaks of mundane tools for managing change. These are such things as calendars, diaries; reports, agenda, public statements, physical settings and the way the manager's personal staff are organized. He gives eight rules for using these tools:

- Spend time. This itself exerts a 'claim' on the decision-making system.
- Persist. Having more patience than other people often results in a chosen course of action (though not always).
- Exchange status for substance. Reward allies with visible tokens of recognition.
- Allow opponents to participate. Often those outside the formal

decision centres overestimate the feasibility of change. They may become more realistic when involved themselves! (This strategy is sometimes called 'co-optation.')

- Overload the system. If a lot is pushed in, something will come out!
- Provide waste bins. Put 'throw-away' issues at the top of the agenda (to absorb debate), saving substantive issues for later.
- Manage unobtrusively. Imperceptible changes may persist with little further attention.
- Interpret history. By giving a particular version of events a leader can alter people's perceptions of what has been happening. (This is why the wording of minutes is important.)

Lateral authority, for example from expert to client group

All the rules suggested by Peters can be used by managers who can only influence through advice given to those of similar standing to themselves, or to those above them in status. People only heed advice when the expert has taken care to see things from their point of view. Much of what is written about selling techniques is pertinent. If persons or groups define themselves as needing what the sales person has to offer, they can see the choice of what to buy, or what to do, as their own choice.

Constitutional authority, for example of voters

Change may be brought about through the ballot box. In between elections, pressure groups, voluntary movements, trade unions, and citizens action groups may seek to lobby their representatives. In some countries people may lawfully take part in demonstrations, 'sit-ins', 'sit-downs', strikes, 'work-ins' and other non-violent methods of protest.

The methods are all diagrammed in Figure 2.4 which shows also some more extreme activities so that we have a picture of 'holding to the mean' at a level within organizations as well as at the level of society. (Refer to Figure 1.1)

6 SUMMARY

This chapter looked at how organizations seek to control themselves and their environment in pursuit of goals. Control was defined as

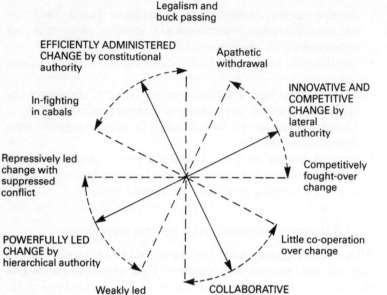

Figure 2.4 Change processes and the golden mean
Note: Compare with Figure 1.1

direction or restraint applied to contingencies. Contingencies are any force or thing. The simplest model of a controlled system is the thermostat. Role cultures have regulations that can sometimes work like thermostats. There are purposes, plans, measurement and corrective action. Power cultures tend to rely on direct intervention by superiors when it comes to corrective action. Both cultures favour *regulation*, which applies restraint. Appreciation, on the other hand, applies forward direction to contingencies. It tends to be favoured in achievement and support cultures. It was pointed out that, although control is usually thought of as keeping events going according to plan, it can be defined much more widely to include applying direction in order to *create* deviation rather than to reduce it. Appreciative methods of control tend to serve this purpose by fostering an ability to 'map' the variety and patterning of the environment. This ability is a matter of trained judgement.

The choice of control strategy does not depend on cultural

preferences alone. Systems theory suggests that variety and variability in the environment call for appreciative control, but regulation can be used for units which are relatively closed. Exchange theory focuses on the part played by reward power in the control of behaviour at work. Other considerations are the leader's style and the degree to which accuracy is possible in assessing performance.

The choice between regulation and appreciation is not a choice that is made once only, however. Methods may alternate between restraint and direction, and so features of the four cultures will predominate at different times in the same organization. This is because new contingencies are constantly arising. Two accounts of control cycles stress recurrent crises. In one case these crises result from past attempts at control. In the other, control provokes rebellion.

Controlled change may be brought about by mutual consent, by direction from above, by adopting expert advice or constitutionally through the ballot box. People carrying out their everyday roles may create evolutionary changes. Boundary roles are particularly suitable places from which to do this.

Although many considerations apply, **culture affects control through preferences for regulation or appreciation.**

FURTHER READING

The following articles are pertinent:

Cammann, C. and Nadler, D.A. (1976) 'Fit your control systems to your managerial style', *Harvard Business Review* 54 (1): 65–72.

Greiner, L.E. (1972) 'Evolution and revolution as organizations grow', *Harvard Business Review* 50 (4): 37–46.

Mant, A. (1976) 'How To analyse management', *Management Today* October: 62–5,130,132.

Nelson, E.G. and Machin, J.J. (1976) Management control: systems thinking applied to the development of a framework for empirical studies', *Journal of Management Studies* 13: 274–87.

Pascale, R.T. (1978) 'Zen and the art of management', *Harvard Business Review* 56 (2): 153–62.

Peters, T.J. (1978) 'Patterns, and settings, an optimistic case for getting things done', *Organizational Dynamics* Autumn: 2–23.

Four books are recommended. The bibliography contains further international references.

Ashby, W.R.(1981) *An Introduction to Cybernetics*, 3rd edn, New York: Harper & Row.

Buchanan, D.A. and Huczynski, A. A. (1985) *Organizational Behaviour: an Introductory Text*, Hemel Hempstead: Prentice-Hall International, especially ch. 22, pp. 451–78.

Katz, D, and Kahn, R.L. (1966) *The Social Psychology of Organizations*, London: Wiley.

Vickers, G. (1973) *Making Institutions Work*, London: Associated Business Programmes.

RECOMMENDED EXERCISE

'Role analysis': This is a chance for you to think about your own role.

RECOMMENDED CASES

'Computerized health records': a problem of introducing change.

'The dilemma of an administrative officer': how to control illicit union activity.

'Theatre problems': how to improve the service to hospital theatres.

Chapter 3

Cultures and organizational design

CHAPTER OBJECTIVES

By the end of this chapter you will be able to:

1 trace the connections between the four cultural types and different organizational designs
2 describe four different decentralized structures
3 distinguish between classic and flexible bureaucracies
4 explain why transnational corporations are regarded with ambivalence by governments
5 apply your knowledge to the recommended cases

1 MODELS FOR DESIGNING ORGANIZATIONS

We have spoken, in Chapters 1 and 2, of organizational cultures, cycles of change and different methods for controlling contingencies. It is now time to look more closely at how these things affect the *structures* of organizations: who has authority, who decides what and who relates to whom. The structure is created by *organizational design*.

We are familiar with designs in architecture, art, manufacturing, civil engineering, landscaping and many other fields. Things are usually designed before they are made. But organizations are designed whilst they operate. Their structure has to serve changing tasks, so we could more accurately speak of an on-going *process* of *re*design. This is usually the responsibility of managers at the top level (see Chapter 8). These managers have to see that the structure is appropriate to such ideological, economic and order goals as are listed in Table 1.2.

Goals of sharing and involvement require a structure where people

Table 3.1 Design tasks for achieving five organizational values

For an EFFICIENT organization	For an INNOVATIVE organization
4 The structure must be such that the organization can formalize working arrangements and keep administrative control, using **role culture** procedures (the 'administrative' problem)	3 The structure must be such that the organization can prepare for future management requirements, using appreciation and an **achievement culture** (the 'entrepreneurial' problem)

5 The structure must be such
that the organization can
achieve BALANCE, shifting
emphasis according to needs

For a PRODUCTIVE organization	For a COLLABORATIVE organization
2 The structure must be such that the organization can obtain operational control over resources using a **power culture** orientation (the 'engineering' problem)	1 The structure must be such that the organization can choose and serve an appropriate clientele using appreciation as in **support cultures** (the 'entrepreneurial' problem)

Notes: The values are in capital letters. The numbers are the same as in Figure 2.2. They represent the stages in Greiner's life cycle when a particular value will be appropriate to emerging needs. The terms in parentheses are those of Miles and Snow (1978).

are COLLABORATIVE. Goals of control and legality require a structure that can marshall PRODUCTIVE resources in an orderly and EFFICIENT way. Goals of competition require that the structure encourages people to be INNOVATIVE so that new challenges can be met.

These requirements are listed in Table 3.1 which also sets out five tasks which organizations must undertake if the values listed in capital letters are to be achieved.

The first *entrepreneurial* task is to secure agreement on what to make or whom to serve. The decision on the product or clientele will include the technology. Second, materials, equipment and workers have to be obtained and used: the *engineering* task. Third, future requirements for staff, equipment and finance must be predicted, and fourth, *administration* must be set up so that regulative control can be maintained as described in Chapter 2.

The importance of the tasks varies in sequence, in what Miles and Snow (1978) call an 'adaptive cycle', in which the entrepreneurial, engineering and administrative problems follow each other as firms seek to maintain or modify their market strategies. The task numbered 5 is therefore to balance the structure to changing conditions. Miles and Snow, like Skinner and Winckler, indicate that cycle duration is variable, so that at times two or more cycles may coincide. In fact all the problems are always present in some degree. The entrepreneurial problems shown on the right involve relations with the outside world, while the problems on the left are internal.

Five types of *organizational design* that help the five tasks just described are shown in Figure 3.1. They refer to the design of a whole organization, rather than to its constituent parts. The examples are discussed in order. We then relate the idea of an adaptive cycle in organizational design to ideas from the previous chapters.

1.1 Entrepreneurial and self-managed forms

Entrepreneurial clusters

According to Jay (1975), the earliest forms of human organization were hunting groups of roughly ten males supporting a base camp of about forty persons. Perhaps the entrepreneurial cluster is the modern equivalent of this band. In the West there have been numerous studies of entrepreneurs, some of which are listed in the bibliography. An entrepreneur gets personally involved in a host of activities while seeking to build a discrete business. However, he or she also needs to involve other people (bankers, customers, suppliers and so on). This is useful in giving the entrepreneur knowledge of possible product markets. Werbner (1985) gives an example – the social network of Manchester Pakistanis.

> Brothers, kinsmen and fellow villagers often follow one another into market trading or manufacturing. They create 'entrepreneurial chains'. Pakistanis of similar origins are concentrated in certain sections of the industry.... Tarik's son had worked at weekends and in the school holidays for various Pakistani rag-trade manufacturers. Several of his school friends came from

Emphasis on internal
stability

Emphasis on external
uncertainty

4 Classic or *full*
   bureaucracy,
   or **temple** HIERARCHY
   (compatible with
   role culture)

3 Decentralized,
   collegiate,
   or **matrix** or
   MARKET forms
   (compatible with
   achievement
   culture)

5 Hybrid or
   multidivisional forms,
   transnational
   corporations
   (compatible with
   mixed cultures)

2 Traditional ADHOCRACY,
   a centralized form;
   the pyramid or **web**
   (compatible with
   power culture)

1 Entrepreneurial
   cluster, or CLAN
   or *implicitly*
   structured form;
   self-management
   (compatible with
   support culture)

Figure 3.1 Models of organization
Notes: The terms in bold type are those used by Handy 1985. Those in italics
are from Pugh et al. 1968, those in capitals from Quinn and McGrath 1985

families that had small factories, so he could buy 'lines' of clothing
at a discount direct from the factory. This gave him the edge in
starting his first market stall.

(Werbner 1985: 411)

Tarik himself was made redundant and handed his redundancy
money to his son to help him to establish himself. Soon the son
co-opted his father into the business. They formed the nucleus of a
cluster, in which relationships are built on trust and people tend, by

mutual agreement, to do what they are best at. Decision-making is intuitive (Table 6.1) and control appreciative (Table 2.3). Co-ordination in such an organization is achieved through informal understanding. Beyond the activities entailed by legal requirements, there is little formal structure. Norms are implicit in what people do rather than explicit in written job descriptions. Pugh and his colleagues (1968) coined the term *implicitly structured* for organizations which scored low on three dimensions which they measured – impersonal control, structuring of activities and concentration of authority. Such organizations do not specialize, standardize or formalize their arrangements. The absence of formality is countered by the strength of personal ties, as between Tarik and his son. Even when entrepreneurs attach themselves as subcontractors (or extrapreneurs) to large sponsoring organizations, the ties are based on trust, as are the ties of an entrepreneur who builds a cluster inside a 'host' organization (an 'intrapreneur'). The activities of the cluster are geared to serving the chosen customers or clients, whether small or large. Decisions are *ad hoc* and taken by persons on the spot. Relationships are friendly. The cluster is consistent with support culture values.

Self-management forms

This form of organization is more self-conscious about its internal structure than is the entrepreneurial. An example is given by Bloor (1986) who worked as a novice staff member in a half-way house for disturbed adolescents in the UK. He says it was permissive and egalitarian.

> The Ashley staff have abandoned supervisory control, but they get the house cleaned by other means. They orchestrate the work group by encouraging resident initiative and self-regulation, by monitoring poor task performance, and by using collective pressure.
>
> (Bloor 1986: 186)

The key therapeutic device seems to have been the morning coffee group (a cluster) where people were confronted with the consequences of their behaviour by other residents, or by staff. Such a unit also has close ties with the outside world from which young people are referred and to which they go.

Another example was suggested in Chapter 1 (Table 1.4), namely

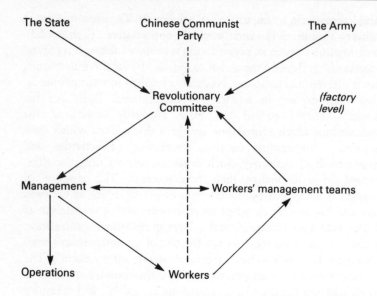

Figure 3.2 Workers' management teams in the People's Republic of China between 1967 and 1970: →, authority link; ⇢, similar link but of weak or unclear kind; ↔, reciprocal authority of workers electing managers who then assume authority over workers
Source: Lockett (1983)

a Chinese factory during the Cultural Revolution. Figure 3.2 shows both workers' management teams at workshop level and the Revolutionary Committee at factory level. The Revolutionary Committee had three links to the outside world – the representatives from the state, the army and the party. The workers' management teams seem to have been clusters in which, according to Lockett (1983), some workers were in charge of equipment and maintenance, others in charge of tools and implements, others of labour and welfare matters and yet others of production planning. These teams exercised some supervision of managers who were expected to do manual work, on a regular basis, in order to appreciate the problems faced by workers.

Here, as in the entrepreneurial forms, authority is diffuse and relationships informal despite a variety of tasks. Status differences are minimized. These conditions are compatible with support culture values.

1.2 Centralized structures

The cluster is often followed by the centralized form. Greiner explained that, as organizations grow, it becomes difficult to resolve internal disagreements unless someone is willing to take a strong line. This central person may be the charismatic founder of the voluntary organization or the owner-manager in the entrepreneurial cluster.

The task that is addressed by centralization is that of gaining operational control. This can be done in several ways. Rezazadeh (1961) suggests that the term centralization (versus decentralization) contains three different ideas. First there is *concentration* (versus dispersal) of authority. There is a single source of authority instead of many sources. Second there is *absolutism* (versus autonomy). Commands or rules are enforceable instead of being optional. Finally the rules have '*universal*' scope. They apply to everyone, not just to particular persons. In practice these three aspects of centralization may be found to different degrees and in different combinations.

The owner who manages the small firm may be the sole source of authority. In the UK most owner–managers are men, but more women are now starting their own businesses. By custom and practice 'bosses' are able to take all major decisions. Though they tend to give orders *ad hoc* as problems arise, they can enforce them. There are few rules, but all the subordinates are known to the boss, and the rule of obedience applies to everyone.

Handy calls this typical power culture structure in a small firm a 'web', with the spider at the centre. Another metaphor is the hub of a wheel from which the spokes radiate outwards. The most common metaphor for the centralized structure is the pyramid, with power at its apex. Where the organization is small enough to be one 'tribe', and the pyramid is relatively flat, such centralization can have a unifying effect. It was common in the West until the middle of this century and, according to Lammers and Hickson (1979) and to Hofstede (1980a), it is traditional in developing countries. The associated values are status, obedience and control (Table 1.1). By the time the organization has grown to about a thousand employees, however, the chief executive is likely to be overloaded, especially if there are external problems demanding attention.

The centralized form keeps internal order through vertical channels of communication, concentrated authority and deferential relationships. But the design has the weakness that a successor to the chief executive may not be found. Managers below the apex have

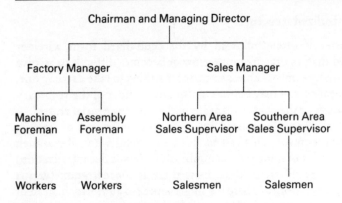

Figure 3.3 A centralized form of organization

been excluded from knowledge of the business as a whole. They have been confined by the structure to a geographical area, or to one function (probably either manufacturing or sales), or to one stage of operations (for example spinning or weaving) or to one product line (for example brand A or brand B). No one but the chairman and managing director has the whole picture (see Figure 3.3). Thus, when change is sought, 'new blood' may have to be brought in from outside if those below the chief executive are unwilling to accept increased responsibility. At all events, the design changes to a decentralized form, and the culture changes also.

1.3 Decentralized structures

The entrepreneurial clusters and self-managed forms (see Section 1.1) operate with dispersed sources of authority, freedom to challenge decisions and limited scope for rules, partly because they are small and partly because they have support cultures which encourage co-operation. We now look at forms of decentralization in larger organizations with achievement cultures, which value creativity, competition and independence.

Decentralized profit centres

A department, division, subsidiary or any unit defined by a market, or a technique to serve that market, can be turned into a profit centre with freedom to decide its own policy and strategies for reaching given goals. The task of the top managers (above unit level) is to

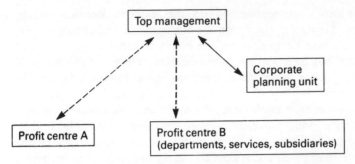

Figure 3.4 A decentralized form of organization; - - - indicates that
top management has only partial control over profit centres

determine long-term policies for the whole company, manage
corporate finances and arbitrate among profit centres (Figure 3.4).
The scope of the autonomy of each profit centre is limited to its own
particular operations, but there it can enforce its own decisions and,
from the parent business's point of view, those decision sources are
dispersed. The advantages of this type of decentralization are as
follows:

- top managers are freed from having to make short-term decisions;
- it provides intrinsic satisfactions to those who head the profit
  centres;
- it is flexible because it puts decision-making closer to the scene of
  action.

There are also disadvantages or difficulties, however:

- it requires capable managers;
- the centre head may maximize short-run profits at the expense of
  corporate long-term goals;
- provision of support services to each centre may add to
  administrative costs;
- there are centrifugal tendencies which top management may not
  be able to curb.

Collegiate structure

This is the form of 'bottom up' decision-making that is found in
many academic institutions. The faculty members serve on
committees which decide the policies for their own departments.

Departments are represented on the supreme decision-making bodies. However, there can be antagonism and 'rubbish bin' decisions (see Chapter 6) to the extent that the term 'organized anarchy' has been applied to universities. Wilson (1985) describes 'Chaos College' where the innovations pursued by each department were at the expense of the integrity of the whole college. Some departments have much more influence than others because of their popularity with powerful outside interests – funding bodies, employers, schools and so on. However, the advantages of the decentralized profit centres can also apply to collegiate forms where major goals are shared.

Matrix structure

The collegiate form has sometimes been combined with the matrix (Figure 3.5). The latter co-ordinates activities at the point where they intersect. Each position in the matrix has at least two reporting links. In a college there may be differentiation by subject taught and by type

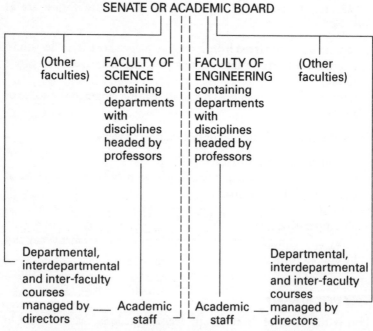

Figure 3.5 An example of matrix structure: ———, reporting relationships; - - - -, upwards representation

of course – undergraduate, postgraduate, short-course students and so on. A teacher of mathematics who is responsible to the professor of maths for pursuit of scholarship in mathematics may be teaching maths to engineers and responsible to a director of undergraduate engineering courses for collaboration with specialists from other disciplines in furthering the aims of the course. The industrial equivalent of the 'subject-by-course' matrix would be the 'functional-by-product' matrix where, for example, a training specialist may report to both a personnel manager and a manufacturing manager. Matrix organizations may have dual assignments for certain managers, or a joint-planning process that spans the parts of the organization that are stable and those that change frequently. The Faculty Boards in the University example deal with five-year plans and frequent redesign of courses.

A power culture, because of its emphasis on central control and superior authority, has difficulty with a matrix structure. Similarly, a role culture does not approve the unscheduled meetings which help the smooth working of a matrix. The support culture may operate within a matrix, but it is the achievement culture which is most compatible with matrix structure requirements. Co-ordination is focused on *unlike* contributions to a common task, for example mathematicians and engineers to a degree course. (A support culture may emphasize the common interest in teaching but not give due weight to the different resource needs of the two subjects.) Galbraith (1971) suggests that a reason for using a matrix form is that previous attempts at co-ordination have not succeeded. The matrix may be used as part of a flexible bureaucracy (see below).

Flexible bureaucracy

Bureaucracy is often thought of as 'rule by bureaucrats' or officials. A 'classic bureaucracy' resembles this image (see Section 1.4 below). But the term 'flexible bureaucracy' is used by Lammers and Hickson to describe an organization where there are dispersed decision sources, local variations in rules and only partial enforcement. Indeed, among units, there may be relations which are similar to market relations in the economy, with parts of the organization charging other parts for services or for goods supplied. Raybould (1985) describes the Coats Patons group of companies in 1985 in terms which suggest a decentralized bureaucratic structure.

More people have had some element of their pay related to individual or company performance, or a combination of the two. The form of involvement varies enormously, from factory floor productivity schemes, added-value schemes, plant-wide profit-sharing and executive bonus schemes to a group-wide savings-related share option scheme.... Local autonomy, organization into smaller units, improved communication and concentration on the personal element in relationships has helped to provide greater awareness ... in the involvement and participation of the workforce.

(Raybould 1985: 42)

This organization would be bureaucratic on measures of specialization, standardization and formalization, developed by Pugh *et al.* (1969), but it is decentralized, not centralized, and the type of culture is one of achievement rather than role. Lammers and Hickson state that the flexible bureaucracy is characteristic of Anglo-Saxon countries, whereas the classic bureaucracy is more characteristic of Latin countries.

Before we consider the classic bureaucracy, let us summarize the design features of decentralized forms, since four variants have been described. What they have in common is that activities are spread across numerous occupations and sometimes across sites also. Dispersed centres of authority get power over their own operating decisions. Specialists of different occupations may be jointly responsible for common tasks, for example through task forces or project teams or committees, and persons may report to more than one superior. Decisions of broad scope which are taken by the top policy makers may still be challenged from below, and the scope of rules may be modified to allow for local circumstances.

1.4 Classic bureaucracy

Classic bureaucracies are said by Weber (1947) to have a *rational-legal* basis. This is because there are rational grounds for the division of labour, and because each official is employed under a contract that is legal in form. Classic bureaucracies grew out of the *line and staff* type of organization which was developed by armies. The front line soldiers do the fighting (called by systems theorists the 'primary task'). They are supported by staff in specialized units who transport and maintain their equipment, cook their food, pay their wages, treat casualties and so on.

Table 3.2 Classic bureaucracy

Possible objectives for jobs	Chain of command	Overlapping functional hierarchies		
National comprehensive service across all relevant fields	Top administrative grades	*Professional grades*		
Regional comprehensive service across all relevant fields	Administrative grades			
Local comprehensive service across all relevant fields	Higher executive grades		*Skilled*	
Systematic provision in one or two fields only	Executive grades			
Provision of a situational response	Clerical grades (counter staff etc.)			*Semi-skilled*
Working to objectives that can be specified completely	Some manual workers (e.g. cleaners)			

Notes: The objectives suggest possible 'horizons' of jobs in the various grades. The hierarchy represents an ascending order of discretion, based on qualifications and training, though the points of overlap are not exact. (There will be unskilled and semi-skilled trades in national and regional bureaux, but the *discretion* exercised in such jobs is less than that of professionals.) The solid line is the chain of authority and accountability.

Most bureaucracies are large and have tall hierarchies (Table 3.2). It is often assumed that they will be government agencies. But they can be found in businesses also when the centralized flat pyramid has grown tall. Pugh and his colleagues suggest that administrative control is exercised impersonally through appeal to procedures, and so a role culture is suitable.

Constas points out that a form of classic bureaucracy has endured for centuries in some societies. She states that the Pharoahs of ancient Egypt, the Chinese Emperors and the Pope all headed bureaucracies that were highly centralized. They did not rely solely on Weber's 'rational-legal' authority, however, nor did they have pure role cultures. It was believed that the rulers were divine or had a divine mandate. The bureaucracy was subservient to the special qualities or 'charisma' of the deity. This was vested in the office of the pharoahs, emperors or popes. The hierarchy of the Roman Catholic Church is still seen in this way, though it also has features of the collegiate structures described above (Section 1.3, 'Collegiate structure').

Elements of power and support cultures are found in these particular classic bureaucracies. Constas argues that this is also true of the bureaucracy of the USSR after 1917. It 'was elaborated after the revolution in which the Bolsheviks seized power and represents the institutionalization of that power'. The revolutionary doctrine provided the charisma that was 'routinized'. For over seventy years, powerful cultural forces prevented the move from a tall centralized hierarchy to decentralization with its attendant power sharing.

Another problem with bureaucracies is described by Lawrence and Lorsch (1967). People whose work is divided into separate specialisms come to have different priorities. They start serving different goals. Some need immediate results, others a long-term perspective. This growing apart is known as *differentiation*. The greater the amount of differentiation, the greater is the requirement for integration, or pulling together, (see also Chapter 9, Section 4.2, 'Differentiation/integration'). The internal boundaries need to be regulated, so that all parts work for the overall goals and not solely for subunit goals. This necessity leads to *hierarchy*. In the army the hierarchy extends from the private to the general. Each officer has his own command and is responsible for unique results. The whole organization has a pyramid shape. Argenti (1968) argues that the pyramid is at its best when it is flat, allowing rapid communication up and down, but many pyramids have grown tall.

> A manufacturing company is essentially an organization that buys components or materials, adds something to them in the production department that increases their value and sells them. These three functions, buying, production and selling, are the activities from which the company earns its profits – in some types of company a fourth activity must be added, namely transporting and distributing. . . . An advisory department's task is to comment upon how these physical operations are being done . . . (as the accounts department does with its costing system), or how it should be done (as the work study officer does) or what should be done in the future (as research, or planning, or marketing departments do). So important is it to choose the right thing to do

and to do it in the right way that the actual task of doing it is
gradually becoming of less importance.

(Argenti 1968: 148)

The number of services has proliferated. There are often several
hierarchies of different lengths, depending on the type of occupation
(Table 3.2). The pyramid cannot easily accommodate them all,
neither can the 'temple' – Handy's (1985) term for a classic
bureaucracy. The pillars of Handy's temple, the different functions,
are kept separate from bottom to top. The board of directors is like
the Grecian pediment, which can unify a stable structure but which
falls when there is an earthquake. Bureaucratic procedures may be so
geared to regulation that the variety in the environment cannot be
met through extra appreciation (see Table 2.4).

Hannan and Freeman (1977, 1984) believe that the past successes
of temple structures are an obstacle to redesign from within.
Upwards accountability means that each level is monitored by the
level above. This hierarchy leads to structural inertia. Performance
which has served in the past gets repeated. For this reason, when
circumstances change, classic bureaucracies do not transform
themselves but may die and be replaced by newer organizations.

Fligstein (1985), however, reports research that suggests that it is
not the inertia of the structure so much as the inertia of those who
occupy the institutional roles in the structure that prevents
adaptation.

Where the classic design ceases to serve, the designers can choose
a flexible form or a hybrid form, and this frequently occurs. Pugh and
his colleagues (1968) used the term 'full bureaucracy' instead of
'classic' because they believed they had discovered several partial
forms. They drew profiles of particular organizations indicating the
degree to which they resembled the classic case. They correlated the
number of employees with their measures of concentrated authority,
impersonal controls, levels of specialization, standardization and
formalization. The more employees there were, the more likely it was
that a full bureaucracy would be found. (Conversely, the fewer the
employees, the more likely it was that the organization would be only
'implicitly structured'.) The classic bureaucracy is, then, an attempt
to control large concerns through hierarchical decision-making and
impersonal relationships. It usually has a role culture.

1.5 Hybrid forms

A hybrid is a mixed form likely to be found in very large concerns. Table 3.1 and Figure 3.1. together suggest that a hybrid is an attempt to achieve balance between preparing for the future (by appreciation) and keeping operational and technical control (by regulation).

National hybrids

State enterprises may be hybrids, as may any concerns that are large enough to be operating in several environments. The activities, decision-making, authority patterns and relationships are all varied. The hybrid concern is attempting to run 'steady state' operations where conditions are stable, while maintaining a readiness to innovate in unstable conditions (see Chapter 10, Section 3.1).

There are many ways in which organizations can grow into hybrids. Public bodies may be set up by legislation and extended through government or local finance. Businesses may plough back their profits into extending their operations, they may borrow more finance, they may take over or merge with other businesses. Some organizations seek to remain distinctive by staying in one industry, and so they grow by taking over their supplier or their outlets (vertical integration). Other organizations may grow territorially, or by extending their clientele, while continuing to provide the same service. Organizations known as conglomerates have grown by diversifying into areas of business unrelated to their previous ones.

A conglomerate may have a holding company form at the centre (a legal device through which a small central office manages the portfolio of investments) and subunits that operate as independent companies. Alternatively, the centre may be the locus for long-range planning and finance, with divisions elsewhere based either on products or territory.

Whatever the design, the directors have to ensure dividends for the owners, who may be large institutions (such as pension funds) whose stake is a purely financial one. 'Critical theorists' (see Chapter 10, Section 2.4, 'Critical social science') oppose such capitalist forms of organization because the legal framework allows the directors (or 'dominant coalition') to sell off businesses over the heads of those who work for them. Ellerman says:

The capitalist corporation is indeed the only major human organization in our present society which has owners who may buy and sell it as a piece of property.

(1983: 271)

Ellerman argues further that it is because employees only have the legal status of hired servants that they have no voice in divestment decisions which harm them.

Without the employment relation, the corporation would be an empty legal shell holding certain assets which could only be remuneratively employed by renting them out. . . . From the viewpoint of organizational democracy, it is the renting of human beings, the employment relation, that is the problem.

(1983: 272)

The problem of organizational democracy, or how the boards of businesses can represent many 'constituencies', is especially acute when the conglomerate is a transnational corporation (TNC), or a multinational enterprise (MNE).

Transnational hybrids

Firms have

initially sought foreign markets for their domestically produced products in order to further utilize productive capacity. If their products sell well in host countries, the parent firm may then establish regional marketing operations in these areas to assure a continuing market. Finally, in order both to achieve transportation economies and to further relations with host governments, production facilities may be constructed in these host countries through direct investment or joint ventures.

(Miles and Snow, 1978: 132)

The TNC which has been successful will move into yet more countries, and become multinational. It is both a strategic and a design decision how far such an MNE decentralizes its operations, training indigenous managers to assume responsibility, and how far it reserves all major positions to nationals of the owning group.

Let us look further at the power which the boards of MNEs can wield. Dunning outlines some of the consequences of the present system. He says that where disposition [of resources] is decided by private capital in promotion of its own goals, it does not follow that the resulting distribution of output will be consistent with that which the countries in which the MNEs operate are seeking. This new international division of labour is certainly accelerating the relocation of some industrial sectors from older to newer industrialized countries.

(Dunning 1985: 15)

The MNE can open up operations or close them down according to the perceptions of its top managers of what will serve its objectives as it seeks global profits for its investors. If it pulls out of a country it can sometimes adversely affect not only its own workforce but also that country's economy. Thus a lot of power is being exercised.

Dunning is particularly concerned with the structural changes at national level in Britain which have been affected by the decisions of MNEs on where, and in what, to invest.

Technological innovation has made communication over large distances quick and reliable. Investment in one country may well be financed from profits made in another part of the world. In what Patterson and Stevenson (1986) call 'the firm of the future' there will be computer integrated manufacturing with a core of 'permanent' staff at any given place, but also a periphery of temporary workers who can be called upon to supplement the core, possibly working from their own homes in another country.

Another fairly recent development is that trade, which used to be carried on between separately owned organizations, can now be conducted under the umbrella of common ownership. According to the United Nations (which created a Commission on TNCs in 1974), over 30 per cent of world trade in 1985 was intra-firm.

Marlow comments:

Multinationals are very nearly in the position of being unloved and unwanted; that this is not quite the case is because of their actual and potential contribution to the provision of goods and services and the creation of wealth so desperately needed by one third of mankind.

(Marlow 1984: 301)

Perhaps the problem is not so much who owns the MNEs as how to make sure that others who have legitimate interests are also influential. This leads to consideration of the role of governments and of the international community.

Dunning points out that in the nineteenth century government intervention helped industry to settle by providing public utilities, but in the late twentieth century the equivalent attractions are airports, motorways, colleges and universities and an efficient economic system. He cites Japan as

> the classic example of a case in which industry and government can work harmoniously together to promote a positive and yet well articulated policy towards both inward and outward MNE activity.
>
> (Dunning 1985: 18)

Many countries do not have the economic power that Japan can wield, which is why the United Nations set up its Commission. That body, at the time of writing, has not been able to agree more than a draft code for regulating the activities of MNEs, though member countries of the Organization of Economic Co-operation and Development (OECD) have signed a code to prevent the worst abuses. It seems likely that MNEs will also find themselves more and more constrained by the 'instruments' that the European Community will develop.

Indeed, Marlow (1984) thinks that a new breed of corporate leaders must reconcile some of the conflicts attributable to the success of MNEs. Part of the design for MNEs in the 1990s should be 'a well-established multi-national secretariat representing the considered views and interests of multi-nationals the world over'. (p. 304).

After the MNE we need to be able to design the 'pro-world' enterprise. The United Nations is a candidate, but its future shape and resourcing is not yet clear. We shall have to learn fast how to tackle global problems and international emergencies.

2 DISCUSSION: A SEQUENCE OF DESIGNS

Quinn and Cameron (1983) summarize eight models of organizational 'life cycles', each of which has an entrepreneurial stage, a collectivity stage (similar to the adhocracy), a stage where structure is elaborated (and decentralized) and a formalization of control (bureaucratic) stage. But there is great variation in how long any stage may last. They comment that

> none of the models is concerned with organizational decline and

death.... This may be because in mature organizations ... life cycle models break down.... In the small group literature however it has been found that groups frequently return to earlier stages.

(Quinn and Cameron 1983: 40)

Discussion of the dynamics of change in small groups can be found in Chapter 7 (Section 3). For organizations we might consider a learning-cycle rather than a life-cycle model. There are experiences to be reflected upon, inferences to be made and modifications to structure to be introduced. These changes form the basis for more reflection. When problems recur, new elements can be distinguished from familiar ones and new solutions tried. A learning cycle is not just 'going round in circles'. It is more like an upward spiral of developing capabilities.

How might the capabilities of organizations be judged? Quinn and Cameron produced a summary of effectiveness criteria which includes the values shown in capital letters in Table 3.1. They think organizations are judged differently at different stages in their 'lives' (or learning cycles). They cite the case of a Development Center for treatment of the mentally disabled. Its first head was a charismatic psychiatrist. The Center was entrepreneurial and the staff had 'almost missionary dedication and zeal'. The Center was praised for this COLLABORATION and for the INNOVATIONs in its programme. However, some years later, a series of adverse newspaper reports criticized the Center for INEFFICIENCY and inadequate accounting for public monies. The New York State's Department of Mental Hygiene, the Center's parent department, intervened, insisting on more formalization. The psychiatrist left soon after, and a more administratively minded person, who emphasized control, was appointed as head. Staff morale dropped and more staff left. The initial support and achievement culture was replaced by a power and role culture.

According to the competing values approach of Quinn and McGrath (1985), two aspects of the environment are critical in determining the most appropriate structure and culture. The first is the degree of uncertainty or certainty, and the second is the degree to which an immediate response is required, the urgency, or intensity in their terms, of environmental demands. The entrepreneurial cluster or clan can deal with high uncertainty, but a more centralized approach is needed to deal with high uncertainty combined with high intensity. A more decentralized approach can respond to urgent operating situations, provided that these are not combined with high uncertainty also. The hierarchical form of the classic bureaucracy is best suited to conditions in which there is neither high intensity nor high uncertainty.

Greiner (1972) (see Chapter 2) suggested that each new design is an attempt to rectify the problems created by the previous one. It is a form of incremental decision-making (see Chapter 6, Section 2.2, 'Incrementalism'). Touraine suggested that the desire on the part of individuals for autonomy to pursue their own self-interests is in conflict with the need for unity in the system, and so the design swings first one way and then the other. Skinner and Winckler (1980) (see Chapter 1) posited three types of goals which are best realized by different types of power. From their descriptions we can surmise that the cluster would be best for ideological goals, the centralized or bureaucratic forms for order goals and the decentralized or hybrid forms for economic goals.

Whoever is taking redesign decisions will be forced to make tradeoffs. Some values can only be realized at the expense of others. A productive and efficient concern may be profitable in the short run, satisfying present customers and shareholders. If it does not organize for new product development, however, it will lose potential customers and decline. Products have a life cycle for which an organization must be prepared. Thus the timing of organizational redesign is as important as the model chosen. There is no perfect or permanent solution, only small or large transformations (see Chapter 9). An organization has many different 'stake-holders' whose interests may conflict. The power to back such interests is unequal.

3 SUMMARY

Organizational design is the creation of structures which provide for activities, decision-making authority and relationships at work. To create the type of organization desired (for example one which is externally and internally innovative, productive, efficient and collaborative) there are four main areas to consider. What is the organization trying to do? How is it to do it? What administrative arrangements does it need now, or might it need for the future? These four areas are addressed through five different types of organizational design: the cluster or self-managed group, the centralized concern, decentralized forms of various kinds, the classic bureaucracy and hybrid forms. Over a long period of time all of these designs may succeed one another in the same enterprise.

The entrepreneurial cluster is suited to close scanning of the market. It is egalitarian, informal and friendly. So is the self-managed group. Both are compatible with a support culture.

The centralized form is an attempt to unify and control operations once the enterprise has too many employees to rely on agreement among them. It concentrates decision-making in one or two offices, has vertical communication and has deferential relationships consistent with a power culture.

The decentralized structures use dispersed decision-making in an attempt to locate decisions near the points where action occurs. Relationships tend to be dictated by the nature of the work being done. Different professions may be expected to collaborate for common goals. The achievement culture is suited to these structures.

The classic bureaucracy uses numerous specialists whose activities are co-ordinated by a hierarchy in which each level is accountable to the level above. Relationships are formal and governed by regulations. The role culture is likely to be most compatible here.

Hybrid cultures are attempts to deal simultaneously with problems of internal control and external responsiveness – issues discussed in cyclical theories. One form of hybrid, the multinational corporation, is large enough to be able to influence national economies for good or ill. International bodies such as the OECD and the United Nations are concerned with the legal framework governing corporations. It is impossible to attain all desired values through organizational design. There have to be tradeoffs. Other things being equal, **culture affects organization design through a preference for centralized or decentralized forms**.

FURTHER READING

A useful general text is:

Child, J. (1984) *Organization: a guide to problems and practice*, 2nd edn, New York: Harper & Row.

More specialized, but readable is:

Lorsch, J.W. and Lawrence, P.R. (1970) *Studies in Organization Design*, Ontario: Irwin-Dorsey.

There are also some large books with useful chapters which you should find in a good library:

Crouch, C. and Heller, F. (1983) *International Yearbook of Organizational Democracy*, vol. 1, New York: Wiley, contains, as Chapter 28, Lockett, M., 'Organizational democracy and politics in China'.
Folkertsma, B. (ed.) (1972) *Handbook for Managers*, London: Kluwer Harrap, is a looseleaf cumulative publication which contains Argenti, J., 'The pyramid, the ladder and the matrix', taken from *Management Decision*, Autumn 1968.
Nystrom, P.C. and Starbuck, W. (eds) (1981) *Handbook of Organizational Design*, Oxford: Oxford University Press.

For some developing country approaches see:

Blunt, P. (1983) *Organizational Theory and Behaviour: an African Perspective*, London: Longman.
Onyemelukwe, C.C. (1973) *Men and Management in Contempory Africa*, London: Longman.
Prasad, G.K. (1974) *Bureaucracy in India: A Sociological Study*, New York: Very.

For multinationals see:

Brooke, M.Z. and Remmers, H.L. (1978) *The Strategy of Multinational Enterprise*, 2nd edn, London: Pitman.
Franko, L.G. (1977) *The European Multinationals: a renewed challenge to American and British Big Business*, New York: Harper & Row.
Stopford, J.M. and Wells, L.T. (1972) *Managing Multinational Enterprise*, London: Longman.

For entrepreneurs see the following book and article:

Deeks, J. (1976) *The Small Firm Owner-Manager*, New York: Praeger.
Johannisson, B. (1984) 'A cultural perspective on small business – local business climate', *International Small Business Journal* 2 (2): 32–41.

RECOMMENDED EXERCISE

'A Social Services Department': You use position titles as a basis for designing an organization.

RECOMMENDED CASE STUDY

'The Student Loans Board': A problem concerning the level in a hierarchy that should deal with sensitive external relations, and a problem of differentiation between higher administrative and lower executive grades within a hierarchy.

Chapter 4

Cultures and the design of jobs

CHAPTER OBJECTIVES

By the end of this chapter you will be able to:

1 cite six design principles
2 distinguish between four major purposes of job design suggested by the cultural examples
3 explain the advantages and disadvantages of keeping jobs simple, and give nine principles for designing work this way
4 cite nine principles for creating complex (enriched) jobs, and explain the advantages and problems associated with doing this
5 explain what is meant by joint optimization of a social and technical system
6 analyse the recommended cases

1 INTRODUCTION TO JOB DESIGN

Technically, 'job design' refers to the planned content of a job. It includes the methods to be used and the layout of workstations. Job designers must decide which tasks are to be isolated and which combined. Will people work alone or in groups? What technology is available? How will any materials needed be delivered and removed? What about the servicing of equipment, and the monitoring of performance? What facilities must be provided for the health and safety of employees? Unique answers will be specified in any comprehensive design, but a consistent perspective is possible as recommended in the first principle of Table 4.1.

This table suggests six principles to guide designers. It also connects these principles with other forms of design. First, consistency is desirable. Previous chapters have indicated that

Table 4.1   Designing a job or organization compared with design in the visual arts

Principles	Applications	
	to a job or to an organization	*to visual arts*
	Form/structure of a job or organization	Photography, painting
1 Work from some consistent perspective (ruling values)	Support, power, achievement or role cultures	Surrealism, expressionism, pop etc.
2 Seek to produce an overall effect	Cost-effective performance, employee well-being	Pleasure, or impact
3 Predict consequences	For labour markets, education, customers	For taste, fashion, styles
4 Respect the constraints which apply	Skills shortages, demand for employment, age structure of the society	Patron's wishes, display site etc.
5 Take reactions of stakeholders into account	Of workers and managers, the public, the government	Of the artists, investors, the public
6 Use knowledge of the behaviour of the resources to be used	Organizational behaviour	Properties of paint, canvas, film

Source: Adapted from Binsted 1980
Note: Compare the organizational development principles in Chapter 9, Section 3.

the values of the organizational cultures serve to provide this consistency.

The second principle speaks of an overall effect. Ultimately this effect is some change in the environment – goods and services sent out, customers satisfied, employment opportunities provided, subscribers prepared to give support and so on.

To implement the third principle, some part of the organization has to be scanning the labour market for signs of skill shortages or surpluses. Before current product brands reach maturity, preparations must be made for the jobs needed to replace the brands with new ones.

The fourth principle suggests that choice of technology (in the broadest sense of 'ways of working') is constrained by such things as the capital available, the skills of the labour force and so on. Internal stability may be upset by technological innovation that has not been properly introduced. External uncertainty may render a given technology obsolete while it is still under consideration.

The stakeholders referred to in the fifth principle are those who can affect the success of the working arrangements adopted. Finally, to design jobs or organizational structures, it is necessary to use such knowledge as we have of how people behave and how enterprises operate.

This chapter directs attention to how the four cultures affect job design, and how the principles in Table 4.1 can be applied. The first two of these principles are interconnected. The perspective influences the effect sought. The purposes of job design can be thought of:

1 from a power culture perspective, as to control a workforce;
2 from a support culture perspective, as to enrich the quality of working life;
3 from an achievement culture perspective, as to match the environment and human being to get results;
4 from a role culture perspective, as to create a sociotechnical system.

We shall consider these in turn and finally (in Section 3) ask about the place of job design in relation to the wider question of employment, noting also the relevance of the remaining four design principles in Table 4.1.

2 TYPES OF CULTURE AND PURPOSES FOR JOB DESIGN

2.1 To control a workforce – the power culture

In eighteenth-century Britain, workers were herded into the new factories as 'hands' whose task was to 'tend' machines. In the woollen and cotton industries men, women and child machine-minders were bullied by harsh supervisors to do as much work as they could physically handle. Control was easy for employers because poverty prevented the workers from complaining (and so risking the loss of their livelihood).

It was late in the nineteenth century, however, that F.W. Taylor deliberately designed jobs according to what he called 'scientific management'. Taylor experimented with the conditions under which a worker could shovel the maximum amount of pig iron, by varying the tools, layout and instructions. After his 'time and motion' study, a worker had only to provide the energy. Tasks of assembling components of manufactured products were (and often still are) broken down into the simplest possible elements, with each element assigned to a different worker. The classic example of simplified work is the assembly line, where each worker performs a single operation on the product as it passes by on the track. Each worker's pace is determined by the speed of the track, which is controlled by management. It was argued that the simpler the job, the greater would be the firm's efficiency because

1 training time is very short, and so training costs are low;
2 it is easy to replace workers without loss of production;
3 consistency of output can be readily checked;
4 aggregate performance can be used as a basis of wages, and so that costs are lower when output is lower:
5 recording of workshop performance for control purposes is easier.

The overall effect that Taylor sought was high productivity from a docile workforce. He believed that if the relationship between effort and reward was clear the average worker would perform so as to earn a reasonable wage. He predicted that the consequences of his system would be increased output, which would be good for employers and for the economy. Opponents of Taylor's work simplification claim, however, that the advantages listed above are outweighed by the disadvantages. People who are used as 'hands' will utilize their brains in ways which may defeat the system. In this they can be very successful. The best known example is the 'bank wiring room' at the Hawthorne plant of the Western Electric Company, studied in the late 1920s, and described by Roethlisberger *et al.* (1939). The small group of men there regularly produced an output of 6,000 units per day, even though they were capable of producing many more. Such collective regulation of output is a common device of workers against what they see as attempts at exploitation. Employers' response to worker 'restriction of output' has sometimes been to create a new job of 'expediter' or 'progress chaser' to hurry jobs through the various stages of production and out to the customer. The employment of such personnel adds to the indirect costs of production, thus decreasing overall efficiency. 'Scientific management' is less successful in controlling a workforce than it claims to be.

A second source of criticism comes from Marxist 'Critical Theory'. As early as 1844, Karl Marx said that the worker:

> does not affirm himself, but denies himself, does not feel content but unhappy, does not develop freely his physical and mental energy, but mortifies his body and ruins his mind. The worker therefore only feels himself outside his work, and in his work feels outside himself. He is at home when he is not working, and when he is working he is not at home.
>
> (Marx, in Burns 1960: 99)

This condition is known as 'alienation'. Critical theorists are concerned both with the dehumanizing effects of alienation and with the ways in which the capitalist class uses job design to dominate the working class. They argue that the attempt to minimize the control which workers themselves exercise over their jobs tends to be more effective when there is a large pool of unskilled unemployed. Sometimes there are 'dual labour markets'; certain jobs are reserved, for example, for men only, or for 'whites only'. Employers uphold social distinctions when they offer alienating work to ethnic minorities or part-time women workers. At all events, argue Critical theorists, employers have only been ready to introduce an improved quality of working life when demotivation or labour shortages have threatened efficiency and profits. For this reason Critical theorists are as sceptical of the philosophy and process of job enrichment (see below) as they are of scientific management. They believe that job enrichment also aims at a docile workforce, but docile by consent rather than docile because of weakness. Job enrichment can be 'part of the subtle apparatus to control by consent with which management attempts to secure hegemony' (Clegg 1983). Let us see how job enrichment differs from Taylor's principles.

2.2 To enrich the quality of working life – the support culture

Davis and Taylor (1972) set out the principal distinctions between simple and complex jobs. These are listed below.

Taylor's principles *Simple jobs involve*	*Job enrichment principles* *Complex jobs involve*
repetition	variety
minimal skill	challenge to skill
minimal discretion	considerable autonomy

confinement to one work
  station
	opportunity to interact
	  socially.

very small transformation to product/service	meaningful, large, visible transformation,
very short cycle time	longer time to complete
constant pace	variable pace
minimal knowledge, planning and control	considerable knowledge, planning and control
predetermined quality standard	quality judgement

The overall effect sought from job enrichment is personal satisfaction for those who do the jobs in question, with a chance for abilities to be used. For this reason it is classed here as illustrating a support culture.

The ways by which greater complexity may be introduced into jobs so as to enrich them are by (a) job rotation, (b) horizontal job enlargement, (c) vertical job enlargement and (d) the creation of 'autonomous working groups'. The provision of more complex work is stated to be required for personal growth and development. Critical theorists argue that such notions play into the hands of managers who will redesign jobs on these lines to get the support of workers. The methods will be described in turn.

Job rotation

Workers can change places from time to time. Under this system the job of each worker may be simple, but variety is introduced as they swap places. In a packaging department, for example, there may be machines for filling bottles, capping them and labelling them, and machines for making cartons. Workers may put the full bottles and any other items, such as leaflets or packing pieces, into the cartons by hand. The last operation may be to erect corrugated containers, pack these with the filled cartons for shipping, seal them and stack them on pallets. These operations are all semi-skilled and may be laid out in a horseshoe-shaped line. Workers can learn to carry out any number of the tasks, instead of staying put at one position on the line.

Horizontal job enlargement

A given workstation may be allocated more to do – thus the cycle time is extended. This change may also mean that the transformation to the product is more obvious. The enlargement is 'horizontal' in the sense that the level of difficulty is constant. The operator may assemble a complete radio instead of only sub-parts, for example.

Vertical job enlargement

All work involves a certain amount of planning and control as well as of execution. Under 'scientific management', however, Taylor (1911) insisted that 'all possible brainwork should be removed from the shop floor, and centred in the planning and layout department'. Vertical job enlargement restores to the worker some of the responsibilities which Taylor removed. It is also known as 'job enrichment' because it contributes to self-esteem. Indeed, the term 'job enrichment' is sometimes reserved solely for this type of design, where added responsibility for planning and for quality control indicates to a person that he or she is being trusted to exercise judgement. A British example of vertical job enlargement can be found in the case study 'Job enrichment in the British National Health Service'.

Autonomous working groups

Group tasks, rather than individual tasks, are taken as the unit for enrichment for autonomous work groups. Such groups can be thought of as part of a decentralized system of roles, so further discussion of them is kept for Section 2.4 below. We turn now to the question of the interchange between the environment and human beings which can occur at the place of work.

2.3 To match the environment and human being – the achievement culture

This perspective does not focus either on controlling people or on helping them to develop in their work. Instead, it focuses on the combined characteristics of tasks and of people. The overall effect sought is high productivity through the best use of people and equipment in suitable surroundings.

Two areas of study deal with the general fit of the environment to human beings. At the broadest level there is human ecology, while at the micro-level there is ergonomics. Each is briefly described. (See Chapter 5 for matching people to jobs.)

Human ecology

Human ecology is 'the study of human organisms in relation to the physical and social environment which constitutes their life space'. It deals with much more than work. It is concerned with the degree to which the total environment is favourable or harmful to humans, with what climatic and other deprivations and extremes humans can tolerate and with how human behaviour changes in new settings. In some parts of the world the livelihood of whole tribes is threatened by natural disasters or human interference. A people may have to change their whole way of life, or become extinct. To a lesser extent, migrants may have to survive culture shock. The issues go beyond job design to lifestyle. Nevertheless, human ecology does impinge on work, and so on job design. Barker and Gump (1964), for example, have studied such matters as the effect of the size of schools on student behaviour. While there are aspects of the natural environment that cannot easily be changed, plans can be made for buildings and for those who occupy them. Physical layout makes it hard or easy for people to meet each other, and the arrangement and style of furnishing encourages or discourages informality.

Ergonomics

Ergonomics is 'the application of the human sciences to the study of work' (and to domestic and leisure activities). It is the Western European name for what Americans call 'human factors engineering', though there are some differences. Ergonomics pays as much attention to health and well-being as to efficiency, and so it incorporates a stronger contribution from anatomy, physiology and medicine. Human factors engineering is more concerned with the efficiency of humans as components of systems – astronauts in aerospace technology for example. Human imagination may be more inventive than machines, yet human error may contribute to accidents which cause damage, injury or loss of life. It is important both to make the most of human capabilities and to get rid of conditions which increase the risks to humans.

The physical aspects of working conditions, such as heating, lighting, ventilation, humidity and noise received attention in the UK during the First World War, because it was necessary to maintain the health and safety of munitions workers if the war was to be won. It was also important to know when work might be impaired through fatigue, and how fatigue might be reduced. Experiments were conducted to find out the total number of hours that could be safely worked, how many rest pauses were needed and how long the pauses should be. More recently, shift-working and jet lag have been examined for any stressful effects. Experiments connecting stress with colour indicated that some colours are depressing and others are stimulating. The wrong background colour can create general malaise, but colour correctly employed can enhance efficiency. It can do so, for example, by enabling workers to distinguish different things they have to use in their work. Electric wiring is a familiar example. Conduits carrying different liquids may also be colour-coded.

Ergonomists hope that knowledge of human physical and mental capacities will be used at the design stage of equipment, machinery and products. The fourth design principle in Table 4.1 is especially relevant. Constraints are imposed by the human sensory and nervous system, mental perception and muscular co-ordination and control. Since many jobs now include the use of monitoring devices such as dials, screens and visual displays, it is important that the technology is 'user friendly'. In the past, engineers often created machines before they considered the job of the machine operator. People could be obliged to make awkward movements or to adopt uncomfortable postures. The interaction between machines and humans is now a key area of ergonomics. Technology, however, is not just machinery. It is the full range of methods employed to produce a given result. In Section 2.4 we consider the jobs done by people from the point of view of systems theory.

2.4 To create a sociotechnical system – the role culture

People relate to one another at work through the roles they adopt, and so a perspective which stresses such linkages can be labelled a role culture perspective, though it is much more than this. It sees the task and person as components of something larger, and so might more fairly be classed as 'integrated'. It does, however, demonstrate a concern for the value of rationality which is a key value in role cultures. The overall effect sought is one in which manual and clerical work is properly connected to other operations so that the organization functions well as a total system. The 'socio' part of the system is the ways in which its human members relate to one another. The technical part is the methods used to convert the inputs into outputs. The interrelationship between the technical and the social is crucial for economic effectiveness. The social should not be subordinated to the technical (as can happen with work simplification) nor should the technical be subordinated to the social (as can happen with job enrichment). Instead, they should be jointly optimized.

Trist and Bamforth (1951), from the Tavistock Institute of Human Relations in London, pioneered the sociotechnical approach in the British coal mines in the late 1940s. The industry had just been nationalized and greater mechanization was introduced. The conventional work-simplification approach (of subdividing tasks) was adopted when the change from hand-got to mechanized conveyor-belt technology made it possible to work long coal faces instead of short ones. The miners, however, lost out because they were deprived of some of their skills and of the types of small-group support to which they had been accustomed. In spite of mechanization, this conventional system was unproductive. Trist and Bamforth demonstrated that substitution of a 'composite' method of working, based on multi-skilled groups, could exploit the benefits of the new technology without sacrificing the social organization. The composite method was much more productive, and there were fewer accidents. The technical and the social could be jointly optimized through locating responsibility for the co-ordination of tasks, and for control over performance, to the people who were actually doing the work.

A colleague of Trist, Ken Rice, was the first to attempt to apply the concept of a sociotechnical system to the design of a production process in India. When he arrived at a mill in Ahmedabad he found that activities were broken down in accordance with work-simplification principles. This fragmentation meant that, in what was to be the Experimental Automatic Shed, there was no collection of workers smaller than the total shift of twenty-eight and no sense of community. Rice's contribution was to reorganize the shift into four groups, each with its own leader. The groups were autonomous in that each had control of its own internal activities while the shift supervisor dealt with 'external relations' with higher management and other departments. Friendships could form within the groups and there was considerable improvement in efficiency and reduction in damage (Rice 1958).

A follow-up study, some fifteen years later, revealed that the group system installed by Rice continued to function in the Calico Experimental Shed where it was known by its English name. (Apparently there is no generalized concept of 'group' in the Gujarati or Hindi languages.)

Miller (1975) concluded that the persistence of Rice's method in the Experimental Shed, but not elsewhere, was made possible by the surrounding conditions. The business environment favoured a 'steady state' here because the cloth woven 'was a product for which there was a reliable market, and in which few if any improvements in quality standards' had been required since 1954. For the other sheds, however, things were different – marginal improvements in output or quality could help the company to secure new markets. Supervisors therefore tended to pressurize workers instead of assisting the group leaders to find solutions for their groups. The single-minded pursuit of efficiency goals led to interventions which reduced the resilience of the groups, and led to their partial disintegration. Most of the workers had, in any case, been taken on since Rice's departure. Individuals in groups which are not successful tend to look for individual recognition, and this further destroys co-operation. (See Chapter 7 for more about groups.)

The concept of managing 'boundary conditions' is important in the idea of a sociotechnical system. If pressures from the outside world become too strong the internal system changes. We turn, therefore, to the question of job design in relation to the whole field of employment.

3 EMPLOYMENT AND JOB DESIGN

The first two principles of Table 4.1 have been illustrated in the preceding sections. Here the broader aspects of work are considered. What employers do has consequences for the level of employment and education (principle 3) and what the age structure of society is has consequences for job design (principle 4). Reactions beyond those of job holders must be considered (principle 5) as must the way capital and labour markets operate (principle 6).

Work can be performed by people or by machines or by some combination of the two. Economic considerations, of the relative cost of alternative methods in relation to the return on investment, determine managerial decisions under private enterprise. State enterprise may be expected to 'break even' over time, that is, to make neither loss nor profit. Loss would have to be made good by tax-payers, and substantial profits would be seen as a burden on consumers. In planned economies state enterprises may have their goals set for them by their political masters. It is against this economic background that we now review the purposes of job design.

3.1 Employment and control

Employers will not normally use labour-intensive methods if it is cheaper to use capital-intensive technology. In developing countries, however, the pool of unemployed is sometimes so large that governments may, for social and political reasons, subsidize employers who engage in overmanning. In India, for example, Glen and James (1980) describe how a manufacturer of metal products wanted, in spite of extra cost, to add a larger-sized product model to a line. It would have been cheaper to take up the sales potential on an existing model through increasing productivity. Glen and James discovered that:

> the new line would permit many more new employees who, although not anticipated to be fully utilized, would nevertheless be on the payroll. Management's preferred solution, therefore, called for a less profitable investment and a resultant increase in 'fixed' labor cost. The government edict to hire more and more people plays havoc with any optimization of Operations Research activities.
>
> (1980: 43)

Operations research (or operational research as it is known in Europe) is one of many techniques that stem from the tradition of scientific management (see Chapter 9, Section 4.1). Job design to control a workforce is associated with work measurement techniques which, it is claimed, can operate within an error tolerance of ± 5 per cent (Smith 1983). If, however, a government pays for people to be under-employed rather than unemployed, there is reduced productivity, and no amount of job redesign or measurement can alter this fact. We can ask, however, whether overmanning will simply result in more idle time, or whether the slack in the system can be used for job enrichment.

3.2 Employment and job enrichment

In many developing countries there is a fluctuating number of casual workers who drift between agricultural and industrial employment on a seasonal basis. Such a state of affairs does not favour job enrichment. Glueck (1977) suggested the following types of hindrances:

1 *Workers*
   do not identify with their place of work
   have low growth needs
   lack confidence and fear change
2 *Resources*
   have been committed to forms of technology which cannot readily be modified, while the organization's ability to deal with new technology is low
3 *Working conditions* are such that
   it would be economically or technically unrealistic to allow variability in the way job situations are handled
   information cannot readily be provided to give feedback to workers because of cost and data collection problems
4 *The organizational culture*
   is power-oriented, concerned primarily with production, regarding job enrichment only as a means for increasing output

Many of Glueck's hindrances to job enrichment can be found in developed as well as developing countries. In the UK, however, in spite of adverse trading conditions, the position is not altogether bleak for those who advocate improvements to the quality of working life. In 1973, a Tripartite Steering Group on Job Satisfaction was set up which had representatives of the Confederation of British Industry (CBI) the Trade Union Congress (TUC), and the Government. It produced a report in 1975 which summarized the benefits which could be obtained from improved job design as follows:

For workers	For management	For both
more interesting work	better quality	improved
scope for development	reduced	industrial
more autonomy	absence/labour	relations
companionship and	turnover	climate
team pride	more flexibility	
share in any employer	higher productivity	organizational
benefits (i.e. higher		growth
pay)		

In the summer and autumn of 1977, a survey was carried out (Ursell 1983) which looked at the views of 185 British managers and 184 shop stewards on the sharing of power and authority in industry. Job redesign, along with work-group meetings, was treated as a 'soft' form of industrial democracy, while the extension of collective bargaining rights and the appointment of worker directors were treated as 'hard' forms. Only 11 per cent of stewards and 27 per cent of managers were against both forms of industrial democracy. Soft forms only were favoured by 34 per cent of managers and 5 per cent of stewards, while a combination of soft and hard forms was favoured by 34 per cent of managers and 70 per cent of stewards. (The remainder favoured hard forms only.) As the Critical Theorists suggested, managers tend to be primarily interested in job redesign for its contribution towards greater harmony at work.

3.3 Employment and matching jobs to people

We turn now to another feature of job design that may increase satisfaction – job matching. We referred above (Section 2.3) to an array of specialists in human ecology and ergonomics. In conditions where labour supply is plentiful, managers may give lower priority to reviewing the health and safety aspects of job design, or to the goodness of fit between the job and the person. (see Chapter 5 for further discussion of this). However, there are often shortages of certain categories of employee even at times of high unemployment, and so pressures towards market competitiveness may encourage firms, especially those with achievement cultures, to see that there are not too many unsuitable jobs. Countries which have high power-distance cultures, however, may use management styles that resemble more closely those used in the early days of the industrial revolution in the UK, where people were just 'hands'. Firms are mostly unconcerned about working conditions as long as people still want jobs with them.

3.4 Employment and sociotechnical systems

What of the sociotechnical purpose of job design? When work groups are given more control of their internal activities, fewer supervisors will be needed, while the work of those supervisors who remain will be upgraded, because they will have time to think and plan ahead. Kemp *et al.* (1980) tell how, in a British sweet factory, the work group began to put pressure on the various management service departments. They wanted smoother planning and better sales performance to dispose of their increased output! Unless sales are rising, managers may be reluctant to embark on the creation of autonomous working groups. Many of the considerations suggested by Glueck above (Section 3.2) also apply.

A comparatively recent form of sociotechnical system is that involved in teleworking, or technology-aided home-based work. Stanworth and Stanworth (1989) discovered that, in the UK, only a fraction of the 2 million people who work at home are teleworkers. The reasons why reality lags behind rhetoric are partly cultural.

> Teleworkers themselves need not only technical skills and knowledge but also psychological preparation – the inculcation of attitudes, values and strategies facilitating the ability to 'self-start', to use 'small business' skills and cope with isolation. . . . Managers need 'socialising' into a new set of role relationships. Just as large organisations attempting to franchise a business chain network out to independent franchisees often encounter massive difficulties due to their 'top down' approach, so will the bulk of conventionally trained managers when dealing with teleworkers . . . this, coupled with the fact that it will be many years before a comprehensive cable 'national grid' is in place, probably explains the current status of teleworking as a relatively rare and novel work arrangement.
>
> (Stanworth and Stanworth 1989: 51–2)

From a cultural point of view, achievement and support are needed rather than a role culture, and the organization will probably become entrepreneurial or a hybrid (see Chapter 3, Sections 1.1 and 1.5). The teleworkers themselves may design their own jobs and sell a 'portfolio' of skills.

4 SUMMARY

Job design is specification of the content, techniques, and relationships involved in doing work. It has been studied by engineers, who have been concerned to make tasks simple in order to reduce certain costs; and by social scientists who have recommended job enrichment to satisfy human aspirations. Another group of specialists has concentrated on the fit between the environment and the human being. Ecologists have macro-level concerns, while ergonomists are interested both in any risks to people, from working conditions or poor design, and in how machines can complement people's abilities. One way of resolving the differences between these approaches is to attempt to optimize both the technical and the social requirements of sociotechnical systems.

Six principles of design were illustrated from the perspectives of the four cultures. It was pointed out that, though employers have a range of options for job design, employment conditions will sometimes preclude designs which maximize productivity but create unemployment. This is a particularly sensitive issue in developing countries. Just as organization designs change over a period of time, so do job designs, sometimes deliberately, sometimes by default as labour markets change. **Culture affects job design through preferences for work simplification or job enlargement.**

FURTHER READING

Books

Burns, T. and Stalker, G.M. (1966) *The Management of Innovation*, London: Tavistock. A classic study, based on Ferranti.
Davis, L.E. and Taylor, J.C. (eds) (1972) *The Design of Jobs*, London: Penguin. Easy to read.

For a critical theory perspective see:

Dunkerley, D. (1980) 'Technological change and work: upgrading or deskilling?', in Boreham, P. and Dow, G. (eds) *Work and Inequality*, vol. 1, London: Macmillan.

The following articles are of interest:

Boddy, D. and Buchan, D. (1985) 'New technology with a human face', *Personnel Management* 17 (4): 28–31.
Buzzard, R.B. (1973) 'A practical look at industrial stress', *Occupational Psychology* 47: 56–61.
Glen, T.H. and James, C.F. (1980) 'Difficulties in implementing management science techniques in a Third World setting', *Interfaces* 10 (1): 39–44.
Handy, C. (1984) 'The organizational revolution and how to harness it', *Personnel Management* 16 (7): 20–3.
Kemp, N., Clegg, C., and Wall, T. (1980) 'Job redesign – content, process, and outcomes', *Employee Relations* 2 (5): 5–14.
Needham, P. (1982) 'The myth of the self-regulated work group', *Personnel Management* 14 (8): 29–31.
Reif, W. and Monczka, R. (1974) 'Job design, a contingency approach to implementation', *Personnel* May–June: 18–28.

Trist, E.L. and Bamforth, K.W. (1951) 'Some social and psychological consequences of the Longwall method of coal getting', *Human Relations* 4: 3–38.

Wall, T. (1984) 'What's new in job design', *Personnel Management* 16 (4): 27–9.

RECOMMENDED CASE STUDIES

'Job Enrichment in the British National Health Service': How a chief management accountant made dull jobs interesting for his subordinates.

'Rebellious Robots' (in a Zambian manufacturing company): A factory owner loses his skilled workers after de-skilling their jobs.

Chapter 5

Cultures and motivation

CHAPTER OBJECTIVES

By the end of this chapter you will be able to:

1 outline a model for matching people and jobs
2 distinguish between an opinion and an attitude, and state the link between them
3 describe how managers in different organizational cultures view motivation
4 outline six types of motivational theory
5 analyse the recommended cases

1 INTRODUCTION

In the last chapter (Section 2.3) the question of matching jobs to human capacities was discussed. Now the question of matching people to jobs is raised. We look at a model to help in this. Then we consider the broader topic of motivation to work. How do organizations with different cultures seek to keep people motivated? We note the theoretical support that is available for the approaches used.

2 JOB MATCH AND MOTIVATION

When a job falls vacant there should be a *job description* which details the work to be done (as per design). The description includes reporting relationships, connections to other jobs, how performance is assessed, the remuneration and so on. There should also be a *specification* which refers to what is required of the person who is to be engaged. The specification may outline qualifications, skills, experience, past achievements, aptitudes, interests and so on. It should be clearly related to characteristics which have distinguished successful from unsuccessful job-holders in the past, or, if the job is new, characteristics of people performing well on similar types of work. In practice, recruiters often tend to go by their personal hunches. Most would agree, however, that motivation, or the *urge to do* the type of work, is important.

There are many specialized texts on recruitment, selection and placement. These are basic topics in personnel management but are only touched on in the present book. Nevertheless, it is worth noting that the idea of selection as 'finding round pegs for round holes' is not an appropriate metaphor. Holes and pegs are static. This is not true of jobs or people. Previous chapters have emphasized cyclical transformations of organizations. People change too. They can acquire new skills and knowledge, they grow older, their domestic circumstances alter, their expectations rise and so on. It would be surprising, therefore, if a person and his or her job were well-matched for long periods of time. The mismatch is often reflected in the phenomenon of *labour turnover*. This represents the proportions of newcomers and leavers to those who stay. Some turnover is usually considered desirable, but very high turnover can be costly in a number of ways. There are not only the costs of engagement and probably training, but also the loss in output and decrease in quality when an experienced person is replaced by an inexperienced one. Low motivation can mean high turnover, especially when labour is scarce.

This chapter discusses motivation, a term which is used of work in two ways. The first is *an urge to work* (and to keep on putting one's energies into working). The second is *a means by which to keep others keen to work* (especially one's subordinates). The word has the same root as motor and motive power. The converse of motivation is *demotivation*, a lack of 'drive'. A mismatch between the requirements of a job and the characteristics of the person doing it can lead to demotivation, shown in poor work and frequent absence. It can develop in people who were previously motivated. Poor work and frequent absence are sometimes symptoms.

2.1 Types of misfit

A crude way of spotting mismatches that may develop has been suggested by Porter *et al.* (1975). Their model, shown in Table 5.1, includes both the work and the type of employing organization. The

Table 5.1   A diagram for matching people, organizations and jobs

Type of job	Type of organization	
	Mechanistic (role plus power culture)	*Organic (achievement plus support culture)*
Simple	1 High	3 High
	2 **Low**	4 Low
Complex	5 High	7 **High**
	6 Low	8 Low

Notes: High, person with a high need for growth; Low, person with a low need for growth (Porter *et al.* 1975). Bold type indicates a compatible placement.

Mechanistic and organic are terms borrowed from Porter et al. (1975) from Burns and Stalker (1966). Classic bureaucracy is mechanistic and clusters and matrices are organic. (See Chapter 3.)

distinction between simple and complex jobs was made in Chapter 4 (Section 2.2). The mechanistic organization is what Chapter 3 termed the classic bureaucracy, and the organic organization is like the clan, cluster or some decentralized forms. Basically the organizations shown on the left of of Figure 3.1 are mechanistic and those on the right are organic.

Porter and his colleagues divide people into those who have a high or a low psychological 'need for growth'. Provided we do not take this to be a permanent distinction but allow for variation in degree and over time, the model indicates possible sources of satisfaction and dissatisfaction. People with a high need for growth will want to be challenged by the chance partly to design their own jobs. They will also value an organization where they are not closely supervised or rule-bound. People with low growth needs are more concerned with a steady job with clear instructions and a familiar routine where they can call on a supervisor for help when they need it.

Out of the eight positions numbered in the table, there are only two where people will be getting what they need – 2, and 7. A person with high growth needs will be unhappy with position 1, for two reasons – the job will not stretch him or her, and the regulations of the bureaucracy will seem confining. A person with low growth needs will feel most uncomfortable in position 8, because the work will overstretch him or her, and the lack of clear rule definition will create anxiety. All the remaining positions have a lack of compatibility, either from the task or from the type of organization.

The process of matching is dynamic. Jobs are simplified or enriched. Organizations move through a cycle of change, and people change too. They are not pegs in holes. Employers and employees need to anticipate and review the 'goodness of fit' throughout a career.

3 MANAGERS' BELIEFS AND PRACTICES

What about other aspects of motivation? Is a good fit between people and their jobs sufficient for the urge to work to remain strong? What else do people look for? Do managers also have to control working habits through incentives and penalties? What can they do about people who are discouraged from working? Are the interests of employees opposed to those of employers, as Marxists believe, or do both have the same interests? To attempt answers to these questions we need to introduce a few definitions.

An attitude consists of beliefs, plus values, plus feelings. A belief is what someone thinks is true. A value is a way of judging the worth of something. It may be general (as in Table 1.1) or quite specific (such as a preference for the taste of tea rather than coffee). A feeling may be pleasant or unpleasant but is often strong. An attitude is therefore deeper, more comprehensive and more enduring than an opinion, though statistical agreement between several opinions about the same issue may indicate the presence of an attitude. Attitudes are connected to motivation since the values and feelings often lead to a disposition to act on one's beliefs. However, it has to be admitted that not all action is guided by belief. We do many things from habit. Those who share the same culture tend to have similar attitudes and to engage in similar practices. We do not know which come first, attitudes or practices, but it seems likely that they reinforce each other. Workers who believe that capitalism exploits the working class are more likely to strike for their rights than those who believe that if a firm prospers all its employees will be better off. Workers who have experienced successful strike action in the past may be more likely to strike again, while workers in a firm with a history of peaceful industrial relations may be disinclined to strike. The model in Table 1.3 suggests,

Table 5.2 Managers' beliefs on how to motivate subordinates

By control	By encouragement
'Work is performed out of a respect for contractual obligations backed up by sanctions and personal loyalty towards the organization or system' (Role culture)	'Work is performed out of satisfaction in excellence of work and achievement and/or personal commitment to the task or goal' (Achievement culture)
'Work is performed out of hope of reward, fear of punishment or personal loyalty towards a powerful individual' (Power culture)	'Work is performed out of enjoyment of the activity for its own sake and concern and respect for the needs and values of the other persons involved' (Support culture)

Note: The quotations are taken from Handy (1985).

however, that *collective* motivation is much more complicated than this. Attitudes and habits do not arise out of nothing. Past and present circumstances are important too. However, we all have attitudes to work which have provided a happy hunting ground for researchers. Handy (1985) has a list of statements associated with the four cultures which can provide a starting point for discussion. The four statements about why people work are shown in Table 5.2.

3.1 Managers' beliefs in role and power cultures

Just as there are similarities in the structures of mechanistic organizations, whether the culture is that of role or of power, so there is a similarity of belief about how to motivate people. The basic belief is that people are naturally lazy, so that their behaviour has to be shaped by sanctions or penalties or by rewards of pay or praise. In other words, people are not self-motivated but have to be prodded by others. This is what is meant by *extrinsic motivation* (see Table 2.3).

Intrinsic motivation on the other hand refers to self-motivation, which is discussed below (in Section 3.2).

Edwards (1979) gives a graphic description of the practices of a Western company which uses the extrinsic rewards of a role culture.

> The company has explicitly moved away from reliance on negative sanctions, on penalising failure, and moved toward positive incentives, toward rewarding co-operation. All elements of control – not only rewards but the very structure of jobs and the process of evaluation as well – have been bent to make these incentives efficacious. . . . The relief from capricious supervision, the right to appeal grievances and bid for jobs, the additional job security from seniority – all these make the day-by-day worklife of Polaroid's workers more pleasant.
>
> (1981: 178)

Since Edwards is a Critical Theorist who believes that extrinsic motivation is a form of exploitation, he continues:

> They function as an elaborate system of bribes. . . . They push workers to pursue their self-interests in a narrow way as individuals, and they stifle the impulse to struggle collectively for those same self-interests.
>
> (1981: 178)

Eastern workers may also be 'controlled' through a bureaucratic system that emphasizes seniority and identification with one's role. An example is that every Fujitsu employee reaching the age of 45 goes into the company college for an intensive three-month reassessment to find out what job he or she ought to be doing next (Hayes *et al.* 1984). The singing of the company anthem in Japan, and political 'study' groups in China, are ways in which workers are encouraged to identify themselves with the company and the country and so to act as is expected of them.

The extrinsic motivation of the power culture is somewhat different. It is based on the view, which McGregor (1960) calls 'Theory X', that the average human being wants security above all, wants to be directed and dislikes responsibility. Edwards describes a Western organization which is based on this theory as follows:

> The owner and top-level foreman rule the roost in direct personal ways, exhorting or threatening workers to produce more, watching closely how hard workers work, assigning workers to

easy or tough work stations depending on the foreman's fancy, and handing out or witholding pay raises, permission to take time off, overtime, etc. . . . Personal despotism rules the workplace.

(Edwards 1981: 163)

Support for the belief that people must be directed is buttressed, in the East, by veneration for seniority and for high office.

3.2 Managers' beliefs in achievement and support cultures

The assumptions which McGregor calls 'Theory Y' assert the opposite of Theory X. The average person learns, under proper conditions, not only to accept responsibility but to seek it. The expenditure of physical and mental effort is as natural as play or rest. If people have become unwilling to work it is because their natural creativity has been suppressed by their experiences. Motivation is not a problem: the problem is demotivation. People have been treated as though they are irresponsible and they have reacted accordingly. What they need is encouragement, not control. The solution is to give people the chance to design their own work, and to generate their own goals. Some experiments along these lines were discussed in Chapter 4 (Sections 2.2 and 2.4). Our interest for the present is in what support is provided by OB theories for the attitudes just described.

4 MOTIVATION THEORIES

Table 5.3 lists some of the more popular theories of motivation which will be discussed in turn. Exchange Theory, referred to in Chapter 2 (Section 4), contains elements of all three extrinsic motivation theories shown, but treats motivation as a *transaction* between the motivator(s) and the person(s) to be motivated. The extent to which the parties have equal or unequal power is important to the theory.

4.1 Behaviourism

Behaviourism is associated in recent years with the name of the American B.F. Skinner who conducted many research studies of animals. Dr Skinner's maxim is that 'Behavior is determined by its consequences'. Animals discover that some kinds of behaviour obtain food or avoid shocks. Actions which result in harm to the individual

Table 5.3   Motivation theories

Suggesting control by extrinsic motivation	Suggesting encouragement of intrinsic motivation
1 Behaviourism	4 Humanistic theories
2 Expectancy theory	5 Personality theories
3 Social comparison theory	6 Transactional analysis

tend not to be repeated, but actions which benefit the individual tend to recur. People are like animals in this respect.

Behaviourists are not interested in what goes on inside people, but in what people do. The question of whether there are mental processes involved, such as calculations of pleasure or pain, is, to behaviourists, mere speculation. Instead they have put their energies into studying when, and how often, to reward desired behaviour. F.W. Taylor (1911), who is spoken of in Chapter 4 (Section 2.1), thought payment for each extra 'piece' would bring the desired response. However, behaviourists have found that behaviour which is rewarded every time it occurs may persist less strongly over time than behaviour which is rewarded only intermittently. The lure of gambling is said to be an example of this. A well-established experimental conclusion is that knowledge of results (or feedback) is essential for behaviour change.

Behaviour modification is a technique based on Skinner's (1973) ideas which is popular in some organizations. One has to be able to specify precisely what behaviour is to be changed and to record what is currently being done and what is reinforcing (rewarding) existing behaviour. Then one has to find out what reinforcements can be used for the desired behaviour. Examples might be praise, privileges or publicity. It is obviously easier to require specific behaviour in connection with such things as timekeeping, or routine tasks, than it is for more complex matters. Remember, the target for change is what people do, not their attitudes. In organizations the number and size of possible reinforcers is sometimes a limiting factor. Marxists have often supposed that behaviour modification can be used by managers to manipulate workers to work hard for low pay and to be satisfied with poor conditions. Ironically it was the Chinese Communists who were most successful in this, though they used 'thought reform', reinforced by group pressures. Study groups at all places of work met to build 'correct' attitudes. The opening up of China to the West has brought changes which include the desire for pay rises. Expectancy theory and social comparison theory are relevant to this phenomenon.

4.2 Expectancy theory

According to expectancy theory, people are able to create 'expectancies' for themselves. The theory states that a person calculates the value of a certain benefit, or set of linked benefits, and then estimates the likelihood of acquiring them through his or her own efforts. The person is only motivated if there is a good chance of getting something that is *wanted*. It was said, for example, that if Westerners had wanted to use money to motivate the Maoris they would first have had to make them avaricious, since they did not value money.

Variants of *expectancy theory* are offered by Vroom (1964), Lawlor (1968) and House (1971). The important implications of the theory for managers are that the incentives offered must be:

1 attractive to the person concerned;
2 conditional upon successful performance of some action;
3 for action within the person's capabilities;
4 given on terms which are clear.

It has been shown, however, that our expectancies are not constant. The importance of money, for instance, will depend partly on how much of it is coming into the household and what liabilities the wage-earner has to meet. Those who have heavy commitments are more likely to respond to monetary incentives than those who do not. The optimism or pessimism which enters into people's calculations can also change their expectations. In times of recession, for example, a person who has been given notice to quit will not believe that hard work will secure reinstatement. Performance may decline during the period when the person is 'working out his (or her) notice'.

Daniel (1972) demonstrates that people's stated preferences will vary according to whether they are thinking of their daily experiences of frustrations and successes at work or whether they think their statements are part of a bargaining situation. Kiely (1981) also stresses variability. The same action can be viewed quite differently by two individuals. The example she gives is of a lateral job move. One manager saw this as a demotion, and regretted the job he had left behind, whereas another saw the move as an opportunity for self-development, and was motivated by the change.

4.3 Social comparison theory

Expectancy theory can be complemented by social comparison theory of which Festinger (1954) is an exponent. Our expectancies are partly formed through comparing ourselves with other people – social comparison. In pay bargaining, for example, trade unions usually refer to the pay received by other groups of workers. People doing similar work should receive similar rewards. This principle was embodied in the UK in the Equal Pay Act of 1970. This Act has now been amended to introduce the more comprehensive idea that work of *equal value* (whether similar or not) should receive comparable reward. It is likely that there will be an increasing demand for more formal ways of setting out how the worth of different tasks is to be determined. Women, and those from minority ethnic groups, will want to know why they tend to get lower rewards than other workers. There are, today, several techniques for deciding the question of the equivalence of different jobs. These techniques are collectively known as *Job Evaluation*. They may involve some form of points rating of the demands made on persons by a given job. Alternatively (or in addition) they may make use of a 'benchmark' job as a standard against which other jobs may be listed in rank order.

From experimental work, Adams (1965) concluded that if persons believe they are underpaid for the work they are doing they will tend to slacken their effort and to be careless, whereas if they believe they are overpaid they will take pains to produce high quality output. According to his *equity theory* their motive is to equate the perceived job demands and rewards. A problem with *equity theory*, however, is whether the rewards should be commensurate with the input (what the worker contributes) or with the output (the quantity and quality of the work produced). Output may be much affected by technology. Under such circumstances the worker's skill and effort may make little difference to output. If input is the criterion, however, it is likely that the skill demands will be the same for those on similar work and people will be forced to compare themselves with dissimilar work. It is likely that equity theory will apply to a restricted range of occupations for which one can see differences in performance that are due to the employee. Personnel texts describe *merit rating* schemes for such cases.

All the theories discussed so far support the idea of extrinsic motivation, namely that it is the incentives provided by others in terms of rewards or penalties that are important. We turn now to a group of theories which are more concerned with intrinsic motivation, and with the circumstances under which a person will be self-motivated.

4.4 Humanistic theories

The motive which these theories emphasize, though the terms may differ, is a human *need* for psychological growth, and so they are sometimes called need theories. Table 5.1 divided people into whether this need was strong or weak. It can be either encouraged or discouraged from infancy. McClelland (1975) thinks people have three types of growth need: for power, achievement or affiliation. The societal culture may have emphasized one or other of these three needs through its child-rearing practices. In Chapter 7 (Section 2) the terms 'tough battler', 'logical thinker' and 'friendly helper' are used for persons who appear to be driven by one of McClelland's three needs; the battlers by power, the thinkers by achievement and the helpers by affiliation.

Argyris (1964) thinks that the natural stages of human life are from total dependence on others as a baby, through the assertion of independence from others in adolescence, to a recognition of interdependence with others in maturity. He considers that many jobs cause adults to regress to babyhood dependence. If persons are to fulfil their potential they must be given encouragement to take responsibility with others for what they do.

Alderfer (1974) is another writer who considers that three needs are basic to human beings. The first is the need to exist, the second the need to relate to others and the third the need to grow. Growth, for him, involves expanding the breadth and depth of one's spiritual awareness, self-understanding, attainments and so on. His (ERG) theory reduces the longer list that Maslow (1965) proposed on the basis of his clinical work.

Maslow's Need theory describes human needs as ordered hierarchically in five categories, as follows:

HIGHEST
self-actualization
self-esteem
social
safety
physiological
BASE LINE

At the base are needs for food, drink and shelter, without which life would be impossible. Maslow believed that a lower need motivates behaviour until it is satisfied. At this point the next higher need becomes the motivator. Once we have the physical necessities of life we are concerned with self-preservation and protection from harm. Safety needs might also include such items as pension rights. The social needs are for companionship and for belonging, while self-esteem requires recognition and respect. If lower needs have not been satisfied, the desire for self-actualization will not be felt. When it is felt it is never satisfied. New possibilities replace those we realize.

Maslow's studies have not received much support from later studies. There is some evidence that the needs do not arise in sequence as Maslow suggested. People 'seem to move up and down the hierarchy, rather than progressing neatly up through it' (Cox and Cox 1980). Individual differences are said to account for this, but there is evidence of cultural differences here too. Nevis (1983) says, for example, that for the Chinese the base of the pyramid is social (belonging) needs, because if you do not belong your physiological needs do not get met!

Herzberg (1968) saw things a little differently. He was interested in demotivation as well as motivation. He called his theory a two factor theory because, according to him, dissatisfaction and satisfaction are not opposites, as we might have supposed, but unconnected states of mind. His research method was to ask people about times in their lives when things were going well and times when things were going badly. People felt good when they had accomplished something or had been praised for their achievements. They felt bad when frustrated by company policy, low pay, poor supervision and such like. From these findings he developed his two factor theory. His critics say that his factors are an artifact of the methods he used, and other studies have not always come up with the same findings (Ejiougu 1983).

Since Herzberg gave the name 'hygiene' to the things which cause dissatisfaction, and 'motivators' to the things which give satisfaction, his theory is also sometimes called *hygiene/motivator theory*.

Managers need to attend to hygiene or harm can result, just as illness can result from lack of cleanliness. But, although avoiding dirt may prevent disease, it does not promote vitality. Likewise, if Herzberg's hygiene factors, such as pay and supervision and the working environment, are acceptable, people will not necessarily work harder. Motivation, according to Herzberg, depends on other things: the interesting nature of the work one has to do and recognition for achievement. The manager who believes in job enrichment can appeal to humanistic theories, but may equally describe what is being done in terms of expectancy theory.

Almost 26,000 people currently in work completed a survey in *The Guardian* newspaper. They were mainly upwardly mobile managers, professionals and executives between the ages of 25 and 44. Of these 41 per cent applied for their present job in order to widen their experience and professional knowledge. From 83 to 88 per cent listed 'respect of people you work with, personal freedom, learning something new and challenge' among their top ten sources of satisfaction. Forty-four per cent did not expect to be with their present organization three years later.

We must be careful, however, not to generalize to all groups of employees or to all countries. For the Chinese, in theory at any rate, it is only through obedience to the command to 'serve the people' that one achieves self-actualization. Indeed the individualism implied in the term 'self-actualize' is foreign to their thinking. (Practice may be different as bureaucrats have had opportunities, denied to the masses, to line their own pockets.)

We need to see people as whole persons, with a life before, after and outside work. We can also recognize that some behaviour may be linked to current domestic circumstances, as Guest and Williams (1973) graphically portray. Hall and Fletcher (1984) estimate that, at any particular time, up to 20 per cent of a company's workforce will have a personal problem which is likely to affect their performance. Each person is unique both in private circumstances and in personality. We turn therefore to see whether personality theories cast any new light on motivation.

4.5 Personality theories

These theories are not primarily concerned with motivation, but rather with describing and accounting for individual differences in temperament, aptitudes, interests and so on. From the point of view of the beliefs outlined in Table 5.2, however, we can ask, 'are there really types of people who prefer to operate under regulative control and others who would prefer appreciative control?' (Table 2.3)

The answer may be 'yes', as psychologists working before the Second World War discovered. They were concerned with the spread of Fascism. They wondered whether certain types of persons were likely to find the intolerance and ethnocentrism (racial exclusiveness) of Fascism attractive. From research in this area, in 1950, the term 'the Authoritarian Personality' was introduced into psychology. Since then, others have defined authoritarianism in terms of rigidity in thinking, a *closed mind*, a preference for clear-cut distinctions and a dislike of opponents, irrespective of the type of beliefs held.

Analysts such as Sigmund Freud suggested that the rigidity of closed minds might be a psychological defence mechanism to prevent the person becoming aware of disturbing tendencies within himself (or herself). He saw personality as composed of an unconscious 'id' which contains repressed wishes, memories and so on, a conscious ego, and a superego which censors what is admitted into consciousness.

Other so-called 'depth' psychologists, such as Adler and Jung, have contributed theories which also emphasize the importance of *unconscious* influences in current motivation and in the appearance of such traits as authoritarianism. Though Jung (1973) himself cautioned that his typology is not to be used 'to stick labels on people at first sight', some of the psychological 'types' derived from his theory of psychic processes can relate to the four types of organizational cultures described in this book (see Chapter 7, Section 2, and Chapter 10, Section 2).

The last theory to be mentioned here, transactional analysis, could have been classed as a theory of personality, but, since it is also a theory of how persons communicate with each other, it is given a separate heading.

4.6 Transactional analysis

Berne (1967), the originator of transactional analysis, asserts that we all carry within ourselves subconscious memories of the parenting we received when we were very young. From these memories we are endowed with three 'ego states' or ways of being in the present. There is the parent (P), with whom we identified. P is concerned with moral judgements (Critical P) and with taking care of ourselves (Nurturing P). We also have an adult (A), which is the part of us that works things out, and deals with information. Finally there is our child (C), based on how we once were. Our 'natural' or 'free' child is fun-loving and creative, but we also have a rebellious C, who fights against P, and an adapted C, who tries to please P. Our ego states play an important part in our work or leisure activities, but they can also give rise to unpleasantness. To explain how this happens we must consider Berne's theory of motivation.

For our psychological well-being as infants we needed to be cuddled or stroked. According to transactional analysis, we still need strokes in later life, in the form of appreciation from others. What we cannot bear is to be ignored. Even abuse is better than nothing. In our early years our C learned to behave in ways that would get attention, whether positive stroking or negative (a kick).

In Berne's theory all three ego states *transact* with each other, not only within a person but from person to person. When two people are exchanging work information the A in each is engaged. However, if our internalized parents and child are bidding for strokes they can play havoc with communication. For example, they will give ulterior messages (often non-verbally or through tone of voice) which differ from the Adult to Adult message. Another way they foul up communication is by crossed transactions. An example is shown below:

	Secretary	Manager
Secretary		
'Is the report to go out today?'	P	P
	A ⟶ A	
Manager		
'Get lost!'	C	C

The secretary's A to A request is answered by an angry P to adapted C. But maybe the secretary 'invited' the rebuff by making her request at a moment when her boss was very busy. She might even have given a non-verbal 'kick me' signal from her 'adapted child' by knocking very timidly before entering.

The authoritarian person, in transactional analysis terms, is one who has a strong Critical Parent ego state. Such a person gets noticed (and therefore a stroke) by a partner who has a highly developed

Adapted Child. The partner also gets noticed. These two can indulge in pastimes which are relatively innocuous rituals, or they may begin a *game*.

A game is defined by Berne as 'a series of moves with a snare or gimmick' which 'hooks' the vulnerable ego state in the other person. The secretary and boss might become involved in 'Now I've Got You Son of a Bitch' (NIGYSOB) if their crossed transactions continue. Games usually end in bad feelings all round. They can even result in physical harm to one or more persons. Fisticuffs, Berne says, may be the only attention you have learned to get, especially if you were physically abused in childhood. Breaking up games, or refusing to play them, can make an organization more efficient. The reason is that games divert energies, which would otherwise be available for work, into scoring points off others. One of Berne's followers, Wojdowski (1978), has written an account of games that are especially popular among bureaucrats.

Training courses are given by transactional analysis consultants to help people at work to recognize the unconscious elements in their own and other's behaviour so that they can find suitable remedies themselves. The remedy suggested by transactional analysis is to find new payoffs to replace the dysfunctional ones that people have been covertly seeking. This should reduce crossed transactions as well as game playing.

5 SUMMARY

One can motivate others (keep them keen to do something, especially work) or be motivated oneself (have an urge to do something, especially work). The urge is likely to be stronger if one is in the right job. A simple model for detecting the beginnings of a mismatch relates need for security or for growth to type of job and of organization.

Role and power cultures tend to stress extrinsic motivation, provided by rewards and penalties. Achievement and support cultures stress intrinsic motivation, a striving after something to satisfy one's inner self.

There are a number of theories that support each of these views. The element common to behaviourism, to expectancy theory and to social comparison theory is that they all suggest *means by which to keep others keen to work*, by shaping behaviour through rewards (and possibly punishments). What the humanistic theories, personality theories and transactional analysis have in common is that they all suggest that some form of placement, encouragement, personal development programme or retraining may bring out the intrinsic motivation, the *urge to work*, that is already there. Personality is relevant not only to placement but also to development programmes which can help people to be aware of aspects of their motivation which had previously been hidden. Inner change may be sought and found by persons who have been unfortunate in their early experiences with others.

Culture affects motivation through preferences for extrinsic or intrinsic motivators.

FURTHER READING

Works covering the main theories are as follows:

Argyris, C. (1964) *Integrating the Individual and the Organization*, New York: Wiley.

Berne, E. (1967) *Games People Play: the psychology of human relationships*, London: Penguin.

Edwards, R.C. (1979) *Contested Terrain: the transformation of the workplace in America*, New York: Basic Books.

—— (1981) 'The social relations of production at the point of production', in Zey-Ferrell, M. and Aiken, M. (eds) *Complex Organizations: Critical Perspectives*, Glenview, IL: Scott Foresman, ch. 8, 156–82.

Harris, T.A. (1973) *I'm OK, You're OK*, London: Pan.

Herzberg, F. (1968) *Work and the Nature of Man*, London: Staples Press.

Lawlor, E.E. and Porter, L.W. (1968) *Managerial Attitudes and Performance*, Homewood, IL: Irwin.

Maslow, A.H. and Murphy, G. (eds) (1969) *Motivation and Personality*, New York: Harper & Row.

McClelland, D.C. (1975) *Power: The Inner Experience*, New York: Irvington.

McGregor, D. (1960) *The Human Side of Enterprise*, New York: McGraw-Hill.

Skinner, B.F. (1973) *Beyond Freedom and Dignity*, London: Penguin.

Vroom, V.H. (1964) *Work and Motivation*, New York: Wiley.

The following articles are helpful:

Ejiougu, A.M. (1983) 'Participative management in a developing economy – poison or placebo', *Journal of Applied Behavioral Science* 19 (3): 239–47.

Guest, D. and Williams, R. (1973) 'How home affects work', *New Society* 18 January: 114–17.

Guest, D. (1984) 'What's new in motivation?', *Personnel Management* 16 (May): 20–3.

McClelland, D.C. (1965) 'Achievement motivation can be developed', *Harvard Business Review* 43 (November/December): 6–16, 20–4, 178.

Nevis, E.C. (1983) 'Using an American perspective in understanding another culture: toward a hierarchy of needs for the People's Republic of China, *Journal of Applied Behavioral Science* 19 (3): 249–64.

Rogers, K. (1963) 'Psychology and the manager', *New Society* 40 (4 July): 19–20.

Schein, E.H. (1968) 'Organizational socialization and the profession of management', *Industrial Management Review* 9 (2): 1–16.

RECOMMENDED CASES

'The Change of Site': Six wards are to be moved to new quarters and staff are fearful of the consequences.

'The Cold War': A new foreman finds a demoralized workforce.

Chapter 6

Cultures and decision-making

CHAPTER OBJECTIVES

By the end of this chapter you will be able to:

1 describe four different decision-making strategies used by individuals under different conditions of uncertainty
2 describe four different decision-making strategies used by organized groups under different conditions of uncertainty
3 explain the meaning of the Japanese words 'ringi' and 'nemawashi'
4 outline the differences between antagonistic and collaborative approaches to decision-making
5 analyse the recommended cases, or take part with others in an exercise

1 INTRODUCTION

Chapter 5 began with a simple model for matching people who want security to simple jobs, but those who want personal growth to complex jobs. What makes a job complex is that more decision-making is required of the worker.

A decision is *the settlement or resolution of some matter*. So decisions play a part in all the topics covered so far: in control, in change, in organizational and job design and in motivation. It is no surprise, therefore, that our cultural typology is relevant to decision-making. It is relevant to the methods used and to the style or manner of using them. But other things are important too.

In the present chapter we examine three of those other things. The first is *uncertainty*. It is harder to resolve matters when there is much uncertainty. Second, we note how *time-scale* affects decisions. Long-term issues are harder to resolve than short-term ones. Finally

Table 6.1 Decision-making strategies and styles according to difficulty

Causal links	Preferences	
	Certain	Uncertain
Certain	(a) (Individuals) maximize and habitualize	(b) (Individuals) use bounded rationality
	Analytical style	**Conceptual style**
Cues can be recognized	(a) (Organizations) programme a routine to maintain present behaviour	(b) (Organizations) (i) reduce uncertainty through interaction for compromise or consensus or (ii) use the dialectic
Uncertain	(c) (Individuals) use implicit favourite to analyse pattern and then select from past strategy	(d) (Individuals) use intuition and inspiration to play best hunch and adapt
	Directive style	**Behavioural style**
Cues are novel	(c) (Organizations) use (i) incrementalism or (ii) the Delphi technique	(d) (Organizations) get results from (i) the rubbish bin or (ii) political games

Note: The styles in bold type are terms used by Rowe and Boulgarides (1983).

we ask whether the decision makers have *common interests* or different stakes in what is to be decided. Culture can unite or divide people.

2 PROBLEM COMPLEXITY AND DECISION-MAKING STRATEGIES

This section is about the nature of the problems. They can be classified according to two kinds of uncertainty. The first is uncertainty about what is really wanted (preferences) and the second is technical uncertainty about what leads to what (causal links). The combinations of these two types of difficulty are associated with four different types of strategy for individuals working alone and with four for 'organizations' (people working together, in committee or informally).

Table 6.1 shows, in parts (a) of the matrix, that there are problems which are easy to solve because we know both what we want and what is likely to be the best way to get it. In parts (b) we do not know what our priorities are but, once we have made up our minds, we can make a technically rational decision. In parts (c) we know what we want but are unsure what will enable us to get it. Finally, in parts (d) a double uncertainty arises: we are unsure of what to aim for or how to achieve our aim.

It is possible to compare Table 6.1 with Table 5.1. Decisions in simple jobs in mechanistic organizations are like (a) above; those in simple jobs in organic organizations are like (b); those in complex jobs in mechanistic organizations may be like (c); while those in complex jobs in organic organizations may be like (d). It is also possible to compare the (a) strategies with those of *regulation* and the (d) strategies with those of *appreciation* (see Table 2.3). We describe the decision strategies in Sections 2.1 and 2.2 below, starting with those for individuals working on their own and going on to decisions made by more than one person. Discussion of *group* decision-making is continued in Chapter 7 (Sections 6 and 7).

2.1 Individual strategies

A strategy is a method, and 'style' is the way in which a method is pursued. Style has been introduced here because it provides links to the four organization cultures. We meet style again in Chapter 8 (Section 3.2) where we consider how leaders lead. For decision-making styles, the descriptions of Rowe and Boulgarides (1983) seem roughly appropriate. The *analytical* style is 'logical, abstract, thinking', which the maximizing strategy requires. It accords well with a role culture. The *conceptual* style is 'spatial, creative and wide-ranging', which sounds like intuitive thinking. Where preferences are uncertain, rationality can only be used up to a point. It is 'bounded'. Beyond that point, guess-work is needed. The achievement culture encourages this style. The *directive* style is 'focused, rigid and results oriented'. Because causal links are uncertain, choice of tactics has to be somewhat arbitrary, and so favourite solutions are chosen. 'We'll do this because I say so' is typical of a power culture. The *behavioural* style is said to be one of 'listening, support and empathy', that is, it pays due regard to feelings. Where there are double uncertainties, feelings can provide some guidance. The support culture respects this style. The strategies are outlined below.

Maximizing

To maximize is to get the greatest net benefit from your decision. Sometimes the word 'optimize' is used, though optimum means 'best' whereas maximum means 'most'. Often the best and the most coincide, but not always. Anyway, neither is possible unless you know what benefit you want, and what will be the consequences of alternative lines of action. The maximizing strategy consists of the following moves.

Search
1 Ascertain the limits within which you are working – what authority you have, what others expect, and so on.
2 Define the problem.
3 Collect data.

Analysis
4 Analyse the data.
5 Consider all the solutions that are possible.

Evaluation
6 Use an appropriate rule to rank the solutions so that you can choose the one which gives greatest net benefit.
7 Implement the solution of your choice, and check the results.

Specialized texts will explain what each of the above seven stages can involve. Sanderson (1979), for example, has seventy-five pages of questions which a problem-solver can ask while following the routine. Computers can be very useful in stages 4, 5 and 6 in the list.

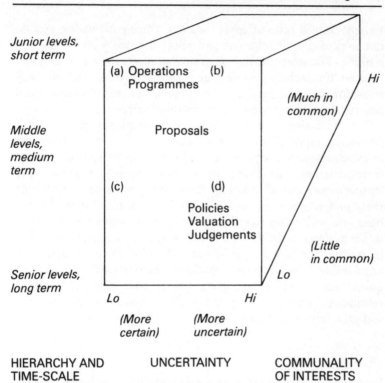

Figure 6.1 Composite framework for decision-making
Note: The letters (a), (b), (c) and (d) connect this figure with Table 6.1

Once a decision has been made, and checked, it can be used for subsequent decisions of the same type. It becomes habitual, or programmed, as do some of the short-term operating decisions shown in Figure 6.1.

Bounded rationality

The term 'bounded rationality' is taken from Simon (1960). In maximizing you are trying to get the best result, but when you are using bounded rationality you are seeking a solution that is 'good enough'. Simon calls this 'satisficing'. At the search stage you only collect data that you *know* will affect the problem. At the analysis stage you do not attempt to consider all possible alternatives. This may be too costly. You select a few alternatives through the use of loosely defined rules of approximation. During evaluation you do not rank order all solutions and select the one with the highest ranking. You select the first solution that meets some base line you have set. If no solution meets your minimum requirements, you may either lower your aspirations or look again. You stop your search and analysis as soon as you have a satisfactory answer.

An exhibition centre provides an example of the bounded rationality approach, using a mathematical model. The problem was to avoid congestion at peak times. The decision-makers had to state their preferences for maximum density (number of persons per square metre) and what rate of flow would be needed. (Note that these preferences were not known fully in advance.) A model was built into which data were fed concerning the number of arrivals at different times of the day and at each entrance. Assumptions had to be made about how long people stayed and what routes they took once inside. The computer calculated the times and locations of queues and overcrowding. Assumptions were changed until the results matched previous experience. Then predictions could be made and preventive action taken.

Implicit favourite

Both the maximizing and the bounded rationality strategies involve consideration of alternatives before settling a matter. With the implicit favourite strategy the matter is 'decided' first, and an alternative is selected afterwards as a means for justifying the choice which has already been made.

Soelberg (1967) explains how job seekers sometimes went for an interview after they had already been offered, and had accepted, an offer elsewhere. The later interview enabled them to tell their friends all the advantages of the place they had accepted compared with the job for which they got the later interview. Selection boards also sometimes seem to operate an implicit favourite strategy! They decide on an internal candidate, but call him to a meeting of the board at which they also see external candidates. This enables them to preserve the appearance of having impartially used the maximizing strategy when, in fact, they have not.

Inspirational/intuitive

Intuition should not be decried. Gore argues that

Almost without exception, a rational decision is preceded by a heuristic decision, traversing the same terrain, but vicariously, and through the emotions.

(1964: 19)

Intuition is akin to the process of 'appreciation' which is 'the selection of what shall be noticed and how it shall be classified, and the way in which it shall be valued'. Intuition is a form of guessing which has its place even in scientific work. However, there is trained intuition and untrained intuition. The former can help in the calculation of a problem. The latter is liable to lead to fallacious reasoning. Redding (1980) remarks that Orientals, more than Westerners, have a tendency to use intuitive sensitivity in making decisions, though many have high mathematical ability also.

Experience, combined with intuition, is sometimes described as a 'flair' for making decisions. Another term is 'creativity', about which Western writers have written much. De Bono (1971) has popularized creative thinking, and Osborn (1981) and Gordon (1961) have developed methods to promote creativity in groups (See Chapter 7, Section 7). These methods make use of the incongruous, the unexpected and the paradoxical. Techniques for extending consciousness were used by Assaglioli (1980). If we become more aware of what is going on, we are better able to choose how to act. Without awareness we do things 'unintentionally', rather than either creatively or rationally.

The four individual strategies have now been described. Much of the time, habit will serve us. When it does not we may attempt consciously to maximize, and, if that is impossible, to 'satisfice' through the use of bounded rationality. We may act on impulse and reflect later (the implicit favourite strategy) or we may rely on trained (or untrained) intuition. We turn now to organizational decision-making.

2.2 Organizational strategies

Routine programmes

We have already seen, in the description of work simplification in Chapter 4, that mental work as well as physical work can be routinized, both for individuals and for groups. Indeed, Gresham's law can be applied to decision-making. Instead of bad money driving out good, we have daily routine driving out planning. This was illustrated in an experiment reported by March (1988). The subjects were made responsible for managing an inventory control system. They had three tasks: (i) to pass on to clerical staff some routine information about inventory levels in various warehouses; (ii) to adjust the allocation of clerks to warehouses so that each group of clerks had a comparable workload; and (iii) to devise new procedures. They were told that all three tasks were equally important, but as the information load increased they did less and less planning for new procedures. An exercise ('Quick containers') is provided in the present book whereby the reader may, with others, try out whether he or she also conforms to Gresham's law.

According to Brown and Steel

> The extreme case of a fully programmed decision, in which all the ingredients are supplied and also rules for dealing with them, is a clerk dealing with routine cases according to the rule book.
>
> (1979: 148)

In a benefit office, for example, all the clerks may decide according to the same routine. The case study 'A Case of Mismanagement' is an example of an office in which there was a routine for the issue of vehicle licences.

Such programmes may also guide meetings of decision-makers. The members do not have to argue about what topics to discuss, because the agenda and papers have been programmed for them in advance. They can quickly get down to business.

Compromise

Organizations with many decision-makers may have to reach compromises between differing requirements. This is particularly so in the case of the trade off between keeping expenses down and providing the services people want. A compromise is reached through negotiation and mutual concession. It may be based on majority pressure, or on a genuine consensus in which the concessions are believed to be fair by all concerned (as, for example, in the Japanese 'ringi' method described later in this chapter). Of course, not all dissensus results in compromise. Something better may be achieved – an 'integrative' solution in which everyone gets a bit more than they had originally anticipated because some new factor is brought into the situation. At all events, co-operation is involved. (For a description of co-operative brainstorming see Chapter 7, Section 7.) A way of handling *dissensus* is mentioned below.

The dialectical method

In cell (a) of Table 6.1 known axioms such as mathematical formulae can be used. It is then possible, following rules of logic, to reason from the general to the particular and deduce a conclusion. In cell (b) one knows the connecting links, as a scientist knows the connection between the measuring instruments in use and the phenomena under observation, but one needs help in deciding what goals to follow. The dialectic has been placed in cell (b) because the method assumes that there is a concealed synthesis (or certain preference) embedded in *competing* assumptions. The decision-makers' task is to help the synthesis to emerge. Mitroff and Emshoff (1979: 5) outline the four steps of the method along these lines:

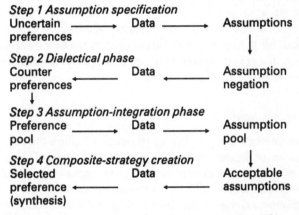

In a debate, proposers and opposers set out arguments for and against some proposition. People thus hear the 'original and counter preferences'. After a debate a vote is taken. In the dialectical method, instead of voting for one side, people look at all the ideas put forward (the assumption pool) from which they develop a synthesis, the integrative solution mentioned in 'Compromise' above.

Incrementalism

Cells (c) or (d) are appropriate for problems which are initially only vaguely structured, with unclear causal connections. The longer title given (by Braybrooke and Lindblom 1970) to this method is 'disjointed incrementalism'. A more popular title would be 'muddling through'. It is used by individuals as well as organizations. The strategy is as follows.

The decision-makers have a sense that something is wrong. To relieve their sense of dissatisfaction they think what might be done to improve matters slightly, without searching for root causes or ultimate solutions. Because it is too costly (in time, energy or money) to delay action until alternatives have been researched, the group implements a decision without having reviewed all consequences. If adverse consequences do, in fact, arise, the group tackles them in a later decision, or hopes that some other body will deal with them. It is assumed that results which are not readily accessible to observation can be disregarded. The preference, in incremental decision-making, is to get rid of something which is disliked, rather than to attain some distant goal. In this sense incrementalism is remedial. The lack of 'cause–effect' certainty means that the decisions are provisional and, because of the risks involved, the decision-makers often only seek to change things 'at the margin'. (If they make things worse rather than better, it is unlikely they will make them catastrophically worse!). A government, for example, may decide to introduce a new budget part way through the year if the consequences of the previous budget were not as satisfactory as had been hoped.

The Delphi technique

The Delphi method involves taking an opinion poll on the problem from a number of persons whose judgements carry weight. Their initial views are put together and circulated to all respondents, and further comments are requested. This process continues until a satisfactory level of agreement is reached (or deviant judges have been eliminated).

The rubbish bin

Cohen *et al.* (1972), the American inventors, call this strategy the 'garbage can'. The basic idea is that several relatively independent things pour into the garbage can or rubbish bin.

The bin contains:

Problems
Solutions (which are somebody's product)
Participants
Choice opportunities

Decision-making is viewed as an activity which absorbs the energy of those available, works on problems and comes up with solutions which are determined in large measure by the random stream of events. Such decision-making occurs in organizations characterized by problematic preferences, unclear technology and fluid participation, which the authors call 'organized anarchies'. They cite universities as an example!

Different energies are required to solve the same problem at different times. As soon as the total of effective energy that has been spent on a choice equals or exceeds the requirements at that particular time, a decision is made. For unsolved problems there will be various energy deficits at the end of a given time period.

Each participant allocates his energy at the start of the next time period to the problem with the smallest total deficit (that is, the problem closest to resolution). Organizational structure influences the process in the following ways:

1 the timing of the arrival of problems, choices, solutions and participants;
2 the energy distribution between the participants;
3 the links established between the various flows.

The authors elaborate the various ways in which they designed a computer simulation, and the varying conditions they introduced. A feature of the model is the partial uncoupling of problems and choices. Choices are made only when the shifting combination of problems, solutions and decision-makers happens to make the action possible. Some decisions resolve problems, but other decisions get taken by oversight (wrong choice) or flight (the problem has gone away, and so the decision came too late). Pfeffer (1981) remarks that the model plays down purpose to such an extent that it is unpopular with those who see decision-making as an essentially intentional activity. The authors claim, however, that the garbage can model does correspond with their observations of university decision-making.

Political games

Allison (1971) substitutes for the garbage can a 'game', though not the same kind of game as the transactional analysis games mentioned in Chapter 5 (Section 4.6). Allison views decision-makers as dealing with many issues simultaneously, as a card-player deals with a hand of cards. He concludes:

Governmental action does not presume government intention.
The sum of behaviour of representatives of a government relevant
to an issue is rarely intended by any individual or group. Rather,
in the typical case, separate individuals with different intentions
contribute pieces to the resultant. The details of the action are
therefore not chosen by any individual (and are rarely identical
with what any of the players would have chosen if he had
confronted an issue as a matter of simple, detached choice).
Nevertheless, resultants can be roughly consistent with some
group's preference in the context of the political game.

(Allison 1981: 147)

In Table 6.1, whose eight strategies we have now described, it
appears as though there are only two types of decision uncertainty.
This is not so. The paragraph quoted from Allison, above, draws
attention to something we have ignored so far – how individuals
relate to other individuals when reaching collective decisions.
Relations are affected by the position of the decision-makers in an
organization, and by their perceptions. To these questions we now
turn. Figure 6.1 provides a composite framework which places the
problem uncertainty already discussed in the middle and adds
hierarchy, time-scale and participant interests as further
complications.

3 THE DECISION HIERARCHY AND THE TIME SPAN OF DECISIONS

Decision-making, according to Simon (1960), is synonymous with
management. That claim will be examined more fully in Chapter 8.
Even if it is true, however, it does not mean that the only people who
make decisions are managers. It was pointed out, in Chapter 4, that
an aspect of job enrichment, and of autonomous work groups, is that
workers are involved in mental as well as manual work. The mental
work is the decision-making about such things as what to do next,
whether to change what is happening, whether adjustments or
corrections are needed to the work in progress, or to the equipment,
and whether everything is satisfactory or not. A feature of these
decisions is that they recur at frequent intervals and so can soon be
changed. In hierarchical organizations recurrent operating decisions
(a) tend to be taken at junior levels (shown top left). Long-term,
non-recurrent decisions (d) tend to be taken at senior levels. Note

that, contrary to what you might expect, the hierarchy axis shows senior levels at the bottom. Only thus can we superimpose the centre of Figure 6.1 on Table 6.1. The time-scale refers to the length of time needed to reach a decision; the time it takes to carry it out; and the length of time before the impact is felt. According to Jaques (1976), these are correlated, and so they have not been separated out in the figure.

Though a decision is 'a settlement or resolution of some matter', it may be only provisional. The matter can be reopened. Figure 6.1 shows policies as long-term decisions and programmes as short-term ones. Proposals are placed in between, as interim decisions, since they usually get incorporated into policies at a later stage in the *process* of decision-*making*.

Brown and Steel describe the different contributions made to this process at different hierarchical levels in the UK civil service as follows:

> Typically, junior members will not question their seniors' definition of the ends to be served, while the latter will assume that factual information reported by juniors is correct. Typically, too, the most senior levels will be concerned with authorization – with the final check that a proposed course of action is consistent with a general system of values – rather than with working out detailed proposals. But they may also take the initiative by setting a broad agenda, or specifying general rules to which their subordinates have to work.
>
> (1979: 179)

What Brown and Steel say also describes company hierarchies. The most important, long-term, decisions are made by those at the top of the hierarchy. Those below are concerned mainly with referring new problems upwards, and with executing the policies that have been made by those above. Of course, there are day-to-day operational problems such as shortages or surpluses of staff, materials or facilities, which can be resolved at junior levels on the basis of past practice, or of specified guidelines and limits. Anything for which no precedent exists is passed up.

For both long-term and short-term decisions staff help may be required. The 'staffers', in the civil service, may be experts in particular subjects which are the stock in trade of a ministry or department. Companies tend to have specialists in money matters (finance and accounting), specialists in making the goods (manufacturing), specialists in personnel matters, marketing and sales, and so on. At the policy level, boards, councils or governing bodies may co-ordinate the specialist inputs to decisions. At lower levels co-ordination may be achieved through having specialists report to a common superior. In self-managed organizations the membership may elect their governing body which, in turn, may appoint professional managers and staff. If the organization is small, it may obtain the services of outside advisers before committing itself to long-term policies.

The greater the differentiation into levels and specialisms, insiders and outsiders, the more likely it is that persons from different parts of an organization, or from different organizations, will see the aims, means and processes of decision-making differently (see Chapter 3, Section 1.4).

4 PARTICIPANT INTERESTS AND DECISION-MAKING IN DIFFERENT CULTURES

Quinn and McGrath (1985) introduce a model similar to Table 6.1 but based on a combination of uncertainty with *intensity* or urgency of the problem. Where interests are seen as disparate, the need to resolve differences may be felt more acutely and contribute to a sense of urgency. Thus, in Figure 6.1 disparate interests are shown as creating harder conditions. What we are concerned with is whether people see themselves as sharing common interests or as having disparate interests. Such perceptions can differ on different occasions, depending on the issue concerned. It is likely that all organizations will sometimes have groups which are competing internally with other groups. At other times the same groups may be working well together. Nevertheless expression of disagreement is permitted more frequently in some countries or organizations than in others (see the 'Rivers State' case study).

4.1 Competing

Some decisions occur as a result of contests and disputes. In role cultures especially the emphasis is on the impersonality of the procedures for resolving such issues. For example, civil courts or tribunals have to decide between claims and counter-claims, and come up with an award. The adjudication may be that one party loses all and the other takes all (a zero-sum result), or that each party forfeits and gains something. Other contested decisions may not be referred to third parties. They may be resolved through a process of bargaining between the parties. Buyers and sellers may reach agreement on the price of goods or services, and employers and trade unions may bargain over work and wages. Political differences may be resolved through appeal to the electorate.

Thus, at various levels, there is structural provision for divided and often opposed loyalties. However, the type and extent to which opposition is allowed varies in different countries, and, because of this, we cannot assume that contested decisions will be made in the same way. Opposition may be tolerated in some matters but not in others. The former Chinese premier, Chou En-lai, gave his view of the position in the People's Republic of China (quoted by Milton *et al.* 1974: 479) as follows:

> The minority which opposes socialism and wants to restore capitalism is intolerable in China. . . . We openly criticize that minority among the masses. With the aid of the masses we isolate them. . . . There is another very distinct type of minority. . . . It exists within the people themselves who support the socialist revolution and the dictatorship of the proletariat but maintain different opinions. Theoretically and philosophically we consider contradictions of this sort beneficial.

In the People's Republic of China the multi-party system, however, like market competition, is seen as part of capitalism. Enterprises are owned by the state, or by some other public body such as a commune. The workers voice criticism not out of self-interest, which is at variance with the organization, but because their factory is not being managed in the best interests of society. Striking is permitted for such reasons.

4.2 Collaborative decision-making

Collaborative decision-making is based on shared interests. Mair (1962) gives an example, from the Karimojong people of Uganda, of collaborative settlement of disputes prior to colonial rule.

> Within a 'neighbourhood' of two or three to a dozen settlements, numbering a few hundred people, disputes are talked out in a gathering of *all the adult men*; and at the end the elders of this small political community pronounce a decision which probably represents a general consensus of opinion.
>
> (Mair 1962: 77; emphasis added)

Ouchi (1981) calls this kind of community 'of individuals who are connected to each other through a variety of ties' a 'clan'. Sometimes a clan is based on blood relationships, but he also applies the term to 'an intimate group of industrial workers'. Ouchi is writing of Japan, where much effort is put into helping all employees to identify themselves with their company to become, in effect, a clan.

Western and Japanese decision-making differ in that, in the West, fewer people are usually consulted. The Japanese attach greater importance to implementation, unlike Westerners who give priority to the speed of reaching a decision. The time to *reach* a decision is increased in proportion to the number of people who have to be persuaded. The time it takes to *implement* a decision, on the other hand, is likely to be shortened if everyone's agreement has been secured. The word for decision-making in Japan is 'nemawashi', which is 'the process of planting a tree – i.e. implanting its roots in the soil so it can grow' (Keys and Miller 1984).

Even when Western managers do seek consensus, it is usually in a small group, whereas, according to Ouchi (1981), in Japan 'a team of three will be assigned the duty of talking to all sixty to eighty people' who may feel the impact of a policy, 'and each time a significant modification arises, contacting all the people involved again'. In Japan, the process of reaching a common mind (through the ritual of 'ringi', whereby the decision is expressed in a document bearing each person's stamp of approval) is less fraught with conflict than it would be in the West. The reason is the existence of the clan in Japan.

Western attempts to involve more people are of two kinds: direct, and indirect. Direct participation, in its stronger form, means that those who have to implement a decision are the ones who make it. 'Autonomous work groups' participate directly in operational level decisions regarding production matters and some staffing matters (see Chapter 4, Sections 2.4 and 3.4). Even bureaucratic organizations have experimented with autonomous work groups. Collaborative working is fostered by the opportunity for all employees in a department to meet with the responsible manager(s).

A weaker form of direct participation for employees is where those affected are consulted. One company defines the requirement as follows:

Employee participation requires an organisation's plans and decisions to take account of the views and experiences of all those affected by the business. Employees should, therefore, have the opportunity to influence and contribute to decisions which affect them. Managers, therefore, whose ultimate responsibility it is to take decisions, will explain intentions and options about plans and activities at their level and involve their employees in decisions and changes that affect them. Managers will have the information and authority to adopt an open style of management.

(Brewer 1978: 28)

Note that such participation does not imply that any action will be decided by majority vote. Action remains the right and duty of the manager, and is compatible with bureaucracy. Chapter 8 describes the connection between participative structures and management style.

In the UK, managers are obliged, by legislation, to consult workers on certain matters such as health and safety, and they usually do so indirectly. Indirect participation refers to a right that people have to elect or appoint a representative to speak for them on some decision-making body which is discussing matters of common interest. Workers may elect members to works councils, or, in some cases (for example British Steel Corporation and the Post Office), to the board which runs the enterprise. There are many variations on structures for employee representation, some being confined to the top levels and others providing representation at multiple levels. Three issues have been the focus of disagreement in Europe: the proportionate representation of different levels and sections, what powers they should have, and how far collective responsibility weakens independent criticism. The European Community may attempt to impose greater uniformity of practice among the constituent countries. There are wider questions of whether customers and suppliers should be considered as 'citizens' of businesses, and whether share-holdings should be acquired by 'owners' who have no stake in a concern other than the financial one.

Chapter 1 introduced the idea of economic, ideological and order goals. Values in these areas can both unite and divide people. In business, the emphasis is mainly on economic and technical matters, but social and political considerations may be just as important if decision-making is to be a collaborative activity.

5 SUMMARY

Problems can be classified according to whether there is uncertainty about aims or about means or both. Situations are simple if there is no uncertainty. This is unusual, however. Under varying degrees of uncertainty, individuals (and organizations) employ different strategies. Strategies described were maximizing, satisficing, implicit favourite, intuition, routines, compromise or consensus, incrementalism, the Delphi method, the dialectic, the rubbish bin (or garbage can) and political gaming. Though these strategies are based on degree of uncertainty, they are also associated with 'analytical–directive' or 'conceptual–behavioural' decision styles. **Culture affects decision-making through a preference for the more analytical or the more intuitive styles**.

Degree of uncertainty is not the only source of difficulty. Two further considerations are the time period involved and whether or not there are common interests. The longer the time-scale of a decision the more likely it is to be taken by senior managers, while short-term decisions are likely to be made by lower level employees. Managers and workers may need the assistance of staff specialists.

Where participants perceive that their interests are antagonistic, machinery for resolving differences may be needed. Where the culture stresses the unity of interests, it may be necessary to find ways in which people can participate collectively. In the West, economic and technical rationality have received much emphasis, but ideological commitment (social, legal and political) may also be important in enabling co-operation in decision-making. **Culture affects perceptions of unity or diversity** in a decision-making body, since values may unite or divide people.

FURTHER READING

Books

Braybrooke, D. and Lindblom C.E. (1970) *A Strategy of Decision*, New York: Free Press.

Castles, F.G., Murray, D.T. and Potter, D.C. (eds) (1971) *Decisions, Organizations, and Society*, London: Penguin.

De Bono, E. (1971) *Lateral Thinking for Management*, New York: McGraw-Hill (reprinted London: Penguin, 1982).

March, J.G. (1988) *Decisions and Organizations*, Oxford: Blackwell.

Sanderson, M. (1979) *Successful Problem Management*, New York: Wiley.

Simon, H.A. (1960) *The New Science of Management Decision*, New York Harper & Row. A classic work.

The following large book has already been recommended:

Nystrom, P. and Starbuck, W.H. (eds) (1981) *Handbook of Organizational Design*, Oxford: Oxford University Press. It has a chapter by Beyer, J.M. 'Ideologies, values, and decision-making', pp. 166–97. You should find the book in a library.

Articles

Algie, J. (1983) 'Budget priority system', *Health and Social Service Journal* 3 November: 1320–1.
Algie, A., Mallen, G, and Foster, W.(1983) 'Financial decisions by priority scaling', *Journal of Management Studies* 20 (2): 233–60.
Brewer, R. (1978) 'Personnel's role in participation', *Personnel Management* 10 (September): 23–9, 45.
Cohen, M.D., March, J.G. and Olsen, J.P. (1972) 'A garbage can model of organizational choice', *Administrative Science Quarterly* 17 (1): 1–25.
Glueck, W.F. (1974) 'Decision-making: organizational choice', *Personnel Psychology* 27 (Spring): 73–93.
Keys, J.B. and Miller, T.R. (1984) 'The Japanese management theory jungle', *Academy of Management Review* 9 (2): 342–53.
Mitroff, I.I. and Emshoff, J. R, (1979) 'On strategic assumption making: a dialectical approach to policy and planning', *Academy of Management Review* 4 (1): 1–12.
Soelberg, P. (1967) 'Unprogrammed decision-making: job choice', *Industrial Management Review* 8 (Spring): 19–29.

RECOMMENDED CASE STUDIES

'A Case of Mismanagement' (in a Nigerian Internal Revenue Office): How to handle a complaint.
'Theatre Problems': How to improve the nursing service for theatres. (Set for Chapter 2, but can be used here to illustrate bounded rationality.)

RECOMMENDED EXERCISE

'Quick Containers': decision-making in a simulated manufacturing set-up.

Chapter 7

Cultures and group behaviour

CHAPTER OBJECTIVES

By the end of this chapter you will be able to:

1 say what is meant by the term 'group dynamics', and explain how personalities affect dynamics
2 give the advantages and disadvantages of united, or cohesive, and fragmented, or non-cohesive, groups
3 recommend actions to take before or during meetings to improve rational decision-making
4 describe how groups may be used in intuitive decision-making
5 indicate the advantages and disadvantages of group working for manual tasks
6 say how small groups can affect industrial efficiency and industrial relations
7 analyse the recommended cases

1 INTRODUCTION

Chapter 6 stated that decision-making is likely to be collaborative when people perceive they have common interests, but to be antagonistic when internal differences are emphasized. Power distance can create divisions. So can personality differences. This chapter looks at how varied personalities can affect what happens in small groups. We examine the dynamics of groups over time, and the advantages and drawbacks both of cohesiveness and of fragmentation. Suggestions are given for making groups more effective in decision-making and work. We are concerned here only with the *primary* group, defined as 'a small number of persons who meet frequently and think of themselves as a group'. Committees and work groups are of special interest. (We are not concerned with the secondary group, where some common characteristic, for example date of birth, may be used as a basis for grouping, even though the persons so grouped have never met.)

2 PERSONALITY AND GROUP BEHAVIOUR

Membership of primary groups in organizations is usually decided on the basis of people's occupation, knowledge, rank or function. However, in addition to their abilities and knowledge, people bring their temperaments into groups. The simplest terms for such temperaments are those used by Kolb *et al.* (1974). They speak of the tough battler, the friendly helper and the logical thinker. Adjectives used of the battler are: energetic, self-confident, enterprising, forceful, quick to act and ambitious. The friendly helper is said to be conciliatory, trusting, supportive, loyal, idealistic, modest, polite and caring; while the logical thinker is principled, orderly, analytic, fair and thorough.

Kiersey and Bates (1978) have measured four Jungian temperaments (see Chapter 5, Section 4.5), with an instrument called the Myers Briggs Type Indicator. SP's who prefer Sensing and Perceiving in dealing with practical problems in high risk environments are the battlers. The helpers are NF people who prefer iNtuition and Feelings, who like helping others but dislike conflict. Kiersey and Bates have two types of thinkers: the SJ who prefer Sensing and Judging in secure environments where they can attend to details and plan well in advance; and the NT who prefer iNtuitive Thinking where they have autonomy and are respected for their ideas and achievements.

Porter and Maloney (1977) call such temperamental characteristics 'strengths', which, if overdone, become weaknesses. They have a measure they call 'the strength deployment inventory' which asks about how we react in good times and in bad times. We tend to overdo our strengths in bad times. The strong points, if carried to excess, can be seen as weaknesses such as arrogance (in battling), gullibility (in helping) and lack of feeling (in problem analysis).

Here we are concerned with the mix of individual behaviour which can help or disrupt the work of a group. Groups need certain types of behaviour from the members if they are to be effective – behaviour which furthers the task and behaviour which maintains goodwill. Bad feeling can spread in a group composed entirely of tough battlers, since they find reconciliation difficult. But a group containing only friendly helpers may be afraid to take the tough decisions required by the task. A group of like-minded logical thinkers may never get around to any action, for the discussion itself may be too enjoyable!

In Chapter 8 we consider in more detail the particular behaviour of group leaders, but here we indicate that while tough battlers may energize a group and keep up the pressure to get things done, they are also liable to engage in self-regarding behaviour such as abusive language when they become impatient with others. Friendly helpers are good at what is called 'maintenance' behaviour, that is, making things pleasant for others through praising their contributions, and helping to settle quarrels. They can be so anxious to please, however, that they take far too long trying to get everyone to agree. The logical thinkers can help clarify issues, weigh options and so on, but they may also slow the group down because of nitpicking or excessive thoroughness. Blends of these strengths and weaknesses contribute not only to the output of a group but also to its dynamics, to which we now turn.

3 GROUP DYNAMICS AND CULTURAL TRANSFORMATIONS

Every group has a certain degree of cohesiveness, or unity, but groups change. When they have a stable and compatible membership they tend to be united, especially if there is an external threat (for example to deprive them of needed resources). Nevertheless, the members respond in different ways. The tough battlers want challenge and competition, the friendly helpers want peace and co-operation, while the logical thinkers want detachment and time to reflect. These preferences generate internal turbulence which may or may not result in adequate response to external demands. The term 'group dynamics' refers to this turbulence – the group's emotional ups and downs. Southgate and Randell (1977) have likened these to the phases of an orgasmic cycle. Tension will mount, reach a climax and subside. The tough battlers help energize the group. The friendly helpers prevent dissipation of energy in rivalries, and allow the group to enjoy the aftermath of success. Fragmented groups tend to be stuck with the tensions, but these do not get satisfactorily discharged. United groups, on the other hand, may either exhaust themselves in an attempt to retain permanent excitement or grow comfortable with the relaxed phase of the cycle and be unwilling to allow tensions to surface again. The logical thinkers cannot play their part if the drive of the tough battlers and the pacification of the friendly helpers are not dominant at the appropriate times.

The 'hidden agenda' in groups is associated with the emotional dynamics just described. Bion (1948) speaks of the agenda in terms of what he calls 'basic assumptions'. The group behaves as if it is helpless, or as if it wants to fight, or to run away, or to pair up, though these assumptions are not discussed (unless the group has been constituted for the purpose of examining its own dynamics, as is the case with the T-group or training group).

Tuckman (1965) has a neat little mnemonic for remembering the first cyclic movement in a group.

1 FORMING (polite reconnaissance)
2 STORMING (the tension mounts)
3 NORMING (targeting, and standard setting)
4 PERFORMING (getting on with the job)

When a group first meets, the members are polite and spend their time sizing one another up, rather as people do at cocktail parties. With work groups, however, members are very dependent on the formally appointed leader, and they often behave as though they cannot do anything for themselves. However, in Western culture particularly, there are likely to be some members (the tough battlers) who dislike this dependence on the leader, and they start to assert themselves and so to move out of the forming stage. Bion speaks of the 'storming' as being a phase of 'counter-dependency' in which the group behaves as if it wished to get rid of the formal leader. If the challenge from the battlers gets too strong, the friendly helpers take fright, and they may push the group from 'fight' to 'flight'. This does not mean members actually run away, though some may absent themselves for a time. There are very may ways to avoid facing up to things, however. Diedrich (1942) lists thirty ways to 'run away from [solving] an educational problem' (for example 'wet nurse' the problem or 'give it a medal'). Discussion may go round and round to keep the problem alive. Some groups oscillate between Bion's 'fight' and 'flight' assumptions and never get to 'norming' or performing.

The 'pairing' assumption is also part of the hidden agenda. The group acts as if it has given up on its own collective attempt to reach a decision, but it is unwilling to follow the present leadership either. Instead, two of the members are allowed to take the floor, while the

Table 7.1 Overt and hidden agenda in groups, with personality types and ego states

	3 Norming	4 Performing
Overt agenda	i.e. setting goals and standards, and information requirements 'Sensing/Judging'	i.e. getting work done 'Intuitive/Thinking'
	LOGICAL THINKERS	THINKERS BATTLERS HELPERS
	Adult	*P, A, C*
	2 Storming	1 Forming
Hidden agenda	i.e. determining who will control whom	i.e. accepting fellow members
	Fight/flight Counter-dependence	**Pairing Dependence**
	'Sensing/Perceiving'	'Intuitive/Feeling'
	STURDY BATTLERS	FRIENDLY HELPERS
	Critical Parent and Rebellious Child	*Nurturing Parent and Adapted Child*

Notes: Kiersey and Bates' (1978) temperaments, based on Jungian psychology, are shown in quotation marks. (Compare Rowe and Boulgarides (1983) decision styles in Table 6.1.)
Kolb *et al.*'s (1974) personality types are in capitals. Berne's (1967) ego states are in italics. Bion's (1948) basic assumptions are in bold type. The numerals give Tuckman's (1965) sequence.

others sit passively watching, or the group breaks up into a number of private conversations between partners. The pairing continues because the members assume, at the subconscious level, that this will produce a supernatural solution in the form of a new saviour, who, of course, never arrives.

Table 7.1 summarizes the discussion above and links it with transactional analysis. We have stated (Chapter 5, Section 4.6) that energies which would otherwise be available for work get diverted into 'games'. It is these 'games' that are associated with Bion's basic assumptions – or hidden agenda. The 'ego states' described by Berne can be associated with the activities of helping, battling and thinking. The friendly helper is using her or his Nurturing Parent ego state most of the time, but may also use Adapted Child quite a lot. The sturdy battler is using his or her Rebellious Child ego state, and also often the Critical Parent. The logical thinker is using the Adult ego state. As explained, effective groups require the use of the full range of strengths contained in P, A and C. In low performing groups, either some ego states are unused or some are used to excess. People's behaviour is self-oriented rather than attuned to the realities of the situation. Hidden agenda interfere with the group's task. However, people can be taught to switch ego states intentionally, instead of doing so unconsciously. Ferrari (1979) says that non-Westerners recognize Berne's description of C as familiar in their countries also. Though the description of P and A is more specifically Western, Ferrari notes that transactional analysis has been of value nevertheless in helping people to understand transactions in groups in developing countries.

If Table 7.1 is compared with Table 3.1 it can be seen that the support culture is relevant to the agenda of forming; storming is related to power culture issues of resource control; norming is needed for role cultures; while performing involves the achievement culture, but also keeping a balanced emphasis (parts 3 and 5 in Table 3.1). All the cultures are relevant to group decision-making as the sections that follow will show.

4 THE ADVANTAGES AND DISADVANTAGES OF COHESIVE GROUPS

4.1 Advantages

When a group is highly attractive to the members and their work is interdependent, they tend to stick together. The term for this is 'cohesiveness', and such united groups are highly cohesive. They have been dubbed HICO groups by Golembiewski (1962), who contrasts them with LOCO groups (those low in cohesiveness). Support culture groups are most likely to be cohesive and power culture groups are least likely. How much cohesion there is in achievement and role cultures may depend on job design and on how long the members have been together. Effective teamwork demands unity or cohesiveness – but how much? It would appear at first that a HICO group has the best chance of fulfilling the requirements for collaborative decision-making. These are as follows:

1 members are aware of a common purpose;
2 members are accountable as a functioning unit within a broader context, and accept some agreed form of discipline or control;
3 members enjoy helping one another, value each other's contributions and have a sense of belonging which satisfies their social needs (see Chapter 5, 4.4);
4 members are ready to disclose information as and when it is needed.

Some HICO groups can achieve these conditions for a while at least. They have the following characteristics:

1 members participate more;
2 members are more susceptible to group influence;
3 members are more satisfied and less anxious;
4 members perform more uniformly, and the standard of performance will be high if the group favours high output;
5 the group tries to convert deviants, and may expel or reject any members who consistently violate its standards;
6 the group mobilizes its energies well in the face of any perceived threat to its survival.

4.2 Disadvantages

A HICO group can work for or against the broader objectives of an organization, depending on the attitudes of its members (see Chapter 4, Section 2.1, for remarks on 'restriction of output'). Members co-operate amongst themselves, but may not co-operate with outsiders. A HICO group is also likely to be resistent to changes, simply because the members get satisfaction from things as they are. Another drawback is that, precisely because HICO groups believe in their own attractiveness, they are liable to illusions of their own infallibility or invulnerability. Janis (1972) says that in such groups discord is frowned upon, and members censor themselves so as not to 'rock the boat'. Some members even act as 'mind-guards' to prevent unpalatable information from being brought to the attention of members. Excessive optimism can develop, because it appears that there is unanimity, when privately there may be divergent views which are not disclosed. Such a state of affairs leads to 'a deterioration of mental efficiency, reality testing, and moral judgement that results from in-group pressures'. This deterioration Janis calls 'group think'. The consequences of group think for decision-making are as follows:

1 few alternatives are considered (see Chapter 6, Section 2.1, 'implicit favourite');
2 the preferred solution is not examined for hidden risks or disadvantages;
3 options initially thought unsuitable are not reconsidered for non-obvious advantages;
4 little information is obtained from experts to improve estimates;
5 when experts or outsiders are brought in, there is selective bias, in that interest is shown in what supports the implicit favourite and anything that detracts from the favourite is neglected;
6 contingency plans to deal with failure or setbacks are not made because the group does not entertain the possibility of either of these occurrences.

McKenna (1978) suggests that group think may be responsible for the failure by some management committees to heed warnings proffered by accountants.

4.3 Solutions

Decisions made by group think do not all turn out to be bad decisions. The intuitions of the members may be sound, or there may be the political will and resources to carry out a decision against the odds. Knowledge of the behaviour of people in a primary group, however, can serve to alert us to what is happening. If a HICO group is lapsing into group think and producing poor quality decisions, it is possible to introduce the role of 'devil's advocate', and to reward people for speaking out instead of for keeping their qualms to themselves. Mind-guards can be punished for concealing pertinent information. The leader can avoid declaring his or her opinions too early, and may even decide not to attend certain meetings of the group to provoke greater spontaneity. Changing the membership of a group at intervals can also prevent the group from becoming too introspective, and can destroy excessive cohesiveness. Care has to be taken, however, not to fall into the opposite danger of creating a dysfunctional LOCO group.

5 THE ADVANTAGES AND DISADVANTAGES OF FRAGMENTED GROUPS

5.1 Advantages

Where the jobs of different individuals are not interdependent, the fact that people tend not to stick together will not be a drawback. Competition among individuals can promote excellence, especially for those who have a high need for growth (see Chapters 4 and 5). At times a committee may benefit from the existence of factions which represent alternative viewpoints. Such groups will not suffer from group think because the pressures to conformity which exist in one sub-group will be exposed by another, or even by a single dissenting individual. Substantive differences may provide the kinds of tensions which enhance creativity.

5.2 Disadvantages

LOCO groups tend to have low morale and not to work as a team. Emotional differences can be a source of evasion or infighting which prevents rational agreement from being reached collaboratively. The differences in viewpoint among the members lead them to be suspicious of one another.

Horvat (1983) observed the following ten ways in which such distrust showed itself in a self-managed work organization with highly educated participants.

1 Someone asks for an unpleasant problem to be raised at the next meeting. It is not put on the agenda. Excuses are made for this.
2 The information needed is not circulated beforehand, and so the council or committee refuses to discuss it.
3 The subject is put to the end of a long agenda. By this time there is no quorum and the meeting is adjourned. (Alternatively, clique members may wait until enough opposition members have left to push through the decision they want.)
4 Several people disrupt the decision-making by raising pointless issues.
5 The decision does not get recorded in the minutes, or it is ambiguously worded.
6 Special studies are proposed which delay the decision until it is no longer relevant.

7 An official claims not to know under whose jurisdiction the issue falls, so several bodies are circulated and confusion created.

8 Materials are prepared on the last day before a deadline so that no substantial revision is possible.

9 The official concerned with implementation does nothing, banking on the fact that there will not be a challenger for the neglect.

10 The official waits until there is a new committee, then re-presents the decision, asking for advice on implementation, and so the whole issue is reopened.

Zand (1972) has shown experimentally how distrust can affect the perceptions of members and militate against effective decision-making. He gave groups of business managers identical information about a difficult manufacturing and marketing policy problem. However, half his groups were briefed to expect trusting (HICO) behaviour, and half to expect distrusting (LOCO) behaviour. The expectations created differences between the two conditions with regard to

1 goal clarification
2 the reality of the information exchanged
3 the scope of the search for solutions
4 the commitment of the managers to implement their solutions.

The groups which expected distrust performed worse on all the above counts.

5.3 Solutions

LOCO groups will become more united if the sources of disruption or incompatibility can be removed. Possible sources are numerous. Members may not share a common goal, so steps must be taken to provide one. There may be incompatible personalities. Skilful assignment of responsibilities may alleviate this problem. People may have false beliefs about one another, misinformation, or misperceptions about individual or group tasks, rewards, circumstances and so on. Reliable information from a respected source can be used to counter this. External pressures can also be a major factor in reducing cohesiveness (as was seen with regard to the Ahmedabad autonomous work groups in Chapter 4). It may be necessary to protect the group from outside interference.

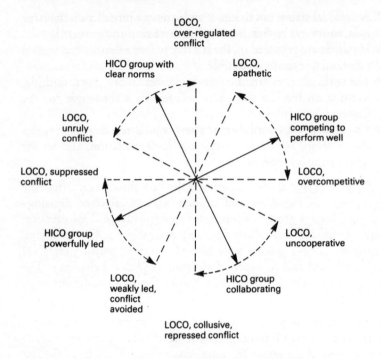

Figure 7.1 Unity and conflict in groups (the golden mean)
Note: Compare with Figures 1.1 and 2.4

Figure 7.1 suggests that, in spite of the disadvantages described in Section 4.2 above, united groups whose high cohesion is based on values from the four cultures *can* be the golden mean that organizations should seek. (Chapter 9, Section 4.4, deals with organizational development which includes team-building techniques for dealing with LOCO groups.)

6 THE USE OF GROUPS FOR RATIONAL DECISION-MAKING

Chapter 6 spoke of decisions being made by individuals or organizations. Often they are made by a committee. Managers may spend some three hours a week in such primary groups, and so it is worth establishing that meetings are necessary. Their value consists in their synergy – that is, the collective product is greater than the sum of the individual contributions. This is the case where people are stimulated to think of things that none would otherwise have considered, or where they become committed to action none would otherwise have undertaken. Meetings may be used to collect or give information, to vent grievances and to solve problems. Meetings are not needed where individuals are authorized to make simple, recurrent decisions for which the required information can be obtained mechanically, electronically or by personal contact. When a meeting is justified, certain preparations are necessary.

6.1 Preparations

The first consideration is who should be invited. Each person who attends must know why he or she is there. All must be able to contribute. It may help to circulate any relevant documents and to verify that key persons will be present and have been adequately briefed. Greater formality is needed with large groups than with small ones. Groups of five or six are often very productive provided they contain persons with the full range of competencies required by the task. If the size of the group is greater than fifteen it is unlikely that all will have an opportunity to speak during the meeting, but people may still contribute by their attention. This is especially true of briefing meetings. Large groups may be appropriate for these. Where people have met regularly over a long period of time it may be wise for them to review their group's composition to make sure that the right people are there for the nature of the decisions being taken. It may be that the business of the group has changed and that the membership should change also.

Choice of location can also merit attention. It may favour those on home ground and put those from elsewhere at a disadvantage. The symbolic significance of the venue must be recognized by the convenor. Attention to physical conditions such as temperature, ventilation and acoustics may also be called for. People must be able to see and hear each other without distraction. The shape of the table and type of furniture also have an impact, suggesting formality or informality. Informality may be better for grievance ventilation, but formality may suit a meeting where recommendations made elsewhere are being submitted for approval. For formal meetings visual aids and stenographic assistance may be required.

6.2 Dealing with the agenda

Further concerns which have to be met during the meeting are shown in the overt and hidden agenda of Table 7.1.

Accepting fellow members

The question of who is present or absent is linked to private concerns about one's place in the group and the value that is placed on one's membership. Introductions may be necessary for people meeting for the first time, or when strangers are present. Subsequent behaviour may also provide cues that everyone is respected. Where persons of different status are present the culture of the organization in which the meeting occurs will influence the extent to which lower status members contribute. In role and achievement cultures people are likely to be invited to speak according to the function they perform. In support cultures status differences may exert a minimal impact, while in power cultures the lower status members may be much more guarded in their contributions, even when invited to speak.

Control

For rational decision-making it helps if meetings start and finish on time. If the estimate of time required is obviously wrong, steps need to be taken to do something about this, such as shortening the agenda or agreeing a fresh time estimate or scheduling a further meeting if necessary. Groups need a procedure for keeping track of time and for seeing that it is used productively. This involves control via 'gate-keeping' – bringing in or shutting out contributions. Disagreement can be productive when it is about substantive issues. If it is not productive it can be reduced by looking for common ground, or by bringing in neutral speakers. Emotional storming tends to be unproductive. It needs to be controlled by removal of the sources of friction, shutting out those whose contributions are generating more heat than light. Attacks can be defused and defensiveness recognized for what it is. In formal groups and in power cultures the gate-keeping is done from the chair. In less formal groups, especially in achievement and support cultures, members may take it upon themselves to do the gate-keeping. In role cultures there may be 'timed items' printed on the agenda paper. For rational decision-making the form of control used must be acceptable to those present.

Setting goal standards and information requirements

People must not only be able to contribute, they must also know what kind of contribution is wanted: factual information, ideas, opinions, reactions,proposals, clarification, support and so forth. Questions are important in getting relevant communication flowing. The right questions must be asked of the right people. If frankness is desired it must be encouraged by commendation and example. It is interesting that people suspect a chairman of bias when she or he shuts them out, but do not have such suspicions when the gate-keeping is exercised through bringing other people in. Different personalities have different fears. Logical thinkers fear that a bald statement may be misinterpreted unless it is placed in context, while friendly helpers fear they will hurt others if they say what they really think. Battlers may think they are being frank when in fact they are being rude. It is possible to state disagreement and difficulties in ways which are a challenge rather than an obstacle to continued discussion. This is a skill which can be learned.

Getting work done

The purpose of a meeting should have been established when it was convened. There are certain kinds of behaviour, however, which help the group to keep at its task. These also can be learned. Some examples are: testing understanding, clarifying statements, building on the ideas of others, and summarizing. It is important that people know what has been decided and what responsibilities each person has subsequently in relation to the decision(s) taken. Next steps should be clear. The date and time of any further meetings may be at the chairman's convenience in power cultures, by regular appointment in role cultures, and *ad hoc* as the need arises in achievement and support cultures.

Trull (1966) suggests that the quality of the implementation of whatever the group decided depends on

1 the authority of the decision-makers;
2 the information available to the decision-makers;
3 the timeliness of the decision;
4 the decision's compatibility with any operating constraints that exist at the time it has to be carried out;
5 the understanding possessed by the doers;
6 the doers not having conflicting loyalties about the decision; and
7 the rewards for doing being greater than the risks.

The above can be affected by the way the decision was reached. In a role culture a majority vote may be regarded as a mandate. In a power culture a minority (even of one) may be able to veto or sanction action. In achievement and support cultures consensus tends to be favoured, with compromise as an alternative. There is further discussion of these differences when we consider styles of leadership (Chapter 8).

7 THE USE OF GROUPS FOR INTUITIVE DECISION-MAKING

For inspirational decisions, there are ways of using groups to generate a greater variety of solutions than individuals alone may do. The best known methods are 'brainstorming' (Osborn 1981) and 'synectics' (Gordon 1961). Saward (1976) gives a great deal of information about synectics as a method for producing creative ideas. Here is an example of what may take place at a synectics session.

1 A person who has a problem is asked to state it in clear and concise terms.
2 Others in the group may assist in clarification of the problem.
3 Group members are asked to go on a short guided fantasy trip to a time and place where the problem is solved, and then to come back to think about possible solutions.
4 Each person is asked privately to write down five or six possible solutions.
5 The first suggestion from one person's list is written up where all can see. People are then asked to call out any ideas that the written suggestions gives rise to for them, without checking whether the ideas are practical or not.
6 The procedure in 5 is repeated for the next person's first idea, and then the next person's and so on, for as long as the group has time for or the person with the problem wishes. The session may end here, or it may go on to stage 7.
7 The problem 'owner' may set guidelines which the group then uses to evaluate each idea in turn. Alternatively, the ideas may be grouped into categories, and the two or three most valuable ideas from each category selected for further work.

Both synectics and brainstorming work on the principle that the generation of ideas must be separated sequentially from any critical examination of their feasibility, since the latter tends to inhibit spontaneity.

Ferrari (see Section 3) concluded that the way in which the opportunity to think freely is accepted and expressed is deeply influenced by the cultural background. He found that Africans tended to use analogies and metaphors from nature, and Asians tended to refer to legends or religious stories. A mixed group gets the best of all worlds. 'The most creative groups were those in which respect for other cultures was highest,' while 'The least creative groups were those in which the members thought their cultural characteristics were the best and in a certain way superior to those of the others.'

The composition of the group can be important in other ways. A synectics procedure will not suffice if the members are not capable of producing ideas, or if they prefer working alone, or if they do not trust one another. It may also be the case that severable able people fail to produce because the dynamics in the group are non-creative. We have already outlined how the emotional life of a group goes through a cycle, or series of cycles, the duration of which will vary from group to group. If a group gets stuck in a particular phase of a cycle it will not perform its decision-making task effectively. The group may be too cohesive, or too competitive, with the drawbacks already mentioned (Sections 4.2 and 5.2 above). We turn now to other types of primary group.

8 OTHER TYPES OF PRIMARY GROUP

8.1 The use of groups for manual tasks

Autonomous work groups have been mentioned in Chapter 4. Much publicity has been given to the experiments in autonomous group working on assembly lines at Volvo and Saab. Such groups have also been used in connection with small batch manufacture, and with continuous process production. Bowey and Connolly (1975) conclude from the European evidence that defining tasks as group tasks, rather than individual tasks, can be beneficial in the following circumstances:

1 when co-operative working is likely to produce a better end result than working separately;
2 where amalgamation of work into a joint task or area of responsibility would appear meaningful to those involved;
3 where the joint task requires a mixture of different skills or specialisms;

4 where the system requires fairly frequent adjustments in activities and in the co-ordination of activities;
5 where competition between individuals leads to less effectiveness, rather than more;
6 where stress levels on individuals are too high for effective activity.

Compare these criteria with the requirements for collaborative decision-making (Section 4.1 above).

Advantages

Under these circumstances the following advantages can obtain:

1 The work, and the relationships, are satisfying to the members.
2 Newcomers are more easily assimilated and trained.
3 From a management point of view, there are fewer units to cope with than previously when there were dealings with individuals.
4 It is easier to arrange coverage for absenteeism or turnover.
5 Changes in production schedules and work allocations can more easily be accommodated.

Compare these with the six advantages of HICO groups (Section 4.1) and of autonomous work groups.

Disadvantages

Some of the disadvantages of HICO groups (Section 4.2) can also apply here; for example, there will be resistance to any attempt to break up the group. Miller and Rice (1967) once considered it would be a good thing if task groups were also friendship groups. (They spoke of 'task boundaries' being the same as 'sentient boundaries'.) In their later work, however, they studied temporary groupings, such as cabin crews and flight crews in airlines, which caused them to revise their opinions. Apparently the airlines had deliberately shifted crew members around to prevent the formation of cohesive work groups, because such groups developed their own private vocabulary of terms and their own habits, and these could create hazards. Replacement personnel, who, by definition, were not 'in the know' might mistake the meaning or actions of fellow workers. To prevent accidents from such causes, the airlines insist on the carrying out of instructions given in the rulebook, and they prevent informal practices from growing up by reconstituting the crew after one or two flights.

8.2   Groups and industrial efficiency

The airline case is a special one. More usually we think of 'working to rule' as being a means of industrial action which slows down operations, simply because the rules which are applied have usually become outmoded. In other words, in the interests of efficiency, there has been an informal use of appreciation and a drift away from regulated practices. 'Working to rule' reinstates the regulations in circumstances where they are no longer helpful (see Chapter 2, Section 1, on control). The point here is that small groups may devise their own modes of operation which may vary from official modes, sometimes to the detriment of the wider organization and sometimes to its advantage. The more cohesive the group, the more likely it is that the members will adopt the (good or bad) habits approved by the group.

Because new circumstances require new actions, the co-operation of workers in solving production problems is sometimes consciously sought by managers. This is a characteristic of the famous Japanese 'quality circles', and Robson (1984) has written a 'practical guide' to European companies on how to introduce them. Employees are given training in group problem-solving methods, and they meet regularly on a voluntary basis to identify, analyse and solve their own specific problems. The leader is usually a first-line supervisor. Interestingly, the idea started in 1949 when an American professor was invited, by the Union of Japanese Scientists and Engineers, to teach statistics to an eight-day seminar on quality control. In effect, people were being given (statistical) tools to do something they wanted to do anyway (improve quality). Where employees are interested in acquiring skills for improving existing methods of working, quality circles can provide the means. These conditions are more likely to obtain where relations between employer and employees are already harmonious.

8.3   Groups and industrial relations

The introduction to this chapter distinguished between primary and secondary groups. Trade unions are usually secondary groups, since they are mostly too large for every member to know all the other members. Nevertheless, there are primary groups within any trade union. Sayles (1958) studied 300 such groups in thirty plants in order to see whether he could account for variation in grievance activity. He came up with four types of grievance behaviour which he termed 'apathetic', 'erratic', 'strategic' and 'conservative'. He thought that the status of jobs, the technology employed, the degree to which jobs were interdependent and whether people at the same workplace used similar or different skills all influenced the type of grievance behaviour adopted. Primary groups are critical, in Sayles's view. Mass production assembly line workers are likely to be erratic; low status and low paid casual workers are apathetic; high paid self-supervised craftsmen are conservative, only engaging in grievance behaviour when their own interests are directly threatened; while key workers who know their own power engage in strategic behaviour, exerting continuous pressure on management. Rose (1978) comments that Sayles does not distinguish clearly between primary and secondary groups, and that he concentrates too much on variables within the employing organization. Explanations drawn solely from job categories, organizational cultures or group dynamics will not do justice to industrial work-group phenomena, whether in Europe, Africa or Asia. What happens in labour markets in the wider society is also important. Where there are seasonal variations in rural and urban work, and where subsistence and monetary economics are mixed, grievance behaviour may take the form of evasion rather than confrontation, for example. Nevertheless, where primary groups are able to establish themselves and become cohesive, they may well form cells of activists, able to respond to provocation or to exploitation by pressing counter claims. The attitudes of employers are, of course, important, and so are the policies of the state, but these are outside the scope of the present chapter (see Chapters 1 and 4 for differences in the importance of groups in China and India, for example).

9 SUMMARY: THE IMPORTANCE OF SMALL GROUPS

Different types of personality contribute to a group. Each person has certain strengths which, if overdone, can become weaknesses. Sturdy battlers are good at keeping things moving, but they tend to get involved in arguments. Friendly helpers are good at pouring oil on troubled waters, but they tend to be nervous in taking risks or a hard line. Logical thinkers are good at sorting out issues, but they may hold up the action with their scruples. The strengths are all needed, since they complement each other, but they are needed in different combinations at different phases in the group's life. A group that lacks insight into its own dynamics may find itself stuck in a stage of dependence or of quarrelling because there is no one to challenge its 'basic assumptions'. It is possible to learn to do this. The hidden agenda arise from members' private concerns about whether they are fully accepted as members, whether things will get out of control or be over-controlled, whether they can contribute in ways which are personally satisfying and whether the group will be sufficiently united to collaborate on a common task while allowing members to retain their own individuality.

Different cultures handle these issues differently, but certain training methods such as T-groups and transactional analysis have proved helpful in many countries. People can learn that aspects of their personalities, the ego states, can be brought partly under their conscious control. It is possible to switch from using one's Free Child in a brain-storming session to using one's Critical Parent when the group is engaged in evaluating the ideas that have emerged earlier.

In rational decision-making it is necessary to prepare beforehand to accommodate the personal concerns of members by paying attention to the composition of the group, the pre-briefing and the venue. When the group meets, there are dangers should it become either too cohesive or too fragmented. There are remedies for both these conditions, but **culture affects group behaviour through preferences for competitive, isolated or collaborative working**.

The behaviour of the chairman will be a crucial factor, especially in power cultures, while in support cultures members may share responsibility for the conduct of the meeting. Gate-keeping, keeping the contributions geared to the task and observing time constraints, is a crucial function whoever performs it.

A group is useful when it has synergy – a surplus above what could be achieved by individuals working separately. In intuitive decision-making this synergy consists in the new ideas which emerge from the stimulation provided by others. The technique of synectics is one way of operating for this purpose.

Group phenomena can also be seen in industrial work groups. There can be synergy when workers' tasks are interdependent and when workers perceive their interests to be the same as those of their employers. But united work groups may develop standards of their own that are contrary to those prescribed by the organization. Such groups may also resist any changes from outside. Conversely, fragmented groups may put up less resistance to change, but demarcations and differentials hinder the performance of the organization as a whole.

Explanations of group behaviour in terms of personality, job category, group dynamics or organizational culture are all partial, but sufficient knowledge is available for training to give some help to those who are frustrated by their experiences in groups.

FURTHER READING

Books

Thelen, H.A. (1954) *Dynamics of Groups at Work*, Chicago, IL: University of Chicago Press. May be out of print. Has some useful ideas but is quite heavy going.

Kiersey, D. and Bates, M. (1978) *Please Understand Me*, 3rd edn, Buffalo, NY: Prometheus Nemisis Press.

Kolb, D.A., Rubin, I. and McIntyre, J.M. (1974) *Organizational Psychology: an experiential approach*, Englewood Cliffs, NJ: Prentice Hall.

Robson, M. (1984) *Quality Circles: a practical guide*, Aldershot: Gower.

Shaw, M.E. (1971) *Group Dynamics*, New York: McGraw-Hill.

Articles

Bion, W.R. (1948) 'Experiences in groups', *Human Relations* 1: 314–20, 487–96.

Bowey, A. and Connolly, R. (1975) 'Application of the concept of working in groups', *Management Decision* 13(3): 181–92.

Burns, T. (1955) 'The reference of conduct in small groups: cliques and cabals in occupational milieux', *Sociology* 8: 467–85.

Elias, N. and Dunning, E. (1966) 'Dynamics of group sports, with special reference to football', *British Journal of Sociology* 17(4): 388–401.

Ferrari, S. (1979) 'Transactional analysis in developing countries', *Journal of European Industrial Training* 3(4): 12–15.

McKenna, E. (1978) 'Do too many nodding heads produce poor decisions?', *Accountancy* November: 48–51.

Tuckman, B.W. (1965) 'Developmental sequence in small groups', *Psychological Bulletin* 27: 384–99; reprinted in Smith, P.B. (ed.) (1970) *Group Processes*, London: Penguin, ch. 17, 322–51.

Zand, D.E. (1972) 'Trust and managerial problem solving', *Administrative Science Quarterly* 17: 229–39.

RECOMMENDED CASE STUDIES

'The Duty Roster': A nursing officer persuades colleagues in a mental hospital to adopt a new rota.

'An Integrated Local Office': Describes how the norms and practices of a local benefit office ran counter to the policies of the then British Department of Health and Social Security.

'Founding of the Kabzeyan Club': Difficulties encountered in founding a women's group for voluntary action in Nigeria.

Chapter 8

Cultures, leadership and management

CHAPTER OBJECTIVES

By the end of this chapter you will be able to:

1 say what is meant by the term 'a leader'
2 describe different situations in which 'charismatics' may become leaders
3 describe what senior managers do, and say how different positions enable individuals to act as leaders
4 give four power bases from which leaders can operate and say how managers lead
5 explain what is meant by the 'agentic frame of reference', its advantages and drawbacks
6 explain why some writers think hierarchy and excessive force provoke non-compliance
7 summarize four types of styles leaders may use in going about their tasks and compare these with the cultural examples
8 analyse the recommended cases

1 INTRODUCTION

A leader takes the principal part in some activity and acts as a guide to others. Many people have led someone else at some time or other, though they may not all have called themselves 'leaders' or been recognized as such.

This chapter looks first at evidence of how people come to the fore through their personal qualities and behaviour. (These are 'charismatic leaders'. Charisma comes from the same root as 'charm'.)

Table 8.1 How people become leaders

	Formal leaders	*Charismatic leaders*
	ARE APPOINTED to an office	CAN OFFER knowledge or skill
Followers accord status out of	respect for the office	recognition of contribution
	(Role culture power base is legitimacy)	**(Achievement culture power base is expertise)**
	ACQUIRE resources to coerce or reward	HAVE personal charisma which symbolizes esteemed values
Followers accord status out of	fear, deference or utility	liking or identification
	(Power culture power base is force or rewards)	**(Support culture power base is *informal* status)**

Note: Compare Table 2.5.

Then we consider leaders who owe their positions mainly to the acts of others, that is, they have been appointed to, or have inherited, their position of leadership. (These we call 'formal leaders'.) Of course, charismatic leadership and formal leadership can be combined, and often are. Nevertheless the distinction is worth making for cultural reasons in both primary and secondary groups. Table 8.1 shows how the different organizational cultures favour different types of leader. The figure is explained in Section 2 below. Then we discuss what leaders do and how their styles of doing it differ in different cultures. Finally we discuss the importance of leadership to organizations.

2 HOW PEOPLE BECOME LEADERS

It so happens that small group studies shed most light on how charismatic leaders emerge. In the last chapter we mentioned that people can bring at least three different kinds of strengths to primary groups – energy, powers of analysis and friendliness. Let us see how these qualities can enable a person to lead.

2.1 Charismatic leaders

In primary groups

In primary groups where there is no appointed leader, it was suggested (Chapter 7) that different persons come to the fore as the needs of the groups change. The leader who is likely to emerge will be the individual whose personal strengths are those which are most desired by the group. The sociable person who is able to tell jokes may take a leading place at parties, the person who has a lot of energy may be asked to lead a campaign group and a logical thinker may be chosen for a group which is engaged on a planning task. The power of charismatic leaders resides in their ability to form good relationships with others by providing what is wanted at the time. Slater (1955) found that, in discussion groups, those seen as leaders tended to contribute more ideas, to talk more and to receive more communications from others. There was a difference, however, between united (HICO) and disunited (LOCO) groups in that, in disunited groups, the highest participator

> apparently does not adjust his amount of participation to the approval and acceptance he receives, but persists in interacting despite their absence. His participation time is determined by his own aggressiveness, by insensitivity rather than responsiveness.
>
> (Slater 1970: 243)

Slater says most of the members in such disunited groups act from personal impulse rather than according to what is in the best interests of the group as a whole. In some cases a single person emerges who can undertake all the types of behaviour necessary for an effective group, and this person will be seen as the leader, whatever the situation facing the group. Borgatta *et al.* (1954) did experimental work which suggests that the presence of an outstandingly capable person in a problem-solving group can raise the whole group's performance. In an achievement culture this leader is likely to be an expert on the type of work being done.

In secondary groups

Although we stated that our knowledge of charismatic leaders comes mainly from small group studies, this does not mean that charisma does not count in larger groups. It does! This feature is illustrated by

Friedland (1964) with respect to trade union leaders in Tanganyika. He says,

> Before the charismatics can emerge as genuine, the social situation must exist within which their message is relevant and meaningful to people. In some, but possibly not all, cases the expression of this message may be viewed as being hazardous and some 'success', as defined by the social group itself, must be registered.
>
> (1964: 25)

Trade unionism started in Tanganyika among dock workers in 1947 and the movement grew during the early 1950s. Westernized educated clerks became full-time leaders. They voiced the dissatisfaction of workers who, hitherto, had not been able to explain their grievances in face-to-face contacts with employers. There were successes in the form of wage increases and improved working conditions. The charisma of the union leaders was their ability to be insulting to employers in ways which nevertheless remained within the laws of libel!

Followers identify with the charismatic leader, and applaud what the leader proclaims. The leader's power derives from the values which he or she symbolizes and expresses (see the bottom right of Table 8.1).

In a political party, however, there will be pressures even on the leader to conform to the party line. Dearlove (1973) cites the vote of censure that can be taken in full council against the elected leader of the majority party in a Borough Council. But Hollander (1964) discovered that a group may allow a leader with a record of demonstrated loyalty to be non-conforming from time to time. Hollander called these concessions 'idiosyncrasy credits'. Despite such credits, it is unlikely that followers will continue to follow indefinitely a leader who is not successful in furthering their objectives unless the leader has some other sources of power. (By the time things start to go wrong, of course, the leader may well have a formal appointment to a very senior post, such as head of state, and have access to military and police forces to prevent the followers from engaging in open criticism. His power base will have shifted from respect to fear.)

The charisma which comes from expertise is most likely to be significant in an achievement culture. The knowledge of a specialist may put him or her in a position to cope effectively with what, for non-specialists, are uncertain and therefore threatening situations. Crozier (1964) showed, for example, that the status of maintenance workers in a tobacco plant was linked with their ability to deal with other people's uncertainties. Other examples of ability to deal with uncertainty are the doctor who knows how to prevent the death of a patient or accident victim and the fireman who deploys people and equipment to bring a fire under control. The power of experts is threatened if their skill is converted to standard routines which can be mastered by anyone, or if there are more experts around than are needed. Whole professions attempt to secure expertise as an asset for their members by creating a scarcity value through restricting entry to the profession. Nevertheless, many specialists are not in a position to dictate their terms to others. On the contrary, they may have to overcome barriers of reluctance on the part of those who are to be 'led'. Expertise can be seen as a threat rather than an asset by clients and customers who are either complacent or unsure of themselves. Experts may need more than charm to take a lead in such cases. They may need to use well-prepared strategies to obtain support, as Pettigrew (1975) indicates. If they are in-house advisers they may work to obtain access to an important policy committee, for example. If they are outsiders they may cultivate good relations with political sponsors on the inside.

2.2 Formal leaders

Experts are often formal leaders. In the hierarchy of a bureaucracy and in countries where resources are concentrated in a few hands, leaders are usually entitled to give instructions and to expect them to be carried out. There have also been attempts to simulate such conditions in small groups (as the following paragraphs describe).

In primary groups

Shaw has reviewed small group research into so-called 'communication nets'. A study by Hirota (1953) using Japanese subjects was included in the review. The communication net contains permitted pathways for the transmission of information in a small group. Four common nets are shown in Figure 8.1: the *chain* represents hierarchy; the *wheel* represents centralization; the *circle* is a closed group; in the *comcon* everyone is completely connected to everyone else. The lines represent the communication channels through which persons can transmit and receive (written) messages. The dots show the positions of the persons in each of the four nets. In these experiments there are five persons, but numbers larger than five have also been used. The

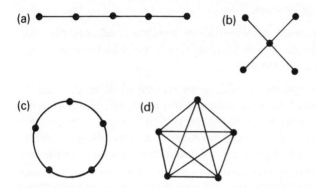

Figure 8.1 Four common nets: (a) the chain; (b) the wheel; (c) the circle; (d) the comcon

experimenter creates (unequal or equal) formal status by the number of channels that are available to each member and by what information he or she is given.

The experimental groups are asked to solve various problems using the information distributed. They may write but not speak. Each group's success is measured by the (shortest) time taken to reach a correct solution, the (smallest) number of errors and the (least) number of messages required.

If we think of formal leadership as stemming from circumstances rather than personal qualities, the information in the experiments can be seen as a chance for any member to reward or frustrate others (lower left power base in Table 8.1). From this perspective the following results from the communication nets are of interest.

1 The person at the hub of the wheel is regarded as the leader by the other persons in the wheel network.
2 For simple problems the wheel is most efficient, and the chain least.
3 The person at the hub is more satisfied than the other members.
4 For complex problems the hub of the wheel can become overloaded and the circle and comcon work better.
5 The chain is least efficient.

The reason why the person at the hub of the wheel is perceived as a leader, and treated as such, in these experiments is that this person has access to more sources of information than any other person, and so has an advantage in relation to the task.

In secondary groups

The communication net experiments simulate conditions that may occur in the design of jobs (Chapter 4) in colonial administration and elsewhere. Moris comments:

> The fastest and most efficient managerial tactic in the colonial situation was for the individual officer to provide all the complex and abstract functions of administration himself. Any complex task was reduced to a set of rudimentary and specific instructions, which the 'centre-post' official could then pass individually to a ring of poorly trained subordinates, each of whom bore only limited responsibility, not requiring much lateral communication (i.e. around the rim of the wheel). By dint of great effort, he [the colonial administrator] was sometimes able to achieve remarkable results, considering the scarcity of resources and the unreliable quality of subsidiary staff.
>
> (1981: 64)

(See Chapter 4 for the advantages of work simplification.) Moris continues:

> The tendency to continue this form of administration as the predominant mode for control is strongly reinforced in contemporary Third World settings. The 'wheel' communication pattern is congruent with the prevailing conceptions of authority in many areas.
>
> (1981: 64)

In role and power cultures formal leaders have two types of advantage. They are strategically situated with regard to superior access to information, and they are followed because their office is respected or feared. There is a range of assets, short of coercive force, which can be used to reward compliance and penalize disobedience. Any incentive which is of value to a subordinate, but which a superior may grant or withhold, gives the superior some power. This power may be constrained by, for example, the law of the land. (In the UK the power to dismiss workers is limited to 'fair' dismissal.) A leader's power may also be constrained by countervailing power on the part of the subordinates to withdraw their co-operation. (One of the reasons why the 'chain' communication structure described above is inefficient is that it is only as strong as its weakest link. One person can block the work of all the rest.) In many parts of Africa and Asia, however, employees fear that they will lose their jobs if they incur the disfavour of even a junior manager or supervisor. They conform in order that they may continue to receive a wage. This is the expedient or utilitarian type of compliance to power indicated in Table 8.1 (lower left).

Though we have indicated that, in power cultures especially, there may be a considerable differential between the resources available to the leader and those available to the subordinates, we have not discussed *how* people become formal leaders. Zald gives some of the possibilities when he says:

Organizational succession systems range from crown-prince systems, in which the chief executive chooses and trains his own replacement, to elective *leadership* systems in which executives serve on short-term sufferance of a politicized, conflict ridden, and involved electorate. Succession systems range from regularized ones, allowing for a chain of successors to be established, to those that take place through spasmodic and clandestine organizational coups d'état. . . . Who chooses key office holders is, in most organizations, a fundamental aspect of constitutions, closely related to constitutional prerogatives attached to specific offices or groups. . . . Most relatively stable organizations develop standard patterns of recruiting key executives. The standard pattern is determined both by the perceived requirements of competence of top officers and the opportunities to develop those competencies provided in organizations.

(1981: 253)

Some formal leaders are invited to apply for their position, while others take part in open competition. They may have to pass various tests, be interviewed by interested parties or obtain sponsorship for nomination. Competence and charisma may be more visible to a wider public after the attainment of formal office than prior to formal appointment, or a formal appointment may be made of someone who has already demonstrated charisma, but, whereas Western leaders are supposedly selected from among the 'outstanding', the Eastern culture values leaders who 'stand in' rather than 'stand out' (Pascale 1978). The group comes first and the individual sacrifices himself for it. Marlow describes the Japanese inheritance from Confucianism and Buddhism as

a philosophy in which learning, living and achieving become one. Hence the holistic and unitary view of life which is expressed in the total commitment of the individual to the objectives of the enterprise at all levels from the president to the shop floor.

(1984: 81)

3 WHAT LEADERS DO AND HOW THEY DO IT

3.1 What they do

From a systems theory perspective, the defining characteristic of a leader is that he or she provides direction for the activities of others. An example provided by Bocock (1971) is taken from the Ismailis in East Africa who have been a separate group from other Indians, Muslim and Hindu, from the 1920s on. 'In matters of finance and the administration of their community they have been pace setters.' He attributes this to the Imam, their spiritual leader. The late Aga Khan was Imam for the first sixty years of the twentieth century. What he did was to educate the Ismailis and to provide funds for many projects through which his wishes could be carried out.

Not all leaders have the assets of a wealthy Imam. Glueck suggests that leading within organizations consists of

a set of interpersonal behaviors designed to influence employees to cooperate in the achievement of objectives

(1977: 183)

In the task area, the leader can set or encourage certain goals, and disallow or modify others. He or she can allocate work and initiate working practices and arrangements, or encourage the subordinates (or followers) to do so.

In the socio-emotional area, the degree of competition or co-operation can be influenced. The leader can promote or discourage the formation of alliances within the group, or between the group and other groups. In general, by example and by what he or she approves or forbids, rewards or penalizes, the leader can influence the norms or standards of those below (see Chapter 7, Sections 4.3 and 5.3).

Top managers and administrators in effect represent the organization in dealings with the outside world. Such managers spend a lot of their time on 'external' relations, trying to ensure that those for whom they are responsible secure the resources and backing they need to attain their goals. They are partly fashioned by, and partly fashioning, the structures (described in Chapters 3 and 4) which make success more or less likely. Vickers says:

the policy maker, whatever the level at which he operates, is also
an artist in the creation of coherent and viable form in human
behaviour; and, like any artist, he must believe in the goodness as
well as the coherence and viability of the design which he is trying
to realise. And even beyond this, he is an artist in shaping the
norms and values from which his policy is made. For he affects
these both directly by advocating his policies and indirectly
through his policies when they are in operation. He thus has scope
for initiation and for creation. So have we all. It is what we should
expect in a human communication system in which every factor is
a function of all the others. But the policy-maker's role magnifies
this scope and makes him more than usually potent for good and
ill.

(1973: 178)

Right across the world, decisions are made by boards of
multinational companies which dispose of assets that are greater than
the gross national product of small nation states. These boards deal
with such issues as the acquisition or divestment of subsidiaries,
assessment of currency exposure by location and overall,
representation *vis-à-vis* governments, divining new applications for
existing products and services, seeking new markets, products and
services, and generally building up, or curtailing, the firm in terms of
a vision of the future. The chief executive plays an important part
here, and several studies have indicated that successful top managers
have two things in common: integrity and an ability to deal with
many different kinds of people (see Margerison 1980; Peters and
Waterman 1982; McCall and Lombardo 1983; Goldsmith and
Clutterbuck 1984).

Mintzberg (1973) observed how such top managers spend their
time. They are dealing with ideological, economic and order goals,
but he classified their work under three major headings:

INTERPERSONAL	INFORMATIONAL	DECISIONAL
Figurehead Inspirational, social and ceremonial role	*Monitor* Checking progress	*Entrepreneur* Responsible for change (directly or indirectly)
Leader Motivating subordinates, and seeking to harmonize their goals with those of the organization	*Disseminator* Transmitting some of his internal and external information to subordinates	*Disturbance handler* Takes charge when the organization or parts of it are threatened
Liaison Bringing together different units	*Spokesman* Public relations, lobbying and acting as expert	*Resource allocator* Sets priorities, schedules work and authorizes expenditure
		Negotiator Trades resources in real time with other parties

Junior managers are much more concerned with internal matters, maintaining the necessary flows of materials, people, equipment and information. These managers will be involved in taking many short-term decisions. In Chapter 6 we noted that, according to Simon, managing is synonymous with making decisions. However, this is an over-generalization. Horne and Lupton (1965), in a study of activity records kept by sixty-six managers for one week, concluded that giving or reviewing decisions accounted for only 8 per cent of managers' time on average, though transmitting information accounted for 42 per cent. At the operating level this information has to do with the work targets, work requirements and work performance. Lawrence (1984), in a study of British and German managers, shows how the information transmission occurs: at formal scheduled meetings, at convened special purpose meetings, in *ad hoc* discussions, by telephoning and by tours of the work areas. Any manager who has immediate subordinates gives direction and guidance to others. This aspect of a manager's work emerged from a study of ninety-three managers from different levels and specialisms

Table 8.2 Organizational cultures and leadership

ROLE CULTURE ASSUMPTIONS	ACHIEVEMENT CULTURE ASSUMPTIONS
4 A good boss is: impersonal and correct, and avoids the exercise of his authority for his own advantage. He demands from subordinates only that which is required by the formal system	3 A good boss is: egalitarian, and can be influenced in matters concerning the task. He uses his authority to obtain the resources needed to get on with the job
POWER CULTURE ASSUMPTIONS	SUPPORT CULTURE ASSUMPTIONS
2 A good boss is: strong, decisive, and firm but fair. He is protective, generous, and indulgent to loyal subordinates	1 A good boss is: concerned and responsive to the personal needs and values of others. He uses his position to provide satisfying and growth-stimulating work opportunities for subordinates

Note: The quotations are taken from Handy (1985).

that was conducted by Hemphill (1959, 1960). From the responses to a questionnaire which contained 575 items, Hemphill extracted statistically ten factors. One of these, which he called 'supervision of work', includes planning, organizing and controlling the work of others. This factor is much more characteristic of junior and middle management posts than of senior managers. Anyone (senior or junior) with responsibility for other people will have to attend to their individual needs (see Chapters 4 and 5) and to their collective needs (see Chapters 1–3). The manner in which leaders perform these various functions is often referred to as their 'style'. Let us examine 'style'.

3.2 How leaders lead in different cultures

On the question of leaders' style there is a confusing variety of terms, and so we look first at how Harrison described good bosses in his instrument for diagnosing organizational cultures. Then we examine the different terms used by other writers for similar concepts. Table 8.2 lists Harrison's descriptions, as cited by Handy. The numbering makes it easy to compare the good leaders with the design tasks in Table 3.1 and with the structures in which they may operate in Figure 3.1.

Table 8.3   Leadership style terms fitted to four cultures

	ROLE CULTURE (logic oriented)	ACHIEVEMENT CULTURE (mixed task and people oriented)
Blake and Mouton (1964a)	Middle of the Road (5, 5)	Team Management (9, 9)
Likert (1967)	–	Consultative (System III)
Lippitt and White (1958)	*Laissez-faire*?	–
Quinn and McGrath (1985)	Empirical Expert	Rational Achiever
Reddin (1970) and Marlow (1975)	Separated	Integrated
Tannenbaum and Schmidt (1958)	Sell?	Consult
See Table 7.1	Thinkers	Combined styles

	POWER CULTURE (output oriented)	SUPPORT CULTURE (employee oriented)
Blake and Mouton (1964a)	Production centred (9, 1)	Employee centred (1, 9)
Fiedler (1967)	Task oriented	Relationship oriented
Fleishman and Harris (1962)	Initiation	Consideration
Likert (1967)	Authoritative (Systems I and II)	Participative (System IV)
Lippitt and White (1958)	Autocratic	Democratic
Quinn and McGrath (1985)	Idealistic Prime-Mover	Existential Team Builder
Reddin (1970) and Marlow (1975)	Dedicated	Related
Tannenbaum and Schmidt (1958)	Tell	Delegate
See Table 7.1	Battlers	Helpers

A simplified way of distinguishing the styles is as follows. In the support culture the leader listens to the views of subordinates and takes them into account. In the power culture the leader tells others what to do. In the achievement culture the leader both gives direction and encourages participation. In the role culture the leader does what he or she is authorized to do.

Table 8.3 lists some of the writers on leadership, together with their terminology. Placement of their terms was based on how well the writers' own definitions fit Harrison's descriptions of good bosses. Blanks indicate that the writers mentioned do not have any term for that area. An additional check was provided by the assumptions about motivation shown in Table 5.2. All the leadership styles listed under the role and power cultures in Table 8.3 rely on motivating people by the carrot or stick, whereas those styles listed under the achievement and support cultures are based on the view that people are already motivated but need encouragement.

This distinction was important in a lot of early work which sought to discover which was more successful in terms of productivity or small group effectiveness, a style which focused on the task or a style which focused on the people doing the task. The results were that, in practice, 'it all depends' on a number of things (of which culture is one). We now give brief accounts of what the writers listed have to say. Note that Fiedler and Fleishman and Harris appear only in the lower half of Table 8.3. Their contribution will be mentioned last.

Writers such as Blake and Mouton and Likert prefer one style *in principle* over the rest. Blake and Mouton's was Team Management. They created what they called a 'managerial grid', formed from two axes, each with gradations from 0 to 9. One axis was labelled 'Concern for task', the other 'Concern for people'. The maximum emphasis on both these concerns was their preferred 9,9 Team Management style. It is questionable whether the style that came half-way along each axis, the Middle-of-the-Road style, is typical of a role culture, but it does not fit easily elsewhere.

Likert speaks of four 'systems'. His Consultative style is like Blake and Mouton's Team Management. He has two Authoritative styles, but his favourite is the Participative style. Leadership styles and control strategies are connected, so two of Likert's terms appear in Figure 2.1.

Lippitt and White carried out an early experiment into leadership in America. They recruited schoolboys to make things in groups in their leisure time. The adult leaders systematically varied their leadership styles and the groups were rotated so each group experienced all styles and all leaders. The results on performance, relationships and satisfaction were noted. The democratic style produced better results and higher satisfaction for most of the boys, though not for all. A few liked autocratic leaders and worked best for them. Chaos resulted from the *Laissez-faire* (or 'leave alone') style. The question mark against this style indicates that it is doubtful whether it should be classed as leadership at all.

Quinn and McGrath have a table which relates their leadership terms directly to their organizational terms which are shown in Figure 3.1. The sections numbered 1–4 there can be compared with 1–4 in Table 8.2. The Existential Team Builder is needed in a Clan, the Prime-Mover in an Adhocracy, the Rational Achiever in a Market and the Empirical Expert in a Hierarchy.

Reddin and Marlow allow for flexibility in style to suit changing circumstances, which, for Marlow, include the dominant culture of the organization. They also describe more effective and less effective variants of each style. The less effective Integrated style, for example, is the Compromiser. He perpetuates mediocrity. He does not expect high performance. He wants to live and let live. The more effective Integrated style is the Executive. Teams lead by Executives work hard but have high morale. They are not sweat shops.

Reddin quotes the Chinese philosopher Lau Tzu as saying, over 2,500 years ago,

> A leader is best when people barely know he exists; not so good when people obey and acclaim him; and worst when they despise him. . . .But of a good leader who talks little, when his work is done, his aim fulfilled, they will say, 'We did this for ourselves'.
>
> (Reddin 1985: 10)

Tannenbaum and Schmidt, in their *Harvard Business Review* articles, list a number of factors which need to be considered in choosing a leadership style. Among these are the personal preference and skill of the leader, the abilities and expectations of subordinates, the type of work being done and the circumstances in which it is being done. Their Tell, Sell, Consult and Delegate styles represent a shifting emphasis from leader to subordinate influence over decisions. The question mark after 'sell' indicates doubt about whether it can be fitted into the role culture position according to the criteria we gave above.

Fiedler includes the leader's 'position power' and 'leader–member relations' in his list of considerations. Although he uses the term Task

Oriented, his description of the style suggests that it is a directive one, and so it has been placed lower left rather than top right in Table 8.3. He argues that when conditions are either very favourable or very adverse for the leader, he or she can use the power culture style. By 'favourable' Fiedler means that the leader is well liked, the task clear and the leader's power high. In that case the Task Oriented style is acceptable; in the adverse case it is necessary. The support culture style works best where situations are moderately favourable to the leader.

Fleishman and Harris found that foremen could combine Consideration with Initiation (pressure to produce) without adverse affects on grievances and labour turnover. They studied subordinate reactions to different leader styles, as did Heller and Wilpert (1981). The styles shown in the lower left in Table 8.3 where there is Hofstede's (1980b) 'power/distance' between leaders and non-leaders are actually preferred in India and the Philippines (see Table 1.1). But subordinates in any country apparently dislike leaders who are unpredictable, inconsistent or vacillating in their approach, and whose style is self-oriented, varying with their own humour rather than with the realities of the task, the people and the culture. Vacillation is not the same as flexibility.

Hofstede's 'uncertainty avoidance' in the wider society suggests that leaders should not 'stick their necks out'. So role culture leadership tends to be invisible. This may partly account for a 'rag-bag' terminology in the top left of Table 8.3. 'Middle of the Road' avoids extremes. 'Laissez-faire' is leaving to others, not leading. Expertise tends to characterize the specialists rather than the 'line managers' in role cultures. 'Separated' leadership is impersonal and even evasive. 'Selling' is an intermediate position between 'telling' and 'consulting'.

Hofstede says, 'The crucial fact about leadership in any culture is that it is a complement to subordinateship.' No one style will be appropriate everywhere. Indeed, there are those who think that style has been over-emphasized in the literature. Perhaps how leaders do, or should, go about performing their functions is not what matters.

4 THE IMPORTANCE OF LEADERSHIP IN ORGANIZATIONAL BEHAVIOUR

Does OB reflect the importance of leadership for organizational behaviour? The very idea that leadership is the performance of a 'function' is disputed. Some OB theorists consider that it is not what is done nor how it is done that matters, but what the leader stands for and who he or she is. They think of leadership as a symbolic activity and also as a form of self-expression. Others think that it is a contribution to the working out of historical processes. Perhaps Shakespeare's words from *Twelfth Night* sum up this view:

> Some are born great, some achieve greatness, and some have greatness thrust upon them.

The search for common characteristics which describe great leaders down the ages has proved fruitless, so most OB writing ignores history. The conclusions about leadership have been based on studies of small groups or on supervisors of industrial work groups, though 'top people' have also received attention. Bryman (1984) reviews the literature on how leaders of large corporations may found a culture, sanction changes in a previous culture or, sometimes, find themselves 'prisoners' of an existing culture. Lieberson and O'Connor (1972) report a major research study to correlate changes in organizational performance with changes in chief executives. They concluded that, despite the many factors that affect performance, leadership alone, in some cases, does make a difference. OB writers who adopt a systems approach, or a critical theory approach, tend to overlook individual contributions by leaders, while those who emphasize individual personality and style generally ignore the importance of systems and history. Cultures and structures can accentuate or diminish the authority of leaders, as the discussion below of some experimental work indicates.

4.1 Obedience to authority

Milgram's (1974) experiments on obedience to authority examined, in particular, obedience to instructions that are morally repugnant to the recipient. He advertised in a New Haven paper for people to take part in a psychology experiment at Yale University. The experiment was said to be to investigate the effects of punishment on learning. Two 'subjects' were asked to draw lots to determine who should be the 'learner'. The learner was actually a confederate of the experimenter, but the genuine subject did not know this. As the person drawing the 'teacher's' lot, the subject was seated at a shock generator. He was told to present to the learner some stimulus words for paired association. If the learner made a mistake, or failed to answer promptly, the teacher was to administer a shock, the severity of which was to increase for every mistake made. Milgram reports that over 1,000 people have served as teachers, and 65 per cent of them delivered the maximum shock, at the insistence of the experimenter, despite the screams of the learner. (The confederate was not really shocked, but the subjects believed that he was. In the standard version the learner was in another room, but some teachers gave shocks of maximum severity even when the learner was in the same room.)

Milgram asks why people were prepared to obey the instructions of a white-coated experimenter who insisted that they had to continue to hurt a fellow human being. His answer is that his subjects were adopting what he calls 'the agentic frame of reference'.

1 The subject has agreed to take part in an experiment, and sees himself or herself as an *agent* to execute the wishes of another person. The experimenter takes responsibility, and the subject is prepared to concede it.

2 Both are acting *on behalf of* scientific knowledge (a source of charisma for the experimenter).

3 The subject has entered, and become part of, a hierarchical organization, and this type of setting evokes an orientation of obedience.

4 When people are inside the system, they cease to feel they are autonomous persons, and they do not see disobedience as a real option. Such an attitude is in certain senses functional for society, as there would be anarchy if everyone followed their own inclinations all the time.

Some critics have said that Milgram perpetrated systematic deceptions himself and, having 'framed' people, he got an inhumane result. Others argue that Milgram's results are not due to his methods. Soldiers, guards and other functionaries the world over have been prepared to commit atrocities when told to do so because they have been taught to obey orders without question. A notorious example is the Nazi, Eichmann, who was tried at Nuremberg for crimes against humanity. His plea that he was acting under orders was not accepted in mitigation. From Article 9 of the European Convention on Human Rights, the Consultative Assembly of the Council of Europe has derived a right to be released from the obligation to perform armed service or to inflict harm on another human being. Conscientious objection to military orders seems to be a special limiting case, however. What about the conditions in industry or commerce? Blau and Schoenherr (1971) argue that power becomes depersonalized in big organizations, and that when the source of instructions is not identifiable people feel trapped in the way that Milgram's subjects did. De Charms and others (1965) concluded, after extensive research, that large organizations are seen as tending to make pawns out of people. So is there a contrary picture to that presented by Milgram?

4.2 Reasons for non-compliance

Charismatic leaders are usually perceived as acting in the interests of their followers, in which case non-compliance is regarded as irrational. However, opposition will develop, informally, if doubts develop as to the soundness of the leader's understanding of requirements.

Etzioni (1974) proposes that leaders who exert either too little or too much power are likely to fail in their objectives. Excessive use of power derived from superior resources alienates those subjected to it, and stiffens resistance. Indeed, if Fox (1974) is right, formal leaders are bound to face opposition, because their discretion limits that of others. Close supervision of people at the bottom end of a hierarchical chain is likely to suggest to them that they are not trusted, and they reciprocate by distrust.

Hill (1974) deals with the kinds of powers available to workers, and with the reasons why some groups are more conscious of their power, and more ready to use it, than are others. Basically, they challenge management when they perceive that their interests are at stake, and that they can do something about it.

Three reasons for non-compliance are, therefore,

1. doubts about the wisdom of the leader's proposals,
2. distrust and hostility provoked by the power distance which exists and
3. perceptions that the interests of the members, followers or subordinates are at stake.

The power of a leader is never infinite. It is limited in a number of ways, for example in

1. the number of persons affected by its exercise,
2. the range of issues affected by its exercise and
3. the ability of others to resist its exercise.

Authority is usually taken to mean power to which a person or group is entitled, and the exercise of authority is regarded as the legitimate exercise of power. Organizational behaviour is affected by the power, authority and styles of leaders, though the recommendations of OB writers on the subject tend to reflect the personal psychological or sociological preferences that have guided their studies. (The final chapter will have more to say about OB theorizing.)

5 SUMMARY

A distinction was made between charismatic and formal leaders, though both types can be found in the same person. *Charismatic leaders* are generally people whose qualities serve the needs of a group, whether primary or secondary. (Such leaders in united groups are acknowledged by popular acclaim, but self-chosen and self-oriented leaders may be found in disunited groups.) The expertise of consultants is a form of charisma. Experts whose skills are not unique, however, may not be 'followed' even where they are formally entitled to be leaders. *Formal leaders* tend to occupy central positions in which they have assets of some kind other than charisma. They may inherit their posts, or be constitutionally appointed. Senior managers may be able to coerce, and even junior managers can reward or punish.

Leaders, by their actions, play a part in setting and enforcing policies and standards for their followers, and in uniting and mobilizing them. Top managers are likely to be involved in external relations and resource procurement. Nine types of responsibilities they have were discussed.

Descriptions of how leaders behave tend to be couched in terms of the degree to which they emphasize people, the task or both. Style preferences differ in different organizational and national cultures. Power cultures are most directive and support cultures are least directive. African and Asian countries on the whole prefer more directive styles of leadership (Hofstede 1980b; Seddon 1985a, b). Thus, **culture affects leaders through preferences for directive or participative styles**.

Followers may obey out of conviction that the instructions are legitimate, or because it is worth their while, or because they like the leader, or because they do not see any alternative. Milgram's experiments suggested a habit of obedience in certain formal settings. Nevertheless, followers may resist informally because of misgivings, or more formally because of distrust or alienation.

Though leadership is an important aspect of organizational

behaviour, the psychological aspects and systemic aspects tend to be treated separately in the literature of OB whereas they are inseparable in practice.

FURTHER READING

Books

Heller, F.A. and Wilpert, B. (1981) *Competence and Power in Managerial Decision Making: a Study of Senior Levels of Organization in Eight Countries*, Chichester: Wiley.

Hunt, J.G., Hosking, D.-M., Schriesheim, C.A. and Stewart, R. (eds) (1984) *Leaders and Managers: International Perspectives on Managerial Behavior and Leadership*, Elmsford, NY: Pergamon.

Mintzberg, H. (1975) *The Nature of Managerial Work*, New York: Harper & Row.

Articles

Bryman, A. (1984) 'Leadership and corporate culture: harmony and disharmony', *Personnel Review* 13(2): 19–24.

Fleishman, E.A. and Harris, F. (1962) 'Patterns of leadership behavior related to employee grievances and turnover', *Personnel Psychology* 15: 43–56.

Hofstede, G. (1980b) 'Motivation, leadership and organization', *Organizational Dynamics* 9(1): 42–62.

Kakar, S. (1971) 'Authority patterns and subordinate behavior in Indian organizations', *Administrative Science Quarterly* 16: 299f.

Lieberson, S. and O'Connor, J.F. (1972) 'Leadership and organizational performance: a study of large corporations', *American Sociological Review* 37: 117–30.

Meade, R. (1967) 'An experimental study of leadership in India', *Journal of Social Psychology* 72: 35–43.

Moris, J. (1981) 'The transferability of Western management concepts: a Fourth World perspective', *Development Digest* 19(1): 56–65.

Pettigrew, A.M. (1975) 'Strategic aspects of the management of specialist activity', *Personnel Review* 4(1): 5–13.

Quinn, R.E. (1984) 'Applying the competing values approach to leadership: toward an integrative framework', in Hunt, J.G., Hosking, D.-M., Schriesheim, C.A. and Stewart, R. (eds) *Leaders and Managers: International Perspectives on Managerial Behavior and Leadership*, Elmsford, NY: Pergamon.

Seddon, J. (1985b) 'Issues in practice: the education and development of overseas managers', *Management Education and Development* 16(1): 5–13.

Tannenbaum, R. and Schmidt, W.H. (1958) 'How to choose a leadership pattern', *Harvard Business Review* 36(2): 95–101; revised May/June 1973, pp.162–80.

RECOMMENDED CASES

'Merivale Electric Plc': Appraisal of a subordinate, with scope for role playing.
'Politics and Business in Malaysia': A Malaysian case dealing with the question of the relevance of a manger's politics to his business performance.

Chapter 9

Cultures and organizational development

CHAPTER OBJECTIVES

By the end of this chapter you will be able to:

1 define organizational development and the conditions which may need to be changed
2 describe the steps involved in organizational development
3 outline six principles for choosing between processes
4 say how the cultures are relevant to organizational development
5 analyse the recommended cases

1 INTRODUCTION: WHAT IS DEVELOPMENT?

To develop is to reach a more advanced or evolved stage. Individual persons can develop, organizations can develop, nations can develop. In the case of individuals, we speak of 'growth' (from infancy to maturity) for the physical changes which occur naturally during the early years of life. We reserve 'development' for the *extra* physical capabilities acquired by, for example, athletes or dancers. They have trained their bodies to perform in ways which go beyond what the average person can do. It is part of the job of a trainer or coach to 'develop' this physical prowess. Similarly, we reserve the term 'management development' for the extra skills which managers acquire from planned experiences, training and coaching. There are four points to be made from these examples.

1 Action is needed to produce development.
2 Development is the process of narrowing the gap between initial capability and desired capability.
3 Some standard is implied by which we can know development has

taken place (for example to run a mile in less than four minutes, to be able to perform the movements specified by the choreographer).

4 In 'systems' terms, what is occurring is increased 'differentiation' (that is, the body can respond in new ways, its range of action is more varied).

Notice that development represents a gain brought about by deliberate effort, whereas decay or degeneration represents a loss. Maintenance, of course, is the intermediate position where nothing is gained or lost. (Athletes, for example, must exercise to keep their fitness.)

The examples mentioned were of physical development. Humans can also develop in other ways, intellectually for example. The goal for intellectual development may be to perform feats of memory, or of calculation, or to be able to carry out research or to write novels. What about moral excellence?

Is there some ideal state for all human beings? Nirvana? Salvation? If so, how is it reached? By work? By karma and reincarnation? By faith? By spiritual exercises? Is it for everyone, or does each person have a different destiny? Is human development completed before death; or in the reception of the soul into heaven; or in freedom from reincarnation; or in what is bequeathed to posterity? Chapter 1 touched on these religious questions. The answers affect behaviour more strongly in countries where a particular creed (for example that of Islam) forms the basis of the society, and where one's eternal destiny is thought to depend upon one's earthly practice. Even in atheistic societies certain things are discouraged, others encouraged.

2 WHAT IS ORGANIZATIONAL DEVELOPMENT?

Beliefs about what an ideal organization is like affect the practice of organizational development. Many Western OD consultants seek to foster achievement and support cultures. Table 9.1, however, lists methods that can be used in role and power cultures also, because the existing culture is the place where one has to start.

Smith (1978) defines OD as 'consciously adopted procedures whereby an organization's overall effectiveness is improved, and the capacity to make future changes is enhanced'. Note that two types of gain are sought:

1 improvement in *overall* effectiveness, not just the effectiveness of

Table 9.1   Organizational development procedures (actions to produce development)

1 Diagnose starting condition in terms of (i) design, technology etc. (ii) skills (iii) information

2 Determine target condition and processes:

Change processes which are	Conditions to be changed		
	(i) Design, technology etc.	*(ii) Skills*	*(iii) Information*
(a) Role or procedure oriented	Operational research	Conventional training	Systems analysis
(b) Achievement oriented	Differentiation/ integration, job design	Behaviour modification, action planning	Survey feedback, management by objectives
(c) Power oriented	Restructuring, replacing key people	Mentor and understudy	Reinterpreting history, survey
(d) Support oriented	Role consultation, job enrichment	Team and interpersonal relations workshops (e.g. transactional analysis)	Career planning counselling
(e) Integrated	Combination of the above	Combination of the above	Combination of the above

3 Implement process(es) agreed upon, and evaluate results

Note: Payne (1991) has a cultural development model in which conception, conversion and consolidation correspond roughly to diagnosis, determination and implementation. He also provides for 'collapse' in the event of failure.

a particular function. (In a hospital this may be some combination of better clinical results, patient care, cost effectiveness and community relations for example.)

2 the capacity to make future changes (i.e. development does not stop after the initial improvement, but the organization is now able to use the procedures again whenever it faces new challenges).

The three OD procedures are shown in Table 9.1. The first is diagnosis, the second target setting and choice of change methods, while the third is implementing the changes and evaluating their effect. We deal with these in turn.

2.1 Diagnosing the starting conditions

First one must define what it is that is currently unsatisfactory, or likely to be so if nothing is done (the starting condition). Table 9.1 lists design, technology, skills and information as areas which need to be reviewed. Sometimes in-house or external consultants are asked to help at this stage. They collect such records and other documents as are available. They may also use interviews, observation, questionnaires or group discussion. Together with senior management they will review their findings and examine what most needs to be changed, and what can most easily be changed (the two may not be the same).

Change will be easier if it is in accordance with commonly accepted values, if the time is ripe, if circumstances are favourable, if the ideas around are feasible and practicable, if the yield in terms of benefit is calculable and obvious, if people feel obliged to make the changes and if the ability and resources are available. Resistance will be less if people experience acceptance and support.

Streuning and Guttentag (1975) summarize the previous paragraph in the following formula:

$$\text{Successful change} = V + T + C + (I \times Y)(O \times A) - R$$

where the letters stand for Values plus Timing plus Circumstances plus Ideas-times-Yield, multiplied by Obligation-times-Ability, less Resistance. The letters can be rearranged to spell A VICTORY. If any of the four items that are multipliers is zero, the whole change attempt will fail. Without practical ideas, benefits, people who care and people who can cope, OD is a non-starter. If these are present, one can agree future targets and suitable processes. Personnel and resources have to be made available, and a timetable must be drawn up with provision for interim and later evaluation.

The sections which follow give an account of some of the problems that can lead an organization to move to the second phase of target setting and choosing from the change processes available, as shown in the cells in Table 9.1.

2.2 Why organizational development is introduced

Diagnosis may reveal that the organization's structure, skills or information channels are not geared up to deal with changes in the environment. Examples provided by Brager and Holloway (1978) are changes in:

- sources or availability of funding
- technology available (for example in electronics)
- 'social technologies' (for example labour market regulations going beyond national boundaries, as the European 'Social Charter' does)
- public opinion (for example on 'green' issues, gender issues or ethnic minorities)
- the power of certain stake-holders (for example investors, consumer groups, state regulatory bodies)
- support for or opposition to the organization's activities (for example sanctions imposed or removed)

Internal problems which may lead top managers to call for OD are the following:

- a lack of any sense of direction or purpose because policies and plans are unclear
- understructuring which leads to confusion over responsibilities so that some get duplicated and others omitted
- concentration on day-to-day matters leading to delay in producing longer-term planning documents
- allocation of responsibilities without any corresponding allocation of the resources to fulfil those responsiblities
- over-staffing or under-staffing in relation to the amount of work to be done so that people are either demoralized or overstressed
- unnecessary expenditure of energy in treating too many signals as emergencies
- rigid demarcation leading to buck passing and delay
- an unbalanced age structure with too few or too many new employees in proportion to total staff
- short-circuiting of established communication channels (which causes dissatisfaction in those who are bypassed or whose work is interfered with)
- too many initiatives introduced which are not followed through because priorities have not been sorted out
- subunits which engage in too much competition for privileges
- lopsided development of the organization (for example with too many specialists compared with generalists)

- expertise at lower levels under used (or, conversely, lower levels take too many important decisions without reference to a wider policy framework)
- a high level of complaints from dissatisfied customers, sponsors, clients etc., or frequent industrial relations disputes
- difficulty in attracting resources (for example qualified people) into the organization, or in retaining the resources already there

All the above are symptoms of problems arising from unsuitable design, information or technology. However, attempts to put one matter right may make others worse. Just as there are open and hidden agenda in groups (see Chapter 7), so there are covert as well as open reasons for the existence of particular designs, technologies and information practices. An overt change may set other difficulties in train. Brager and Holloway tell of a human service organization whose stated objective was to specialize in 'difficult' cases. In fact there was a covert bias in its client selection procedures which screened out the most difficult cases. This bias served to protect the staff. If the selection procedure were changed to conform with the stated objectives the staff would need a lot more support than was available. Naturally, resistance from staff could be expected.

Rather than attempt to deal piecemeal with problems, managers may choose OD to look at the hidden purposes served by the status quo. It is then possible to adopt procedures which are comprehensive, by using a diagnostic format similar to that in Table 9.1 (whose column headings are suggested by the work of Bowers *et al.* (1975) and whose row headings use the now familiar cultures).

3   PRINCIPLES FOR CHOOSING BETWEEN ORGANIZATIONAL DEVELOPMENT PROCESSES

Marlow (1975) describes cultures in the same terms as he and Reddin (1970) use for leadership styles (see Table 8.3, and Chapter 8, Section 3.2). He suggests six principles for choosing OD interventions:

1 congruence
2 predisposition
3 succession
4 anticipating resistance
5 effective learning
6 total forward projection

These principles will now be described. (They might be compared with the design principles in Table 4.1.)

3.1 The Principle of Congruence

The principle of congruence asserts, *Start with a method that is compatible with the existing dominant culture.* If a method that conflicts with the culture is used the programme as a whole will be rejected. However, since transformation of values is desired, it may be possible to switch rows in Table 9.1 (for example, from (b) (i) to (d) (iii)) once some progress has been made with a problem indicated by the column headings. Such a move can be helped by the fact that no organization is completely homogeneous. A secondary culture usually exists alongside the dominant one. This secondary culture can assume increasing importance as the OD programme progresses. Bennis (1959) speaks of change happening through a process of 'unfreezing' existing values and 'refreezing' when new values have begun to form. Thus the dominant culture is gradually melted as problems are worked on. A boundary change may start a thaw (Table 9.2). The secondary culture begins to solidify around the new solutions. But it is no use attacking a 'frozen' culture with an axe!

Table 9.2 Organizational cultures, their values, and the significance of boundaries

	ROLE CULTURE	ACHIEVEMENT CULTURE
VALUES	Rationality Legality Orderliness	Creativity Competition Independence
Boundaries	Give certainty and status	Aid task and occupational identity
	POWER CULTURE	SUPPORT CULTURE
VALUES	Strength Loyalty Control	Sharing Involvement Friendship
Boundaries	Are defences	Create in-groups

3.2 The principle of predisposition

Though OD is aimed at the total organization, it cannot affect all parts at once. Decisions have to be made about where to begin. The principle of predisposition asserts that *those parts which are already predisposed towards change should be sought and selected*. Boundaries are likely to be good places to start. Afterwards one can move towards the centre of the unit, or units, involved.

3.3 The principle of succession

The principle of succession asserts, *'Take one step at a time'*. This is because time has to be allowed for the melting of frozen attitudes.

3.4 The principle of anticipating resistance

It is not only culture clashes which cause resistance to change. Marlow charted a number of change efforts, using a diagramming method that is familiar to systems analysis. Along the bottom he plotted time, and on the vertical axis he showed the levels in an organization's hierarchy that were involved. Symbols were used to represent the type of activity that was going on and whether it was 'official' or 'unofficial'. He concluded that the intensity and extensiveness of activity and of resistance varies over time. There is a slow and sporadic start-up during which resistance is chiefly directed towards testing out the role of any consultant employed. This may last for as long as six months. It is the equivalent of Tuckman's 'forming' stage in a group (see Table 7.1). Resistance during the next stage may be more intense and hostile ('storming'). Some people may refuse to shoulder responsibility. This is Bion's 'fight/flight' mode (Table 7.1). Finally, as a secondary culture moves into the dominant place, people become afraid of the possible consequences of what seem to be irreversible changes. The principle asserts that *the timing and sequence of intervention techniques must allow for the dynamics of resistance* just described.

3.5 The principle of effective learning

The principle of effective learning asserts that *learning situations must be neither too comfortable nor too threatening*. People must have a chance to re-examine current methods, practices and attitudes; to experiment with new ways in a safe environment. Learning takes place at unconscious as well as conscious levels. There will be little learning if difficult issues are avoided altogether, but emotional blocks will prevent learning if issues are handled insensitively. Skills and techniques should be taught in such a way that people can test them out, practise them and acquire confidence in their use.

3.6 The principle of total forward projection

A period of five years may not be too long in which to move from the starting point to the arrival point. The principle asserts that *a forward plan, guided by the principle of succession, must be budgeted.* The OD programme needs to be costed from the start so that the accomplishment of interim objectives against cost can be recorded. Then the forward projection can be adhered to or revised as appropriate.

4 ORGANIZATIONAL DEVELOPMENT PROCESSES

The techniques from which selection can be made will now be described, following the row order in Table 9.1. The techniques can in some cases be used not only to implement change but also to collect information to diagnose needs or evaluate results.

4.1 Organizational development processes in role cultures

Operational Research (OR)

The name 'operational research' seems to have been coined just before the Second World War when it was used in connection with RADAR installations. It uses the maximizing or optimizing decision processes shown in Table 6.1. It can suggest solutions to problems where information is available, or can be created, for statistical manipulation. It has been put in the 'design and technology' column because problems of the design of transport, distribution or manufacturing systems lend themselves to this approach. Van Rest (1982) gives an example from the coffee industry of Puerto Rico. The question was whether to mechanize the picking of coffee beans. The researcher found that it would be more profitable to concentrate on improving access to the crops and mechanizing the sorting process rather than the picking. Operational research on its own would not satisfy the two criteria given in Smith's definition of OD because, although overall effectiveness (for example of the coffee plantations) could be improved, there may be no enhanced capacity for future change unless additional learning takes place. This is true of the other processes in isolation.

Conventional training

Most people think that conventional training means sending individuals away on courses. It can mean this but, in the context of OD, it may mean training at the place of work, sometimes for a whole work group. A deficit in knowledge, skills or attitudes may be indicated which conventional training seeks to rectify. The organization may have a well-established training department which can tailor its internal programmes to the new needs including on-the-job instruction. Alternatively, or in addition, the organization may use external suppliers. There are various forms of open learning packages which people can study in their own time or at work. These may involve computers and video recorders as well as written materials. Whatever methods are used, it is crucial that they are relevant to the real objectives of the organization, that the trainees are well prepared and motivated, and that other employees are supportive. Training takes time which may well put an extra burden on fellow employees and on supervisors and managers. The learners need the encouragement of positive feedback on improvements in their skills and performance. For more senior employees this may involve one-to-one coaching or project supervision. The data collection required for an OD exercise can itself be used as a training vehicle if it is undertaken by a group of managers with professional assistance.

Systems analysis

The objective of systems analysis is to develop effective procedures and systems through the formal analysis and examination of existing and proposed systems. The analyst has various ways of charting flows of materials and information, both computerized and manual. The remit may involve improving on speed, accuracy, relevance, timeliness, cost, employee satisfaction and so on. This may involve locating sources of error or ambiguity, spotting bottlenecks or other holdups, noting which parts are overloaded and which are under-employed and so on. A change of system may be introduced which has little impact beyond a particular department. If so it is not OD. Nevertheless, it may be *part* of OD.

OR, conventional training and systems analysis are all compatible with role cultures because they all stress logical methods for introducing change. Their use may pose problems for individual office holders, but the new systems can still be run by the bureaucratic hierarchy. Because they rely on experts, however, they may not be fully understood by those affected, and there are many examples of new systems failing to gain staff acceptance. A British computer company discovered that though it was demonstrating to customers a computerized production control system, its own production managers were not using it themselves! The training department then had a brief to run events for analysts, programmers and production personnel together, and so that they would learn to appreciate each other's problems and viewpoints.

4.2 Organizational development processes in achievement cultures

Differentiation/integration

This OD procedure is a means of keeping the design of the organization under review. As new problems arise, new specialisms are invented. This brings differentiation. In the UK, for example, in 1959, the nursing specialism of 'infection control' was introduced to deal with hospital-acquired infection, because regular nursing staff had neither the time nor the knowledge to cope with a problem that had grown more serious as new medical treatments were introduced. But, to achieve goals, such new specialisms must be properly integrated into the overall design. Lawrence and Lorsch (1967) maintain that the greater the differentiation the greater the need for integration, and the harder it is to achieve it (see Chapter 3, Section 1.4).

Differentiation

The OD procedure of 'differentiating and integrating' involves looking at the ways in which work is divided up and co-ordinated and considering whether improvements can be made. Chapters 3 and 4 dealt with designs that might be chosen. Now we are considering modifications, and so it is helpful to have a list of options for dividing up work. Some are set out below, using a hospital as an example:

1 by function (for example medical, nursing, administration, support services)
2 by type of customer, client or patient (for example men, women, children, the old)
3 by serial stages in the work (for example admissions, treatment, convalescence, discharges)
4 by territory or catchment area (for example regions, districts)
5 by type of 'transformation' effected (for example surgical, orthopaedic, obstetric)
6 by time (out-patients, shortstay, long stay)
7 by stability or variability of workload (emergencies, acute or chronic conditions)
8 by status or seniority. (See Table 3.2)

In the example of infection control, a new function was introduced. It is a support service, since the infection control nurses do not do any nursing themselves but visit hospital sites to advise on potential sources of infection and to help where cases of infection have been reported. The status, or seniority, given to this specialism depends on the level in the hierarchy of the hospital at which it is introduced. The higher the level, the more authority these nurses have.

Integration

An OD programme may involve decisions about where such new posts should be slotted in. Other forms of integration occur through combining departments or tasks. Some hospitals have experimented, for example, with a change to 'total patient care' whereby ward nurses are given responsibility for particular patients for whom they undertake all the nursing needed. Formerly they carried out a limited set of nursing tasks, but for all the patients.

Table 9.2 reminds us, however, that the boundaries of jobs or departments have more than structural significance. A lot of painstaking preparation may be needed before changes are accepted. Cross (1991) describes how Shell UK's Stanlow plant introduced major changes following deals negotiated with the trade unions on flexibility and productivity. During the move towards 'multi-skilling' the culture had to shift from 'being very short-term, confrontational and autocratic to one in which joint problem-solving is the norm' (that is, from power to task culture).

In both the total patient care and oil refining examples, what had formerly been discrete tasks were integrated into new ways of working. How else can integration be increased?

Integration by bureaucratic means

Cross describes the setting up, at the Shell refinery, of a Joint Review Board (JRB) which consisted of four managers, four craft shop stewards (union representatives) and two OD consultants (one internal and one independent). This body set and communicated the objectives, provided resources, defined progress measures, promoted positive attitudes, identified and resolved problems and got the deal implemented in the Engineering Department. It used the existing management information systems and also *ad hoc* surveys. After some years the JRB became the Stanlow Working Arrangements Group, with all fifteen departments on the site as its clients.

This is an example of integration through centralization of the source, scope, and enforcement of the 'rules' for implementing the deal (see Chapter 3 Section 1.3).

Integration by clans (or tribes)

This method can work within groups of like-minded people. Co-operation is achieved through what social scientists call 'socialization', which means that people have been brought up to share the same goals and values and to want the same things, and so they co-operate spontaneously and voluntarily. However, while integration may be strong internally, integration across groups is weak. According to Warren (1971) different clans only enter into concerted decision-making with other clans under those circumstances that help each to keep or extend their own spheres of influence.

Socialization is a long-term process, but, in the shorter term of OD, integrated decision-making between clans is possible when there are tradeoff inducements. Arrangements can be made for

1 direct contact – if the physical layout permits units which are interdependent to be sited adjacent to each other, with free access between them, personal contact is easier;

2 overlapping memberships – some persons may belong to both the units between whom co-operation is desired;
3 task forces to be created to work on particular problems and to recruit from several interested units;
4 liaison persons, or liaison units.

Liaison jobs involve mediating between groups, and so it is helpful if persons appointed to such jobs are familiar with the tasks, beliefs, methods, goals and time-scales that apply to the units to be co-ordinated. The infection control nurses are given special training in inter-personal skills in addition to knowledge about hospital-acquired infections. They have a co-ordinating job, trying to prevent the spread of infection across units by persuading others to take action.

The international discipline of infection control now has a world-wide membership. Integration across national boundaries is attempted through learned journals, international conferences and visits by experts to one another's countries.

Integration by 'markets'

It is possible to arrange for units within organizations to buy services from one another and to sell services to one another. In this way units whose goals are different may enter into arrangements which further the goals of the wider organization.

The three types of integration described can be used in an OD programme as a means to help bring about change and as an objective for change.

Behaviour modification and action planning

Behaviour modification

Behaviour modification is a motivation technique which was des-cribed in Chapter 5 (Section 4.1). It aims at better performance (for example through rewarding higher output or fewer rejected products). It can be used as part of an OD programme for improving skills. However, some OD consultants are opposed to this and other techniques associated with the role, achievement and power cultures. They will only use the techniques shown in row (d) of Table 9.1. Other consultants take a more pragmatic view and will accept contracts which involve any technique that suits the client and seems likely to have the desired effect.

Action planning

This technique focuses upon the organization's mission, that is, what it is trying to do. Since the possibilities for accomplishing the mission are affected by the environment, action planning considers what are the likely external helps and hindrances that might be met. Chapter 1 suggested that 'mission' might be seen in terms of three types of goals: economic, ideological and order goals. Action plans look at the economic effects that the organization is seeking (for example in terms of sales volume, market share, buildings constructed, value added) and whether the environment will be susceptible to these effects. They look at the shifting availability of funds and of sources of funding. The ideology of the organization may be vulnerable to changes in public opinion, to pressure group activities and to government policies (for example on defence matters or pollution). The order goals will be affected by the possibilities for internal and external conflict connected with other aspects of the mission. The points at which pressures are being felt are brought into focus. Opinions are sought about likely trends in the relevant areas and what will happen if the organization does nothing. Opinions are also sought on how the organization can alter the pressures that are being brought to bear on it. In some ways action planning resembles systems analysis or operational research, but it has been put in cell (b) (ii) because, once the mission has been identified, the plan concentrates on the human skills that will be needed to cope with the difficulties that are foreseen, and with how to prepare staff at all levels for the actions the organization will need to take. These actions may include building up skills in public relations, fund raising, customer service, new manufacturing technologies, foreign languages, new styles of leadership and so on.

Survey feedback and management by objectives

Survey feedback

Survey feedback is a way of collecting and collating information about the organization and letting informants know what has been discovered. Baumgartel (1971) speculates that the sort of information which is most useful for inducing change is

1 quantified and 'objective' in the sense of having a reference point outside itself (for example 'at this site' and 'at that site', 'before' and 'after');
2 unexpected (for example that older workers are producing more than younger ones);
3 a pointer to the causal links between means and ends. (see Table 6.1).

Since the present book has stressed culture, it is worth mentioning that Harrison designed a survey instrument specifically to ascertain which of his four cultures is dominant. For other ready-made questionnaires see Lake, Miles and Earle (1973). In OD it may also be felt necessary to obtain some indicator of morale or job satisfaction. If this cannot be obtained unobtrusively through records of absence, turnover or grievances, a survey can be undertaken. Such a survey, if well handled, can shed light on the reasons behind recorded figures.

It is important that, whether the questionnaires are purchased or specially designed, whether completed during interviews or 'mailed', there should be someone with the necessary expertise to analyse, interpret and communicate them. The feedback part of the exercise is as vital as the collection of the data. This feedback should safeguard the anonymity of individuals unless persons have consented to be identified. It is likely to take place in briefing sessions at which questions and discussion are invited.

This OD method is classed as task oriented because it is concerned with letting people know how the relationships at work are seen by others so that plans can be made to deal with issues that are causing trouble.

Management by objectives

Management by objectives is routine in some organizations, though others may introduce it as part of OD. It is a means whereby superiors and their subordinates sit down together to analyse their work to find out how it contributes to the mission of the enterprise. Having determined why they are doing things, they seek to quantify the results they should obtain. They clarify who is responsible for what and by when. The objectives are more important than the means by which they are achieved, and so the method allows discretion to subordinates in how they work, as long as they get the desired results.

Management by objectives can apply to any manager at any level, but the key to success is when groups and individuals mesh goals and efforts to succeed in the situations in which they find themselves. The results are regularly and jointly reviewed and fresh objectives are set. As part of an achievement culture, management by objectives can both change an organization and help it to learn how to continue to change. There is a danger, however, that, in role or power cultures, management by objectives may degenerate into a ritual in which the decisions are actually one way, from boss to subordinate, and the performance measures are 'doctored' by the subordinate to fit the results the boss wants.

We turn now to techniques which can work in power cultures, though some OD consultants would prefer the term OD to be reserved for the techniques shown in rows (b) and (d) only.

4.3 Organizational development processes in power cultures

Restructuring, replacing key people

An organization is not just the means to the achievement of goals (see Table 1.4). It can also be seen as a system of government which, in power cultures, is autocratic, with authority vested in the top executives. One of the rewards of deferring to the leadership is that lower ranks are absolved from some of the responsibilities of leading. The leaders can also be a defence against outsiders and a source of 'we feeling' for insiders. However, when organizational restructuring occurs it is imposed from above (though leaders may have used some of the techniques already described). A new design is selected and persons who do not have the skills to work within it are often dismissed and replaced. Restructuring is often linked with take-overs, when duplication of jobs leads to many job-holders being made redundant. Even when there is no merger, restructuring alters the size of departments and the status of individual managers, and hence their power. It is therefore likely to provoke resistance. Tables 8.1 and 9.2 indicate what can be at stake.

In a power culture those with highest authority are expected to curb strife at lower levels. Mintzberg (1973) indicated that 'disturbance handling' is a function of managers 'at the institutional level' (see Chapter 8, Section 3.1). If the conflict is to be handled so as to develop the organization rather than destroy it, the managers should be aware of conflict-handling techniques. The leadership does not want the new design to alienate persons whose skill and knowledge are vital to the continuance of the organization. Sometimes outsiders are asked to help.

Sheane (1979) writes about how third parties, such as OD consultants, can act in power conflicts. He says anybody who wants to influence the participants must be clear about

1 the issue to be influenced;
2 the power figure (or power group) that must be worked with, worked through, worked against or worked round;
3 means of access to this figure or group;
4 the sorts of activity which would start influencing the chosen issue;
5 the decisions the intervener wants the power figure or group to make;
6 how, pragmatically, preliminaries can be started.

He gives examples of 'making an entry', breaking down big issues into smaller manageable ones, making or breaking coalitions, using new proposals to break the 'threat/counter threat dynamic', making specific, credible and relevant offers, building trust and so on. The process of breaking deadlocks may include small-scale experiments, joint visits, 'behind the scenes' conferences and special assignments. The longer the conflict has been going on the more entrenched the positions will be, and the more difficult it will be to find a face-saving formula. It is easier to deal with conflict constructively by intervening early before it spreads.

Mentor and understudy

Plato (427–347 BC) said there would be no very good government until philosophers were kings or kings philosophers, and Alexander the Great, as a boy, was indeed tutored by the philosopher Aristotle (385–322 BC). In the 1980s and beyond, Marlow (1984) believes that the philosopher–manager is needed. Such a manager could teach his or her subordinates through example and through coaching. One way of teaching subordinates new skills is through role negotiation.

Role negotiation

Role negotiation may be linked with role consultation (see Section 4.4 below). Harrison (1972b) suggests that the process of sending and receiving demands, or role pressures, can be made quite explicit, especially where problems are the result of overload, ambiguity or incompatible expectations. Suppose, for example, that a manager, Harry, has two subordinates, Sam and Matthew, who are working on a report. Harry wants to bring forward the deadline for submission of the report. He is revising his expectations of how they will perform their work. If Harry uses the technique of role negotiation he will find out how the revised deadline will affect them, and allow them to stipulate some concessions they require from him in return. They may, for example, ask to be excused from attendance at certain meetings to give them more time to work on the report.

Strauss argues that:

> Negotiation is not merely one specific human activity or process, of importance primarily because it appears in particular relationships (diplomacy, labor relations, business transactions, and so on), but is of such major importance in human affairs that its study brings us to the heart of studying social orders.
>
> (1978: 234)

He admits, however, that negotiation may be intertwined with coercive, manipulative and other processes. We turn now from skill development to how a power culture may use information to bring about change.

Reinterpreting history

Pettigrew argues that:

> Entrepreneurs may be seen ... as creators of symbols, ... rituals and myths, ... stylistic components of a vision which may .... include the presence of a dramatically significant series of events, rooting the vision back into history.... Visions may contain new and old terminology, sometimes using metaphors and analogies to create fresh meanings.
>
> (1979: 574, 578)

A new vision of the organization cannot be imposed from the top, but the top managers have a unique role and leverage in the process of establishimg and changing beliefs. Peters (1978) suggests that there may be up to nine years involved in the transition from one 'era' to another in the history of an organization. Managing the meanings assigned to situations is an on-going process which may bring about a reversal in perceptions of past history and a commitment to a different future. The old vision is gradually dropped and top management can focus attention on some new vision whose emergence has been fostered for some time. Finally, this vision becomes taken for granted, as a survey could demonstrate.

The use of surveys has already been touched on in connection with achievement cultures. Questionnaires and interviews can be used to gather data in any culture. In a power culture the top members of the organization would decide who should be privy to what information before and after the survey. They may wish to release only such findings as suggest the time is ripe for an OD transformation.

4.4 Organizational development processes in support cultures

Role consultation

In role consultation, the focus is on confidential and individual meetings between members of the organization and an independent consultant. The technique provides a vehicle for self-examination, and it has also been used in counselling employees. It involves listing the members of one's 'role set', that is, those with whom one has dealings both on and off the job, and the expectations one believes that each has. One can then ask what are the most important expectations, what are the consequences of not meeting these, and how one's own part can be redefined to give greater satisfaction (see Mant 1976). The consultant assists in this process. The 'Role Analysis Exercise' provides a do-it-yourself version.

Kahn *et al.* (1964) describe a number of possible types of *role conflict*. Chapter 2 (Section 5.3) mentions how the conflict arises. It is possible for different 'senders' to make incompatible demands (inter-sender conflict) or even for a single sender to be inconsistent. (Is a warder to behave towards a prisoner as a custodian or as a friend? Superiors may sometimes expect harshness and sometimes friendliness.) People can also suffer from role overload – they just cannot satisfy all their role senders! The person caught up in role conflict may be able to take the initiative and get others to adapt. Failing this, the person may cope by ignoring some of the pressures. If neither of these strategies is possible the person may show symptoms of psychological distress unless the role changes. When distressed, a person may repress certain thoughts or feelings. Feelings so pushed out of awareness can surface in ways that are not under the person's conscious control. (The best-known symptoms are 'introjection', 'splitting' and 'projection'. In introjection one attributes another's good points to oneself. In projection one denies one's own bad feelings by seeing them in somebody else. In splitting, one compartmentalizes one's existence so that one can be, for example, a model employee yet a bad father.)

Role consultation is a person-centred technique in that it seeks to remove from the role the sources of the psychological distress. The method is shown under 'design' improvement rather than skills, since role sets are part of organizational and job design. Used within an OD programme, role consultation may help those whose roles are being altered, by improving the fit between the design of the new jobs and employees' preferences (see Chapter 5, Section 2).

Job enrichment is also shown in Table 9.1 as an attempt to improve the organization's design or technology. As it has already been described in Chapter 4 (Section 2.2) the reader is referred to that chapter.

Team and inter-personal relations workshops

Chapter 7 described how personality can affect behaviour in groups, or teams, and how a group develops its own dynamics over time. That chapter also explained how cohesion or disunity affects work and decision-making. Training workshops allow participants to experiment with their own styles of behaviour in a safe situation where feedback can be readily accepted. Usually the trainer provides some terms so that people have a language for describing what is happening. A transactional analysis workshop would use the Parent, Adult, Child terms introduced in Chapter 5 (Section 4.6). Other consultants may use observation schedules, such as Bales' (1950) interaction process analysis, which provide cues as to what to look for and how to quantify improvements. One can count the frequency with which certain types of behaviour occur and deliberately seek to reduce or increase this frequency. One might look for fewer interruptions and more 'building on the ideas of others'. The workshop leader can demonstrate that certain behaviour leads to better group performance. The technique described in Chapter 8 (Section 2.2 'In primary groups') for linking performance to 'communication nets' can also be used to link performance with the frequency of helpful behaviour. A workshop may use video cameras so that the interactions may be preserved on tape for subsequent playback and comment. Leaders can try out new styles (see Table 8.2) in relation to the tasks set during the workshop. Those running the workshops seek to increase openness and trust, and so the method is very definitely person centred. It may be used in OD to increase commitment to working as teams to bring about a revised organizational design, especially where the move is towards greater decentralization.

Career planning and counselling

During the course of OD a number of people may find that the familiar avenues of promotion have changed. Part of the strategy may be to replace key personnel with outsiders. If people are to be made redundant an organization may give such persons access to recruitment consultants with a view to discovering the most likely source of future employment, or to retirement specialists who will advise on financial, health and leisure problems.

Career counselling may be required for those who are to be retained, whether it is proposed to promote them, move them sideways, demote them or leave them where they are. Some companies make use of *assessment centres* to provide relevant information for career counselling, for manpower and succession planning, and for management development.

At an assessment centre participants may complete a battery of psychological tests, take part in group activities which are observed by assessors, and be counselled at an interview at which their performance and work record are discussed. When a person has information about his or her own strengths and weaknesses and about likely changes in the organization, decisions about the future can be made on a mutual basis.

Not all career planning and counselling involves assessment centres or consultants. Managers may have been trained to develop their own subordinates through the method of regular information exchange. This may be similar to the 'mentor and understudy' system already described, except that the subordinate may not be groomed to take the boss's place but may be counselled to seek alternative employment in the organization. Indeed, organizations in the UK now sometimes encourage subordinates to take the initiative in planning their own careers, rather than waiting for proposals to be put to them. Such a policy may motivate certain types of personality, notably the 'battlers'.

We have now dealt with rows (a) to (d) in Table 9.1. Row (e) suggests a combination of strategies, which is perhaps the most usual since it was pointed out that OD seeks comprehensive changes.

The last stage in OD stage 3 in Table 9.1, is to implement and follow up the methods chosen at the second stage. The evaluation consists in checking at intervals how close the results of the changes are to the targets set. Not all OD programmes go smoothly. Some of the six principles cited under Section 3 above are ignored in practice, and some countries are less favourable to OD than others. There are failures as well as successful change attempts. We look now at OD in the UK.

5 ORGANIZATIONAL DEVELOPMENT IN THE UK

The *Institute of Personnel Management* in the UK commissioned a study of cultural change. The authors, Williams *et al.* (1989), present fifteen case studies of changes which took place over periods of from three to five years. However, in those fifteen organizations they conducted only two interviews, each of one and a half hours. The organizations themselves were allowed to edit the reports, adding or deleting as they wished. One reviewer (Chambers 1990) comments that it is, naturally, satisfactory performance results that are reported, but she doubts if the *cultures* changed much. Nevertheless, she tells student readers not to

> get too obsessed by the notion of culture change. It has probably become fashionable because of the recognition, very late in the day, that rational analytic approaches to performance improvement [are] either spat out or digested by the body of the organization so that no noticeable impact [can] be discerned after about a year.

(Chambers 1990: 69)

Steele (1977) states that his exploratory discussions about doing OD in the UK have never got past 'the gastronomic stage'. He lists seven assumptions of American style OD, and cultural blocks in the UK to each of these (Table 9.3). Perhaps the tradition of adversarial collective bargaining in the UK should be added to Steele's list. As the boundaries between nations in Europe are weakened, however, the UK culture itself may be subject to transformation. Change in organizations may then be planned rather than piecemeal. OD stands the best chance of success where the principles listed above are

Table 9.3 American style organizational development and UK cultural blocks

OD Assumptions	UK cultural blocks
'Doing better is a good thing'	'We must be doing all right now or we wouldn't be here'
'The facts are friendly'	Norms about avoiding certain topics
'People should be consulted before anything in their personnel records is disclosed to a third party'	British class structure and the hierarchical authority system
'An adaptive system is a good thing'	'We like to carry on as we always have done'
'Change does not have to be haphazard'	'If it hurts it must be good for us'
'The results of change are not always predictable'	'Prove it will be practical'
'Social science can contribute to organizational health'	Mistrust of professionals and respect for gifted amateurs

followed. There are, in any case, alternatives to OD – what Peters calls 'mundane tools' for making minor changes on a day-to-day basis. (see Chapter 2, Section 5.3).

6 ORGANIZATIONAL DEVELOPMENT IN OTHER COUNTRIES

Many OD consultants prefer to work in national cultures which score on Hofstede's dimensions (see Table 1.1) as follows:

Uncertainty avoidance	Low
Power distance	Low
Masculinity	Low
Individualism	Medium

The Scandinavian countries come closest to these values. The relatively more feminine scores of these countries have meant that group working, where friendly relationships matter, tends to be used for job enrichment (see Chapter 4, Section 2.2, 'Autonomous working groups') within OD. Countries with higher masculinity scores tend to use other forms of enrichment, such as increased individual responsibility.

In Germany uncertainty avoidance is high, but the German scores on individualism are low. It was possible there to use management by objectives on a team basis which reduced the uncertainties for individuals. The French are accustomed to high power distance. Although some organizations in France intended their management by objectives to be participative, in practice it was often introduced by fiat.

Survey feedback has to be sensitively handled where there is high uncertainty avoidance, high masculinity and high power distance. In several Latin American countries the consultant becomes a go-between in the process of conveying information across the power distance divide, reducing its uncertainty and helping organization members to save face.

OD successes have been reported in India using leadership training which follows a 'nurturant-task leader' model which preserves the power distance of the culture. Although the leader is encouraged to take an interest in the well-being of his subordinates, and to develop them, they remain dependent on him for their progression.

The principles set out above (in Sections 3.1–3.6) apply with reference to the national setting within which it is proposed to introduce OD, as well as to the organization itself. The techniques mentioned do not exhaust the possibilities. The interested reader is referred to the further reading at the end of the chapter.

7 SUMMARY

OD was defined as consciously adopted procedures whereby an organization's overall effectiveness is improved and the capacity to make future changes is enhanced. Sometimes it is a response to recognized weaknesses, an attempt to deal with contingencies while following the golden mean, and sometimes it anticipates a future ideal. In both cases **organizational culture influences decisions on ends and means for OD**. Indeed, most writers restrict the title OD to a philosophy and methods that are strongly associated with achievement and support cultures. Changes brought about using a power culture approach are termed power/coercive techniques (for example mass sackings and replacements of key personnel). Changes associated with a role culture are termed rational/empirical (for example operational research plus conventional training).

OD involves not only individuals but also groups in the change process, for the effectiveness and capacity of the whole organization depends on collective effort. An OD programme has a typical sequence. There is diagnosis of the initial conditions in terms of design, roles, technology, relationships, skills and information. Goals are set and suitable processes agreed upon and implemented. Results are monitored and evaluated. For each of the stages suitable techniques were described.

The results of research into the efficacy of OD are equivocal. Cultural reasons for success or failure were suggested. Where success for OD seems unlikely, there are less ambitious ways of bringing about change.

FURTHER READING

Articles

Alderfer, C. (1977) 'Organizational development', *Annual Review of Psychology* 28: 197–223. A state of the art report up to the mid-1970s.
Blake, R. and Mouton, J.S. (1964b) 'Breakthrough in organizational development', *Harvard Business Review* 42 (November/December): 133–8. An account of the authors' own work.
Cross, M. (1991) 'Monitoring multiskilling: the way to guarantee long-term change', *Personnel Management* 23 (3): 44–9.
Hofstede, G. (1980b) 'Motivation, leadership, and organizational development: do American theories apply abroad?', *Organizational Dynamics* 9 (1): 42–62.
Jaeger, A.M. (1986) 'Organizational development and national cultures: where's the fit?', *Academy of Management Review* 11 (1): 178–90.

Books

Levinson, H., Molinari, J. and Spohn, A. (1972) *Organizational Diagnosis* Cambridge, MA: Harvard University Press (reprinted 1977). A source book for ideas on how to diagnose.
Marlow, H. (1975) *Managing Change*, London: Institute of Personnel Management. An account of how the author manages change using measures of four leadership styles.
Mirvis, P. and Berg, D.N. (1977) *Failures in Organizational Development and Change*, New York: Wiley. Stories of OD failures.
Williams, A., Dobson, P. and Walters, M. (1989) *Changing Culture*, London: Institute of Personnel Management. OD success stories.

RECOMMENDED CASES

'Innovation at a Technical College': The structure of a technical college is geared to traditional teaching according to subject specialisms. The college is now required to teach courses which cut across disciplines and which use changed teaching methods.

'Trouble in the Registry': A set of examination papers goes missing. This is a symptom of deeper problems from a 'failed' reorganization and ethnic rivalries.

RECOMMENDED EXERCISE

'A Social Services Department' (see also Chapter 3): An exercise in differentiation and integration.

Chapter 10

Organizational behaviour and the discipline

CHAPTER OBJECTIVES

By the end of this chapter you will be able to:

1 examine the grounds for comparing values at the personal level with cultures at the group, organizational and societal levels
2 decide for yourself which of four research positions you favour
3 explain what is meant by homeostasis
4 describe three theories of change
5 summarize this book and evaluate the usefulness to you of the discipline of OB

1 INTRODUCTION AND CONSOLIDATION

1.1 Introduction

The intentions of this chapter are:

- to consolidate what has been said about organizational behaviour
- to point out that writers on OB are themselves affected by the culture of the scientific community to which they belong and
- to suggest ways forward from this introductory text.

1.2 Consolidation

Typical values found in both societal and organizational cultures are shown in Figure 10.1. It was argued, in the opening chapters, that 'golden means' are sought as objectives at national level, in the management of an economy, in the maintenance of law and order and in social policy. In later chapters it was claimed that the

Figure 10.1 The golden means of selected values and virtues
Note: Not all cultures have a religious core, but see Chapter 1, Section 5, on cultural strength and intensity.

Table 10.1 Examples of types of researchers

Method centred and detached	Problem centred and involved
1 Abstract thinker Favours a theoretical deductive approach (e.g. mathematical models of communication nets)	**3 Intuitive synthesiser** Blends induction and deduction according to intuition (e.g. studies of organization structures and contexts)
2 Experimentalist Favours an empirical approach (e.g. the experimental studies of leadership styles, and some survey research)	**4 Qualitative researcher** Feels 'it is high time for scientists to realize that their subjective feelings and emotions deeply affect their so-called objective studies' (e.g. participant observation studies)

Notes: The names are based on those used by Mitroff (1974) who links his typology with Jungian (1) thinking, (2) sensing, (3) intuiting and (4) feeling types. (Compare the Kiersey and Bates temperaments in Table 7.1.)

For those who like to think of research as a form of investigation, Thorpe and Moscarola (1991) have similar categories which they illustrate with the names of famous fictional detectives: (1) theoretician (Hercule Poirot); (2) scientist specializing in careful measurement (Sherlock Holmes); (3) mixed tool-kit expert (Columbo); (4) ethnologist (Maigret). They add a maverick, Dirty Harry, who 'pushes to provoke a response'.

decision-making of managers and the dynamics of groups are also imbued with the same values. Not all cultures have a religious core, but see Chapter 1.5 on cultural strength and diversity.

The shortfalls and excesses shown are hypothesized to be triggers for change. (See Figures 1.1, 2.4, and 7.1, where the values are also placed as 'golden means' between extremes.) Change which corrects a shortfall or excess is remedial. A gradual change from one culture, or golden mean, to another is evolutionary. A sudden change of culture is revolutionary (in the sense of overturning an existing state of affairs).

What is the evidence that a culture extends to all parts of society? What evidence is there for evolutionary or revolutionary change?

To answer these questions we need to look at different schools of thought among OB writers, since what is admissible as evidence depends partly on the values of those who collect and present that evidence.

Table 10.1 is a typology of social researchers adapted from one used by Mitroff (1974). He examined the values of the natural scientists who were studying fragments brought back from the moon by American astronauts in the Apollo space programme.

2 TYPES OF ORGANIZATIONAL BEHAVIOUR RESEARCHER

2.1 The abstract thinker

The evidence that would satisfy abstract thinkers would have to be collected for theoretical reasons. What they scornfully refer to as 'data dredging' is ruled out because a collection of data cannot be understood without a theory. The word *theory* is sometimes used very loosely to mean 'speculation or conjecture'. Abstract thinkers prefer a tighter definition which insists that concepts are rigorously defined and that propositions about the concepts are spelt out in detail. Their goal is 'a statement of what are held to be general laws, principles or causes of something known or observed'. Experimentalists would argue that a general theory which purports to account for known facts is only acceptable *after* 'the lower-level propositions deduced from it have been confirmed or established by observation or experiment'. Abstract thinkers, however, enjoy the process of constructing theories. They may leave the data collection to others.

Talcott Parsons (1902–79), a sociologist, was an abstract thinker who attempted to construct a general theory of society to include what he called 'the personality system, the social system, and the cultural system'. He put forward a similar idea to that of the golden mean, namely that all systems have to guard against imbalance or serious disturbance (Parsons 1951).

A collaborator of his, Bales (1950), provided data which seemed to support this part of Parsons' theory. Bales developed 'interaction process analysis' which is a way of recording 'positive' and 'negative' behaviour in small groups. He found, in the groups he studied, that the probability of positive actions outweighed the probability of negative actions. (Too many negative actions would seriously disturb the group.) He wrote: 'accomplishment and satisfaction levels can only be maintained in a steady state if ... positive reactions preponderate'. Abstract thinking has been applied to other particular matters referred to in this book. An example is mathematically calculated propositions about 'communication nets' (see Chapter 8, Section 2.2, for small group experimental work with such nets). The properties of larger communication networks have also been measured (by sociometry). The findings are relevant to organizational design.

Negotiation is another topic that lends itself to abstract formulation. It has been approached through game theory which was developed by von Neumann and Morgenstern (1944). Game theory must not be confused with the games in Berne's transactional analysis (Chapter 5, Section 4.6) nor with Allison's ideas about political gaming (Chapter 6, Section 2.2). Von Neumann and Morgenstern deal with issues in which the stakes can be quantified. In one type of game the rules specify that one party's loss is another's gain (the two-person zero-sum game). Another game has a matrix of payoffs such that, if one player is to get the maximum, the other must act 'unselfishly' and sustain a loss; however, if both act 'selfishly' both will lose and if both act 'unselfishly' both will gain something, though not as much as either could get at the other's expense by being 'selfish' when the other is not. Experimental groups can be assembled to play by the rules so that the theorizers can modify their predictions on the basis of observed play.

Walton and McKersie (1965) built a complicated game for which they quantified various types of gains that negotiators in industrial relations may seek and losses they may wish to avoid. Their type of theory-building is intended to offer prescriptions for actual negotiators faced with situations similar to those encountered in their games.

Theories provide a framework. This book has provided a framework too, but only a rudimentary one. The implicit 'grand theory' about cultural connections and transformations has not been fully developed. The problem with abstract theories is that, while they are elegant, the real behaviour they seek to explain is usually messy. So we turn to the contribution of the experimentalist.

2.2 The experimentalist

Abstract thinkers may follow up their thinking by collecting data, sometimes by experiment (for example, with game players or small group nets). As indicated in Table 10.1, however, the experimentalist is less concerned with making *a priori* deductions for subsequent verification and more concerned with acquiring data from which to make inferences. This is what is meant by 'an empirical approach'.

Laboratory experiments require random assignment to

'treatment' and control conditions. Alternatively the people who are 'subjects' may be matched with those who are not given the 'treatment'. The variation in the 'treatment' (which is the independent, or causal, variable) has to be controlled by the experimenter. Since the results can also be affected by 'noise' or 'nuisance variables', background conditions must be kept constant, and anything which is not relevant must be excluded. If this is not possible, allowances have to be made. Experiments are easier with rats or pigeons, but one may question how far generalizations based on studies of animals apply to human behaviour. Where people are recruited as subjects for laboratory experiments, ethical questions may arise. (An example was the work of Stanley Millgram on obedience, which was cited in Chapter 8.)

A number of so-called field experiments have been conducted with groups *in* organizations. One of these was the early study by Lippitt and White of leadership in clubs of 11-year-old boys (see Chapter 8, Section 3.2). There are also examples of field experiments *with* organizations, but Seashore acknowledges that there are not many and that none

> fulfill[s] the canons of experimental design to the degree ordinarily expected in laboratory or field experiments with small groups.
>
> (1964: 165)

However, Wootton, citing Ritchie, points out:

> The difference between controlled experiment and uncontrolled observation is, in fact, one of degree. 'Observation that depends upon a definite interest and involves selection from the whole that is presented in experience is always of the nature of experiment, assuming that by an experiment is meant a *controlled observation such that the number of variables is finite and known*. The ideal of experiment is never attained. It would mean that the whole universe proceeded uniformly while we varied one ingredient'. In practice we must recognize a scale from the almost wholly uncontrolled to the almost wholly controlled; but naturally, the degree of probability attaching to the results is likely to correspond to the position on this scale of the observations upon which these results are based.
>
> (Wootton 1950: 27; emphasis added)

Survey-type research such as Hofstede's might be classed as experimental in that he was seeking to find variations by country while keeping the employing organization constant. He and other survey researchers have been able to 'control for' unwanted 'contamination' in their results by statistical techniques. It is possible, for example, to find that three variables are all correlated (variation in one affects the others). One can then use statistics to test various hypotheses about *how* variables A, B and C might be associated.

To satisfy the experimentalist, the cultural variables listed in Figure 10.1 must have been measured in some way which enables inferences to be made about them. Earlier chapters have indicated that research has, indeed, been carried out with the four types of national cultures and with the four types of organizational cultures. What has not yet been attempted is any form of test for the way in which these particular national and organizational cultures might be associated.

The important thing which separates the researchers on the left side of Table 10.1 from those on the right is that those on the left seek to follow the so-called 'natural sciences', where theory is elaborated for the purpose of explanation, prediction and *control*, while experimentation is conducted as a way of gathering support for theories, or of declaring them false, and as a basis for further theorizing. Abstract thinkers and experimentalists are positivist in the sense that they stress the connection between scientific knowledge and control. They believe the observer is detached from what is being observed, and they seek objectivity through the use of appropriate methods to assess 'the facts'. Mitroff's natural scientists knew that passionate belief is necessary to motivate the scientist to carry on during lengthy periods of uncertainty, but knew also that self-criticism and acceptance of criticism from others are needed too. Nevertheless, abstract thinkers and hard experimentalists try to keep their feelings out of their research.

2.3 The intuitive synthesiser

Both intuitive synthesizers and qualitative researchers believe that total objectivity is impossible. The intuitive synthesizer in Mitroff's typology

> feels that hard data gatherers have a tendency to go on collecting data forever because they lack the intellectual or emotional fortitude that would permit them to extrapolate beyond their always limited sets of data. He also feels that abstract theorizers are

equally limited, for example, their overly formalistic ways of conceptualizing phenomena prevent them from appreciating characterization of problems that are not easily, if ever, susceptible to formalization. (Humanistic Scientists he tends to dismiss as irrelevant.) His general attitude is that intuition and a global approach produces the best ultimate understanding of scientific problems.

(Mitroff 1974: 172)

The present writer was privileged for a time to belong to the research team which worked intuitively to produce *The Aston Studies*, published in four volumes. The research synthesized disparate positions. Pugh and Hinings (1976), comment on the fact that, over the years since 1963 when the Aston programme began, there have been trends in sociology away from a functional systems approach towards concepts of social action (away from environmental causation and towards causation by the actions of organization members). The Aston group aimed 'to bring together system and action, not to see them as theoretical alternatives to be battled over in terms of "correctness" of viewpoint' (Pugh and Hinings 1976: 176).

The description which follows suggests further reasons for describing the researchers as 'intuitive synthesizers'. Perhaps the group's main achievement was in the development of measurement scales that are not based on opinions but on published information, records, organization charts and other documentation, supplemented by the knowledge of senior informants. Characteristics that could be counted were extracted from the materials collected and then grouped conceptually into scales which were tested for statistical coherence. The scales were further grouped mathematically into factors. Causal models were constructed, but it was not claimed that these were the sole ways of interpreting the data. The technique of 'path analysis' can actually show that the data support a variety of different interpretive models (Hilton 1972). It is the researchers' belief that many of the debates in OB to which they addressed themselves 'can be pushed forward only by dynamic studies involving continuous monitoring over periods of time' (Pugh and Hinings 1976: 177).

At first, the theoretical content of the Aston research was 'contingency theory'. It was assumed that certain variables were contingencies (see Chapter 2, Section 1.). These variables were called 'contextual' and treated as causes. The remaining variables were called 'structural'. (See also Chapter 3, Section 1.4) They were thought to be the 'responses'. The chief findings were that as the number of employees grows (a contingency) the structure changes. However, the ideas of those who thought that technological changes would also influence structure (the 'technological determinists') were not supported. Later work incorporated cultural variables (measured by the business organization climate index), group and role variables and performance indicators.

The Aston researchers offer their work as 'a useful taxonomic framework'. The data they collected were placed in a databank which can be drawn upon for secondary analysis (reworking) by others. Cross-cultural studies have been carried out in the United States, Canada, Germany, India, Japan and Sweden as well as in Britain.

From the above research, what can we say about culture? First, it is difficult to know where to set boundaries for sampling. Cultures may be strong or weak, unified or pluralist. We are speaking figuratively when we describe the 'levels' from society to persons. Suppose we give a questionnaire to all the employees of two organizations to assess their cultural values. We may find great similarity of answers in one organization (a unitary or integrated culture) but a great variety of answers in the other (a fragmented culture). Hofstede found, in a multinational firm, that national values were held by employees. However, Mansfield and Payne (1977) suggest that there are likely to be cultural variations even between lower and higher levels in a single hierarchy. The more senior the employees, the more likely it is that their views will be 'golden'. Gordon and Cummins (1979) have also found differences according to type of industry. A society is even more likely to have fragmented values. It may be exceptional to find the same societal values reproduced in organizations and their sub-units. So Figure 10.1 is just a convenient starting point for further enquiry. Might this be by qualitative research?

2.4 The qualitative researcher

Mitroff, in his study of natural scientists, found few of what he called 'humanist researchers'. The discussion which follows departs somewhat from his terms and definitions so as to accommodate viewpoints unique to those interested in social phenomena. (A 'participant observer', for example, joins in the activity being observed, whereas a natural scientist cannot, except in imagination, become an electron, a chemical element, a microbe or whatever.) The researchers to whom we apply the term 'qualitative' oppose positivism. They argue that natural science methods are not appropriate. Because researchers are themselves human they cannot study other people in the same way that a geologist might study rocks. The very presence of a researcher or of the research 'instruments' affects the persons studied. The researcher should therefore continuously reflect on his or her own behaviour and assumptions.

Qualitative researchers use archive materials and on-going events. They analyse the contents of documents, tapes and audio-visual material, they may produce case studies and they may engage with others in the activity to be understood. Instead of trying to distance themselves from others by observing from the outside they believe that the researcher should learn from the inside, or at least see research as a joint endeavour with the people involved. There have been historical and participant observer studies in organizations but, because they have had a different focus from the present book, they have not been described here.

Let us look at two types of qualitative research described by Habermas (1968). Both types reject what Habermas calls empirical-analytic science (on the left side in Table 10.1).

Historical-hermeneutic science

Hermeneutics is 'the art or science of interpretation'. Historical-hermeneutic science is concerned with interaction (it might ask how people experience cultural harmony or strife in their encounters with one another). The meaning of the phenomena is of greater concern than their predictability. The key issue 'is whether the results of an inquiry fit, make sense, and are true to the understanding of ordinary actors in the everyday world' (Psathas 1973).

Anthropologists have described societal cultures, and OD consultants can vouch for organizational cultures. Historical-hermeneutic researchers have added theorizing of their own. Space does not permit a detailed description here, but you will find references if you look up 'symbolic interactionism' and phenomenology, which are two major schools of thought with historical-hermeneutic values.

Critical social science

What is known as Critical Theory is based on the Marxian approach referred to in Section 3.3 below. Marx himself studied how early forms of craft manufacture gave way to capitalism, and he used dialectical reasoning (see Chapter 6, Section 2.2, 'The dialectical method') to deduce that capitalism would in its turn be replaced by common ownership of the means of production. Critical theorists consider that empirical-analytic research methods are part of the powerful forces which support capitalism. The conventional boundaries between, say, national governments and other formal organizations depend on special interests and power relations, which are embedded in society. Critical theorists want to expose these power relations to enable those constrained by them to rise above them.

Habermas thought the critical method is like psychoanalysis. Inquiry in psychoanalysis is strictly personal, aimed at rediscovery of self, and confirmed as correct in its interpretation only by the patient. The key to self-discovery for the individual, or for society, is the restoration of undistorted communications (communication without fear and without repression). The remedy for the distortions, according to Critical Theorists, is research which educates people to determine what their true interests are and what is blocking those interests.

Because critical social science addresses the question of social power it might ask how culture maintains or subverts the powerful. While Figure 10.1 draws attention to power, Critical Theorists would not approve of a power distance type culture being described as a golden mean.

2.5 Organizational behaviour scientists?

Table 10.1 mentions 'scientists' only once. The substitution of the word 'researchers' in the title was deliberate, so as not to beg the question whether OB is a science. For many people, 'research' simply signifies 'inquiry', whereas science is careful observation, theory construction, laboratory testing, publication of results and verification by others. Even in the natural sciences this is a simplistic account of what really happens, as Mitroff's study shows. However, the alternative to positivism is not that 'anything goes'. Each attempt at understanding organizational behaviour, whether qualitative or quantitative, has its own criteria of acceptability, and each has to be undertaken with integrity. Methods must be appropriate to the type of results sought. Falsification or invention of data disqualify anyone from professional status. Nevertheless, choices about what to study, why to study it, where to look, what methods to use and so on are in part ideological for both natural and social scientists. Sponsors and pay-masters obviously have the right to stipulate certain conditions, and human 'subjects' also have rights. Whether one restricts the word 'science' to the empirical-analytic type of work or whether one extends it to cover clinical, historical-hermeneutic and critical studies is a question of definition.

OB is 'a recognized department of learning' within academic institutions in many countries. OB researchers have produced evidence for the existence of cultures, but evidence of linkages from personal temperaments to societal cultures is patchy. It is persons who hold the beliefs, attitudes and values which collectively make up a culture. Without a group of some kind there cannot be a culture, since, by definition, it is *shared*. But not all groups in a single organization share the organizational culture, and not all organizations in a particular society share the societal culture. So there is theorizing to be done about cultural diversity as well as about common cultures. Is there a connection between diversity and theories of transformation? We think that there is.

3 CHANGE THEORIES

We shall discuss three types of change theory.

3.1 Systems theory, change and diversity

Systems theory is abstract, and so it is easier to start with a parable of an organization to which the theory can be applied. Let us assume that there is a craft co-operative whose purpose is to enable previously unemployed workers to make and sell a product. It has to buy raw materials, convert them into goods, price them and sell them. It has a strong support culture. The problem of 'group think' (see Chapter 7, Section 4) prevents the group from noticing, until late, that the sales of its wares are declining. A battler comes to the fore who is prepared to 'rock the boat' in the interests of getting action on the sales front. The group has got into a mess because it does not have adequate records of the kind of people who are its present and potential customers. A thinker now introduces some procedures to improve on the collection and dissemination of this kind of information so that the group can take the right action. It is found that customers have been lost because standards of quality have declined, so an achiever starts a competition for high quality. The sales recover. So the group lives happily ever after? Not necessarily. The workers pay themselves from sales revenue. Their employment is in danger if sales fall off again for other reasons, and so the co-operative must continue to be vigilant. In the parable, it is saved by the diversity of temperaments among its members which enables it to make changes. The explanation given by systems theory is that

> the only way in which an organization can offset entropy (decay) is by continually importing material, energy, and information in one form or another, transforming them, and redistributing resources to the environment.
>
> (Kast and Rosenweig 1981: 51)

The environment places constraints on organizations to which they have to respond. A *decider* has to interpret important incoming signals and see that adjustments are made between subsystems and components. The 'law of requisite variety' (Ashby 1981) states that the decider must be capable of a variety of responses which can match the variety of environmental information. In a social system, such as a business, the decider may well be the chief executive, though it could be a board of directors or, in the small co-operative, a meeting of all the members. The adjustments are made to preserve the status quo, or, in the terms introduced here, the golden mean (or means). Systems theory uses the term *homeostasis* for the preservation of a constant state in the face of variability and variety. This constant state is one of balance or equilibrium. It is possible, however, for the system to return, after disturbance, to a new point of equilibrium. More recently, the idea of equilibrium as a normal state has given way, in some quarters, to the idea that continuing fluctuation is more normal. Shifting equilibria represent evolutionary change.

A societal example of evolutionary change is given by a founding father of OB, Max Weber (1864–1920). Precapitalist forms of organization were patrimonial or feudal, and relied on tradition for their authority. As trade expanded, larger-scale production required funding from accumulated savings. Feudal beliefs that usury is sinful were replaced by a 'Protestant ethic' which sees interest on loans as a reward for hard work and thrift. This new cultural ethic undermined traditional authority. At the same time, capitalists introduced new structures for their enterprises. Feudal and patrimonial organizations were replaced by bureaucracy which is based on the new form of authority which Weber called 'rational–legal'. Weber predicted that bureaucracy would spread because it is suited to modern economies, though he foresaw that the effects would not be wholly beneficial (see Chapter 8, Section 4.1).

For systems theory, change is a form of adjustment to external conditions. If the system is already internally varied its capacity for change is greater. The change from feudalism to capitalism has been evolutionary in some societies. In other societies, such as Japan since 1945, change has been more revolutionary.

3.2 Autopoiesis and change

Maturana and Varela (1980) coined the term *autopoiesis* for the capacity of systems to 'produce themselves'. According to autopoiesis, a system's interaction with its 'environment' is a reflection of its own organization, so the 'environment' can be considered as an extension of the organization itself, not something separate. The source of change, according to this theory, is random variations that occur *within* the total system of the organization and all entities with which it has, or could have, relations. Such random events can trigger massive changes. Whether or not they do will depend on whether the present identity of the system will dampen the effect of the events. Morgan (1986) cites an example from nature in which random behaviour can lead to major change. He says that termites deposit random piles of dirt. When a deposit becomes large it attracts the attention of other termites which transform the dirt into elaborate structures.

In human organizations a critical level of support is sometimes needed before coherent action is taken. Chapter 6 outlines the 'rubbish bin' theory of decision-making which describes how the flow of problems, solutions and energies may come together randomly at first, but, later on, people will devote their energies to those issues which are closest to resolution. Chapter 9 emphasizes that organizational development is 'consciously adopted procedures' that improve performance and teach the organization to change itself (that is, to be autopoiesic in making the most of chance opportunities). Exchange theorists are interested in whether there is power to reward people appropriately for instituting change.

3.3 Change and the dialectic

The dialectic stems from the philosophy of Hegel (1770–1831) but was used by Karl Marx to develop his theory of social change. Hegel supposed that, through the use of his dialectic, reason would discern cosmic forces behind the facts of history. For Marx, materialism (the means by which humans produce their material requirements) was such a force. There are three basic ideas about change in dialectical reasoning.

1 Phenomena change themselves as a result of tension with their opposite.
2 Change may be evolutionary in the sense that, though each 'negation' rejects the previous form, it also retains something from that form.
3 The process of negating each previous negation continues until such switches are no longer possible. There is then a new phase of collaborative or destructive activity (the revolution).

Both Hegel and Marx thought of history as moving towards the 'development of humanity itself', but Hegel's interpretation of this was idealistic while Marx's was materialistic. Marx maintained that, in capitalism, the interests of employers in making profits and the interests of workers in improving their wages are in basic conflict. Marx thought this contradiction would eventually lead to revolution after which the two classes (the proletariat, or working class, and the 'bourgeoisie' or capitalists) would be replaced by a classless society.

Touraine's idea of 'contradiction' is derived from Hegel and Marx, as a reading of Chapter 2, Section 5.2, indicates. Also Skinner and Winckler's idea that committed, indifferent and antagonistic behaviour cannot coexist (see Chapter 1, Section 3.2) could be developed dialectically.

The Chinese philosophy of the Tao, or 'Way', developed in the fourth or fifth century BC, preceded Hegel by many centuries in its account of primeval opposites (Yin and Yang) from whose interaction all things have evolved and which continue to guide all change. So this theory of change has a long ancestry.

Figure 10.1 can be interpreted by theories of systems change, autopoesis or dialectical change. It presents a kind of intuitive synthesis which makes use of the concept of 'culture' taken from writings which have been selected for their coverage of topics which crop up in OB syllabuses. The diversity of OB has therefore been under-represented, but this is true of any introductory text.

4 MOVING ON FROM HERE

There are two ways in which you may wish to take matters further. The first is to go deeper into topics already discussed. The second is to branch into adjoining areas which have not been treated here.

4.1 Exploring deeper

Kinds of knowledge

The question of how we come to know anything is the subject of *epistemology*. The four types of researchers in Table 10.1 follow different 'inquiring systems'. These are shown in the Appendix. The names of the philosophers who have contributed to building the inquiry systems are given so that you may delve deeper into epistemology.

Measuring cultures

Does culture permeate such organizational behaviour as controlling, designing, motivating, deciding and leading? There is evidence to suggest that it does. Harrison, Hofstede and the Aston researchers have operationalized and tested some of the ideas in this book, but not all of them. You may want to check from the bibliography to find how they went about measurement. The exercise 'Culture Sort' is based on part of an Aston measure, the business organization climate index. There are many other measures of cultures or 'climates', some of which are readily available if you want to assess the culture at your own place of work.

The cultural values selected by writers in OB may not be those which a moralist, politician, citizen, manager or worker would have selected as important. Are they values you would propose? What alternative or additional values would you suggest could be important in organizational behaviour?

Positivists strive for each term to have an exclusive content, to prevent any overlap between one term and another. They also seek exhaustiveness, to make sure that no relevant concepts have been left out. Do you think measures of culture can satisfy these conditions? If not, does it matter?

Change theories

Some people think change is linear. The Victorians thought of change as 'progress'. Nations are referred to as 'developing' or 'developed', with the implication that the former are moving towards a goal that other nations have reached. This book has used the word 'development' in a special sense of organizational transformation through organizational development. But it has also favoured the idea that change is cyclical rather than linear. However, a series of temporary shifts looks like permanence. In most societies and organizations, elements of all the cultures are present at the same time, since all the values they represent are desired in some degree. So is cyclical change an illusion? Is it just an aspect of diversity?

A mono-culture would be as dull as a game in which one side always wins. Harmony and tension are found together. Rules can be both fixed and elastic. At any given time the moves of individuals depend, as in such sports as football, on a pattern which is constantly evolving. To achieve a golden mean between violence and dullness in sport involves trying out new game manoeuvres and making new rules that permit both order and excitement. Is this change or homeostasis?

The golden mean

Whether organizations pursue golden means as goals is uncertain. Much may depend on definitions. The golden mean does, however, provide a useful metaphor for linking some disparate topics in OB.

We need, nevertheless, to be on our guard. Perhaps some extremes are good. Maybe we can never have too much prosperity, for example. Also this book is not advocating that expediency demands that we be only moderately truthful, moderately honest, moderately just and so on. Nor do we argue that integrity should be sacrificed to expediency. Ethics helps us to answer questions about what is right or wrong. These questions must be faced by individuals, by businesses, and by societies. The further reading mentions some works to take you further. The next section is about how to expand your knowledge.

4.2 Topics of relevance to organizational behaviour

Business ethics

It was stated in the preface that this book aims to 'provoke thinking about values', but it is not a business ethics text. You can now study business ethics as a subject in its own right, as well as indirectly in connection with marketing, finance and accounting, operations management, personnel management and OB.

A report of the Business Roundtable (1988), published in New York, states that 'a culture in which an ethical concern permeates the whole organization is necessary for the self-interest of the company'. So, many companies today are drawing up 'codes of practice' to indicate what behaviour they expect of their employees, and how they propose to be 'socially responsible' to their customers and to society. The director general of the Royal Institute of Public Administration in the UK points out, however, that conflicts of interest will still arise.

> In any organization there is no *inevitable* congruence between an employee's material self-interest, the dictates of his conscience, the instructions of his superiors, the objectives of the heads of the organization, the interests of the organization's customers or clients and the interest of society at large.
>
> (emphasis added)

Ethics can be studied in relation to government as well as to business. It covers questions of human rights, such as freedom of speech. Power distance cultures sometimes maintain themselves by denying freedom of speech to opponents. Ayittey, a Ghanaian, points out that, in 1990, only six out of fifty-one African countries had a free press and tolerated criticism of government policies. Modern African leaders 'model themselves on their colonial forbears', whereas traditional chiefs tolerated and solicited dissenting opinion. He opines that

> One of these days, Africa's peasants, chanting kirikiri and waving cutlasses, will march to their state capitals and ask their vampire élites a few questions about their Swiss bank accounts.
>
> (Ayittey 1990: 9)

The United Nations produced a Declaration of Human Rights which is a standard to which all signatories are expected to conform. However, breaches of these rights are extremely common. Here questions of politics and economics arise.

Political science and economics

Politics and economics are highly relevant to OB. The values in Figure 10.1 can be held in capitalist, socialist or mixed economies. But both political science and economics have their own theories of change.

Everyone in the world is affected by the actions and omissions of governments. Governments can, however, be changed. The last quarter of the twentieth century has seen the fall of a number of Eastern European regimes, the growing economic indebtedness of many nations and the dawning recognition that the future of planet earth is at stake unless creditors and debtors unite to save it.

Supra-national collaboration on an unprecedented scale is required. Without some common values, this collaboration will not happen. Organizational behaviour was defined as 'how enterprises work and how the people associated with them act' (Chapter 1, Section 1). Whether the United Nations can be the means for resolving the acute supra-national problems of the world and its outer space depends on the will of the citizens and governments of the member nations. So how strongly do we believe in the values embodied in the United Nations charter: in peace, human rights, respect for international law and fullness of life for all?

5 SUMMARY

Previous chapters described people in organizations as seeking such values as order, efficiency, economic innovation and collaboration. What evidence is there that these values are golden means affected by national cultures of power distance, uncertainty avoidance, individualism and femininity? What evidence is there for corresponding types of cultures in organizations (power, role, achievement and support)?

Three sorts of transformations have been described: remedial change which corrects a shortfall or excess; evolutionary change where a culture is gradually replaced by another; and revolutionary change where an existing culture is suddenly overturned by another culture. What is the evidence for these?

These questions are answered differently by different writers. Those who study organizational behaviour are themselves affected by culture, the culture of the academic community to which they belong. In the social sciences **academic cultures tend to favour** either 'analytical-empirical' values or 'critical-hermeneutic' values. The distinction is between those who would copy, and those who would avoid, the methods of theorizing and experimentation used in the natural sciences. The former tend to be abstract thinkers and experimentalists; the latter tend to be qualitative researchers. Intuitive synthesizers pragmatically occupy an intermediate position.

Abstract thinkers require logically consistent theoretical formulations, preferably formulations which are mathematically testable. Game theory and sociometry were cited. These examples could also satisfy experimentalists who require that observations be made for verification, preferably through controlled experiments, but minimally through statistical procedures which control for error.

Intuitive synthesizers take a pragmatic approach, recognizing that methods may have to be tempered by circumstances and that there may be several different explanations for social phenomena. Some support for the speculations in this book has been derived from this type of research.

Qualitative researchers are not concerned with prediction and control, but rather with understanding the subjective experiences they are attempting to describe. Notions of cultural differences have support from qualitative research.

Critical theorists think that those who use natural science methods to predict and control social phenomena are really helping powerful élites to stay in power. Critical theorists seek to expose how scientific 'imperialism' can be used to keep the poorer classes in a society ignorant of where their real interests lie.

The degree to which ideas expressed in this book carry conviction thus depends upon the OB perspective adopted. Three types of change theory can all be accommodated within the framework presented. Systems theory draws attention to the importance of environmental turbulence in inducing organizational change. Autopoiesis draws attention to random variation, coupled with the building up of a critical mass of support for change. Marxist and Hegelian theories emphasize historical contradictions which will culminate in revolution.

An introductory text such as this cannot do justice to the range of issues which have a bearing on organizational cultures and transformations. Suggestions were made whereby the reader can probe deeper, or broaden out his or her own investigations. The 'global village' presents us with a challenge to design and manage organizations which cross traditional frontiers and cultural divisions.

A universal religious core of faith in truth and love could give more hope than our current excesses and deficiencies.

APPENDIX: EXAMPLES OF INQUIRING SYSTEMS

In the four inquiring systems below (based on Mitroff 1974), a subject is presented with (1) to (4) as stimuli. As responses a subject is required to produce (1) to (4).

Leibnizian
(1) A set of primitive (unde-fined) formal elements (symbols)
(2) A set of explicit, formal rules or operators for forming –
(3) A model or single set of complex relations (propositions) that can be . . .
(4) Explicitly shown to follow from (1) by means of (2)

Kantian
(1) At least two alternative (com-plementary, but potentially divergent) sets of Leibnizian elements and operators
(2) A set or sets of Lockean primitive experiential elements such that . . .
(3) When each of the Leibnizian element and operator sets is applied to the Lockean element set(s), a set of multiple integrative models (interpretations) is produced such that
(4) The interdependence between the Leibnizian and Lockean elements is explicitly demonstrated and the multiple interpretations are made available for choice.

Lockean
(1) A set of primitive (undefined) experimental elements (sensory qualities, observations or data)
(2) A set of agreement-producing experiential operators (inclu-ding expert judgement, group decision-making) for forming . . .
(3) A consensual position or a single set (linkage) of factual propositions that can be . . .
(4) Explicitly shown to follow from (1) by means of (2)

Singerian Churchmanian
(1) A set of models such that
(2) Any model may be recursively applied to any other model (including itself) for the purpose of . . .
(3) Elucidating the distinctive characteristic assumptions underlying each model and the entire inquiry process so . . .
(4) The more nearly scientific features can be integrated with the ethical features of inquiry

The names are those of the philosophers to whom the inquiring systems owe their origins: Gottfried Wilhelm von Leibniz (1646–1716), inventor of the differential calculus; John Locke (1632–1704), who spent seventeen years producing his *Essay on Human Understanding* (1690) which inaugurated the 'age of empiricism'; Immanuel Kant (1724–1804) who wrote *The Critique of Pure Reason* and *The Critique of Practical Reason*; C.W. Churchman who after Singer's death, edited his *Experience and Reflection*, published in 1959 by the University of Pennsylvania Press.

FURTHER READING

This Chapter has raised the question of whether or not OB is scientific. The late Professor Barbara Wootton held that social science can (and should) be empirical and analytical. Her book may be available in libraries.

Wootton, B. (1950) *Testament for Social Science*, London: Allen & Unwin.

Mitroff's book can put her position in a wider context of more recent thinking.

Mitroff, I.I. (1974) *The Subjective Side of Science: A Philosophical Inquiry into the Psychology of the Apollo Moon Scientists*, Amsterdam: Elsevier.

Kuhn wrote a popular account of what is 'normal science' and how 'scientific revolutions' occur.

Kuhn, T.S. (1962) *The Structure of Scientific Revolutions*, Chicago, IL: University of Chicago Press.

An interesting 'do-it-yourself' suggestion for getting the flavour of scientific thinking is:

Gibbs, G.I. (1974) 'Scientific concepts and gaming', *Programmed Learning and Educational Technology* 11 (1): 32–8.

An account of recent scientific thinking is found in:

Gleick, J. (1987) *Chaos: Making a New Science*, London: Sphere.

The following article looks at systems theory from an unusual angle:

Lilienfeld, R. (1975) 'Systems theory as an ideology', *Social Research* 42 (Winter): 637–60.

For historical-hermeneutic theorizing see:

Meade, G.H. (1934) *Mind, Self and Society*, Chicago, IL: University of Chicago Press.

Schutz, A. (1967) *The Phenomenology of the Social World*, London: Heinemann.

For a work in the Critical Theory mode see:

Beynon, H. (1973) *Working for Ford*, Wakefield: EP Publishing (reprinted 1975).

Qualitative studies

For factories in America see:

Dalton, M. (1959) *Men Who Manage*, New York: Wiley.

Roy, D. (1960) 'Banana time: job satisfaction and information interaction', *Human Organization* 18: 156–68, 205–22.

For factories in Asia see:

Abbeglen, J.C. (1958) *The Japanese Factory: Aspects of Its Social Organization*, Glencoe, IL: Free Press.

For a co-operative in the UK see:

Eccles, A. (1981) *Under New Management*, London: Pan.

For measures of culture see such reference works as:

Lake, D.G., Miles, M.B. and Earle, R.B. (eds) (1973) *Measuring Human Behavior*, Columbia, OH: Teachers College Press.

On the question of ethics there is now a large literature. Two books and one article are suggested here.

Heidenheimer, A.J. (1970) *Political corruption: Readings in Comparative Analysis*, New York: Holt, Rinehart and Winston.
Hoffman, W. M. and Moore, J.M. (1988) *Business Ethics. Readings and Cases in Corporate Morality*, New York: McGraw-Hill.
Pocock, P. (1989) 'Is business ethics a contradiction in terms?', *Personnel Management* 21 (11): 60–3.

No particular exercises or cases have been selected for this chapter as all the cases are relevant. The Appendix supplements Table 10.1.

Case studies and exercises

I am indebted to the following students for these case studies: F.O. Ajayi, Musa Amadu, S.T. Anga, Marian Bolam, Duncan Cadbury, Jean Cox, Judith Davies, John W. Gray, Charles Jenkins, Helen Johnson, Hannatu Kayit, Dominic Magbor, Nsirim Evans Ogoloma, Colin Ovenstone, A.H. Sidik, I. Sonnar, C.A. Torti, Nigel Woodcock.

A CASE OF MISMANAGEMENT

Introductory remarks

Nigeria became independent from British rule in 1960. The background to this case is that the country, since independence, has suffered from widespread corruption, so much so that the 1975 Corrupt Practices Decree puts a heavy burden on defendants by creating a presumption that favours received by officials are in return for corrupt acts.[1] Fraud, intrigue, bribery and false evidence are practised by entrepreneurs and businessmen as well as by officials. Brownsberger,[2] however, believes that this type of behaviour was not normal in the tribal society prior to independence; he also believes that, since most Nigerian observers agree that corruption should be attacked, it will be attacked, and, in the longer run, such an attack on corruption will succeed. He states, 'The Organization of African Unity went so far as to name a break with materialism as one of its goals for the year 2000.'[3]

There is no space to outline Brownsberger's argument here but, according to him, corruption is associated with Western materialism, and dazzling inequality. 'Traditional community leaders recognise fiduciary duties, and ... they are morally predisposed to execute public responsibilities honestly. Moral men are not pure maximizers that behave corruptly as soon as the net discounted payoff exceeds zero.' Of course, vehicle licence offences are common in developed countries, but the moral concerns of Mr Adu and Mr Obi in the following case need to be seen against the background just described.

The case

In 1973 the Internal Revenue Division of the Ministry of Finance opened a branch office in a small Nigerian village. It was thought that decentralization would improve administrative efficiency. The branch was assigned responsibility for issuing and administering vehicle licences for the region.

An executive officer, Mr Obi, was put in charge. He had no academic background, but had risen through long years of service. He was also approaching retirement. Under him there were a Chief Clerk, some clerical assistants, typists and a cleaner – about ten staff in all.

Six months after the office opened, a clerical officer, Mr Adu, was posted from the main office to join the staff in the village. Mr Adu was a young man without any work experience. He had just left school. However, he was diligent, and took an interest in the work, and he quickly mastered the job. He was assigned the responsibility for issuing vehicle licences. The Chief Clerk's task was to collect and bank all cash payments. As the office was small, the staff formed a close-knit group and acted co-operatively. The exception was Mr Obi. He took little interest in the job, and constantly absented himself from the office. He did, however, form a close relationship with Mr Adu – so close that the staff viewed them as 'Godfather and Son'. Although the staff, and especially the Chief Clerk, disliked the way Mr Obi ran the office, they could not talk openly about this in front of Mr Adu. There was nothing they could do about it.

One day a middle-aged man called at the office to complain that police were harrassing him because of a mutilated vehicle licence issued by this Internal Revenue branch. The man wanted a replacement licence, and was advised to await the return of Mr Adu who was just having his tea break. After waiting some minutes, the complainant became impatient, and charged into the Executive Officer's room to complain. The code of practice for the issue of licences does not permit defective licences to be issued to any member of the public. The practice was to cancel any defective licence and, for security reasons, details were entered in triplicate and recorded in the record books. The complainant demanded a fresh licence as of right. At this Mr Obi became very upset, and started to shout that he was the victim of a disloyal and dishonest clerical officer. He behaved, in the hearing of the rest of the staff, as though he believed the licence had been issued fraudulently.

When Mr Adu got back from his tea break he realized from the uncomfortable atmosphere in the office that something was wrong. Suddenly, Mr Obi called him into the Executive Officer's room and yelled at him, in front of the claimant, as though he had committed an offence. 'You are dishonest! You have disappointed me!' he cried. Then he ordered Mr Adu to issue the man with a fresh licence, without having first confirmed that the original was fraudulently issued. This was quite contrary to the rules which governed the office.

Mr Adu took the licence, and looked at it closely. He recognized his handwriting, but wondered if he had done anything amiss. He was calm for a moment, and quietly looked through the books and duplicates for confirmation. Fortunately for him, from the duplicates and records, there was no sign of mutilation. The licence had in fact been issued for a motor cycle, and not a car. At this point the claimant announced that the licence was taken out for him by an insurance agent, and the agent may have done the mutilation so as to defraud him. This was a serious offence, one that was notifiable to the police.

Mr Adu, having just been publicly humiliated by his superior, now lost his self-control and also began to shout. He insisted that the police should be informed. Mr Obi, however, preferred to handle the matter softly. At this point the Chief Clerk entered the fray and took the side of the clerical officer. The Executive Officer probably realized that he was in the wrong but, to avoid loss of face and to preserve the dignity of his office, he would neither take advice nor apologize to his subordinates. On his instructions the complainant was issued with a fresh licence. As a result of this incident the relationship between Mr Obi and Mr Adu became so strained that the latter asked for a transfer. This was refused and so Mr Adu resigned from the service.

Questions

1 How many decisions can you identify in this case?
2 Refer to Table 6.1 in the text. What type(s) of decision-making did Mr Obi use? What type(s) did Mr Adu attempt to use?

3 Comment on the quality of the resolutions of the problem wanted by each man, stating what criteria you are using.

4 Would you have reported the matter to the police? Why, or why not?

5 Suppose you were the person in the main office who was responsible for posting Mr Adu to the branch. If you heard beforehand of his intended resignation, would you take any action? How do you make up your mind?

6 Has the introduction provided for this case affected your answers in any way?

Notes

1 This is stated in the *Supplement to Official Gazette Extraordinary* (Lagos), 2 December 1975, A172, Section 4.

2 Brownsberger, W.N. (1983) 'Development and governmental corruption – materialism and political fragmentation in Nigeria', *Journal of Modern African Studies* 21 (2): 215–33.

3 Organisation of African Unity (1980), *What Kind of Africa by the Year 2000?*, Final Report of the Monrovia Symposium, Addis Ababa.

THE CHANGE OF SITE

Introductory remarks

This case involves questions of what will motivate staff at each of two hospital sites to co-operate with a proposed change instead of resisting it.

If you attempt the case after reading only the first two chapters of this book, you will be able to make assumptions about the cultures at each of the sites and for the whole hospital. Chapter 2 will also alert you to contingencies for which plans need to be made, and to conflicts that may arise. You will suggest what the Senior Nursing Officer (a manager) might do, in the light of these considerations, to reward people for co-operation.

If you use the case later, when you have read more about job design (Chapter 4), motivation (Chapter 5) decision-making (Chapter 6) and group behaviour (Chapter 7), you may include assumptions about how the work of the nursing staff may change in the modern surroundings, what decisions need to be taken, and how, and which groups are likely to be in existence, or specially created.

If you have read Chapter 8 on leadership, you will be able to help the Senior Nursing Officer cope with the various group influences that may be operating.

The less you have read, the shorter your report is likely to be. If you have studied all the chapters, your report should be very comprehensive and you will be able to include a lot of assumptions of your own.

The case

The City Hospital was created some fourteen years ago from a merger of two smaller hospitals a quarter of a mile apart. There were then approximately 1,200 beds.

The main East site had formerly been known as Littlewich Hospital. It contained most of the acute work and specialties, with their backup facilities and services. The West site, at the Green, had been a sanatorium. At the time of the merger it concentrated on chest medicine, chest surgery and tuberculosis. It also had a purpose-built geriatric unit of seven wards and a day hospital.

Last year, at the East site, building work commenced on a new ward block of twelve wards, with an impressive theatre complex. It has been decided that all acute work should be concentrated there, so that services for patients can be rationalized and improved. The buildings will be ready for occupation twelve months from now.

Six wards from the West site will have to be moved. They are as follows:

C, P   Two male chest wards
D   One male chest surgical ward
G   One female chest medical ward
T   One female chest medical and surgical ward
M   One chest 'overflow' ward ('loaned' from geriatric)

At the East site, only five wards will be made available for those moving from the West. Two will be in the new complex, and the other three will be in the older East building. Their former occupants will have left them to go into the new buildings themselves. It is intended that three of the five chest wards at East site will become mixed-sex wards.

At the Green (West site), the buildings are old and have been relatively untouched except for the geriatric block and the addition of a new kitchen and a dining room. The nurses there have always been a close community, both on days and on nights, and the atmosphere is unhurried, traditional and friendly. Most of the trained night staff are middle-aged women who have been on their wards for some years. In general, they resent the planned move and wish to stay as they are, though they recognize that, especially for patients, there are gains to be made. Staff also fear that the new equipment and procedures will be difficult for them.

A Senior Nursing Officer, Night Duty, has just been appointed. She and the four night Nursing Officers are to formulate a plan so that the move can be accomplished smoothly, in stages.

Assignment

Write a report on the human considerations that will face the Senior Nursing Officer prior to, during and immediately after the proposed move. (You may imagine that you are the Senior Nursing Officer herself, or an outside adviser, as you wish.) Your report should also contain recommendations based on your analysis. You may make any additional assumptions you like, provided they are consistent with the information supplied.

THE COLD WAR

Introductory remarks

This case is in three parts. To get the most out of it you should *not* look at Part II until you have answered the questions for Part I. Likewise, please attempt the questions for Part II *before* you look at Part III.

The events take place at a depot where frozen food is handled and stored. The issue is one of motivating a workforce. The case is therefore recommended for Chapter 5, but may also be attempted after Chapter 8 on leadership.

The case – Part I

After I had worked for about eighteen months with one of the leading frozen food companies in the country, I took a job as foreman of a cold store depot in Edinburgh. Before taking up the post I was given a week of training at one of the Company's other depots to familiarize me with the products and the paperwork. I was then 23 years old.

The Edinburgh depot consisted of an office block, three large cold rooms, the trailer parts of two refrigerated lorries and a big yard. The depot held large stocks of ice-cream – plain, flavoured, family and catering sizes, chocolate-covered ices, cakes, iced lollies etc. A complete range of frozen foods was also held, both for retailing and for catering.

The products were brought to the depot from factories in the south. It was usual for two refrigerated articulated lorries to travel daily, but on at least one day per week there would be three lorries.

The products were sold by a telephone sales team of four, two sales representatives on the road and a sales manager. The day's sales were processed and allocated according to ten areas, each of which was covered by a refrigerated van. The vans were loaded by a night shift and were ready to go by 06.00 hours, although they did not leave the depot until 08.00 hours.

My job, as foreman, was to control both the intake to the depot during the day shift and the loading of the delivery vans on the night shift. I also had to keep up-to-date stock information, and so I took a physical count of the stock in all the cold rooms every other day. I was given a free hand in the way I ran the job and in the hours I worked. Basically, I was on days, but I could go onto the night shift and take days off. I could also work a full day, and then return for an hour or two in the middle of the night to see how things were going. I could give the storemen overtime, or work myself, as I thought necessary.

There were six men on the day shift, in addition to myself. Their duties were to tidy up the cold rooms after the night shift and to make space for the day's intake in such a way that stock was being continually rotated. When the intake began to arrive it had to be unloaded and put away in the cold rooms. The produce was contained in large wire-mesh pallets, like cages. There were twenty-four of these to a lorry. They were unloaded by means of fork-lift trucks, hand-operated lifting forks and a lot of pulling, pushing and cursing!

The night shift consisted of four men. They had to make up the orders and load them into the correct vans, according to area, ready for delivery next morning. Both shifts were responsible for keeping the yard and cold rooms clean and tidy. The work did not require much intelligence.

It had been left up to the men themselves to decide who was to work which shift. The four men on nights were more or less permanent, but they would swap occasionally to suit themselves.

The depot manager was in his early fifties. He did not like going into the cold rooms, and so he delegated all his responsibilities to the foreman. He was, in fact, a very weak manager.

When I arrived to take up the job, the place was a shambles! The stock was all mixed up, nobody had the remotest idea of the stock levels and the amount of damaged stock in the cold rooms was phenomenal. The whole place was filthy, and dripping pipes had caused ice to form all over the cold room floors. The morale of the men who would work under me was very low, and their commitment to the organization was nil. The only reason that the depot could function with such high damage levels was that it was carrying at least 50 per cent more stock than was necessary! This I discovered after I had taken a few stock counts and observed what was going out daily. For four months prior to my arrival, one of the workers, who had five years of service, had been acting as foreman, and it was obvious, from the condition of the depot, that the task was beyond his capabilities. The other men were aged between 23 and 35 and their service ranged from a few months to five years. They thought the insider should have been promoted and they resented an outsider of my youthfulness being brought in as foreman.

When I took charge and gave out tasks for the men to do, they were very slow and unco-operative in carrying them out. After two days I got them together, and told them that, whether they liked it or not, I was in charge. I then asked them what grievances they had that were making them so unco-operative. From this meeting I discovered that they considered their pay was too low. The day shift was getting £65 per week basic pay, but there was extra for overtime. The night shift had only a basic wage, of £70 per week. The job did not require skill, but was hard manual labour and the conditions were uncomfortable. I thought they deserved more.

Some questions on Part I

1 How would you describe the culture at the depot?
2 What could the foreman do to restore morale and to motivate the men? (He has no authority raise pay himself.)
3 Can you account for the behaviour of the depot manager?

DO NOT CONTINUE READING UNTIL AFTER YOU HAVE CONSIDERED THE ABOVE QUESTIONS.

The case – Part II

I asked the men why they had not asked for a rise. There was a lot of shuffling of feet and incoherent stammering. From what I could make out, they had asked for a rise a few months earlier and had been refused. They were too frightened to ask again. I asked why they did not leave and get other work. They said jobs were hard to get, and anyway they were used to this job.

Something had to be done, and so I suggested that I would ask for a rise for them, but they would have to back me up by threatening to withdraw their labour if they did not get the rise. They all agreed to back me up, and we went upstairs to see the manager. I put it to the manager that the men deserved a higher wage and would strike if they did not get it. He turned to one of the men and asked him if he would strike. He looked down at his shoes, mumbled 'No', and left. This happened five times more, until I alone was left with the manager.

Questions on Part II

1 What would you do now if you were the foreman?
2 Why would you do this?
3 Why do you think the men did not keep to their side of the agreement?

DO NOT CONTINUE READING UNTIL AFTER YOU HAVE CONSIDERED THESE QUESTIONS.

The case – Part III

I had decided to ask for a rise myself, as the place was in such a mess and did not fit the description given to me at the interview. I told the manager I would leave if I did not get a rise. I said that, if he did not want the depot to fall apart during the coming summer season, he needed me. He agreed, gave me my rise, and also gave me the power to sack any man who did not do as I told him.

I returned to the yard and found all the men busy working. I called them into my office and 'read the Riot Act' They had not only let me down, but also themselves. They were all very sheepish when I told them what I thought of them. From now on, I said, they would do what I told them, when I told them and in the way I told them, or they would be sacked on the spot. This seemed to win their respect and the job of cleaning up the mess became easy.

I got the leaking pipes repaired and set the men to work to chip the ice from the floors. The day shift did overtime at the weekend and got the stock sorted out. There were three storerooms. All the damaged goods were taken to number three store. They nearly filled it!

Meanwhile I worked out a storage system to rotate the stock in such a way that the products coincided with the order forms and stock sheets. I worked on the night shift on Sunday and Monday and showed the men the new system. I told them how I wanted the cold rooms to be left when they finished. I took Tuesday off, and when I went in on Wednesday morning, the yard was clean and the cold rooms were tidy. I took two stock counts that day – one of all the saleable goods and one of everything that was damaged. This work took me the whole of Wednesday, and so it was Thursday morning before I saw the manager. When I showed him the stock counts he nearly had a fit! The damaged stock represented nearly a quarter of the total. I took him down to the cold rooms to let him see for himself. We would need the space in store number three, I told him, when the summer season started in two to three weeks from then. I suggested that he write off the damaged stock and that we should dump it. He said the quantity was too large to write it all off at once. I said he could write it off in any way he pleased, but I was going to dump it, and that none of it would appear in any future stock counts that I took.

We did dump a large quantity of ice-cream products, but I kept the frozen foods, and the storemen and I took home parcels every Friday. The parcels, and the fact that the job was now done in an orderly manner and was therefore easier, contributed to an improvement in morale. The storemen got a rise a few weeks later, and the depot ran like clockwork.

Questions on Part III

1 Do you agree with the foreman's assessment of why the depot 'ran like clockwork'?
2 Could anything else have contributed to the successful conclusion of this case?

COMPUTERIZED HEALTH RECORDS

Introductory remarks

This is a UK example of how the *support culture* of professional health visitors (HVs) was threatened by *role culture* values. The HVs are nurses who have midwifery experience and who are trained in preventive medicine. By law the HVs have to find out where all new-born babies are living, and they keep an eye on children in their own homes until the children are 5 years old. The HVs are employed by District Health Authorities which, at the time, were located within Area Health Authorities (subsequently abolished). The case is written from the perspective of the immediate superior of the HVs, the Nursing Officer for Health Visitors (NOHV).

The case

Blankshire Area Health Authority wished to introduce its Child Health Scheme, involving computerized recording, for the following reasons:

1 to provide statistics for studies of epidemiology (outbreaks of diseases). Knowledge from such studies can help to reduce childhood illness and deaths. No identification of individuals is required for such work.
2 to provide a detailed profile on any child's health and development to assist any child health advisor (such as HV, family doctor and school doctor).
3 to assist HVs by providing rapid access to all relevant medical data whenever they make a follow-up visit.
4 to increase the take-up of immunization facilities by providing systematic records.

The scheme was planned over a period of two years, and was to begin with the birth notification and immunization records. Two months after this part was supposed to come into operation both HVs and family doctors, or general practitioners (GPs), were refusing to co-operate, or threatening non-co-operation.

In October 1977 the Local Medical Committee (which represented GPs) expressed concern about information being recorded on a computer without the written consent of the parent. It was explained that, whether records were kept in manual or

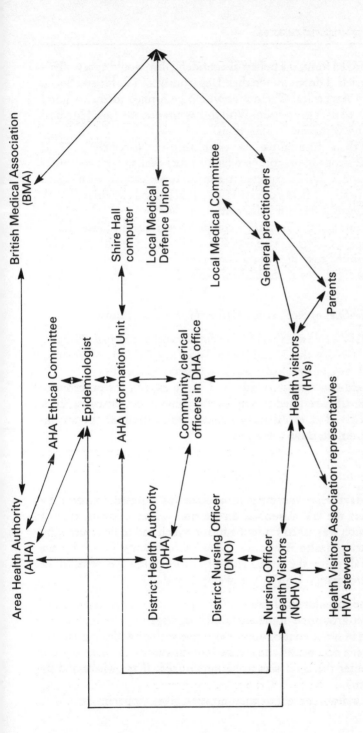

Figure C1 Parties with an interest in the Child Health Scheme, November 1977

Notes: Arrows represent information flows. The Local Medical Defence Union provides insurance for doctors. The Health Visitors' Association is the Union which represents these employees

computerized form, the policy of confidentiality would apply. (This policy was laid down by the then Department of Health and Social Security.) An Ethical Committee would be formed to ensure good standards of data protection. With this assurance, the Local Medical Committee withdrew its objections.

The Ethical Committee was established in November 1977. It produced a code of practice to which all staff dealing with computer information would be expected to adhere. It was explicit with regard to security among fieldwork staff (such as HVs) and clerical staff both in the District Health Authority and within area information departments and the Blankshire computer centre at the Shire Hall.

The epidemiologist, who was also a community health specialist, was appointed custodian of the computer.

Figure C1 shows all the parties involved.

Responsibilities of the Nursing Officer for Health Visitors

The NOHV's role was that of co-ordinator with the District Nursing Officer (DNO), the Area Health Authority (AHA) Information Unit and the epidemiologist. She also supervised the HVs.

She held consultations with the HVs to explain the procedures. These meetings resulted in helpful and constructive criticism. Each HV was given an explanatory booklet which outlined the way in which questions should be asked.

Responsibilities of the health visitors

Eleven days after the birth of a child (as notified to them by midwives), the HV was to call on the family. The following type of information was asked for in the forms which had to be returned to the District Health Authority (DHA) Community Office by the fifteenth day after the birth. (This office would pass the forms to the AHA Information Unit by the twenty-first day.)

1 Name and address of child
2 Ethnic group and dominant family language
3 Type of home conditions (for example with or without garden)
4 Father's occupation and mother's occupation
5 Whether the child was to be immunized. If so, where and by whom?
6 Was written consent to immunization given by parents?

The crisis: opposition from the health visitors

In January 1978 an individual HV approached the NOHV complaining that she was being used as nothing more than a clerk. Why should she have to state the exact size of the garden, if there was one? If the father was an engineer, why should she have to find out what type of engineer? Her intimate relationship with the parents was threatened. The anticipated benefits were not worth this price.

The following day the Health Visitors' Association (HVA) steward requested a special meeting with management about the computer. She raised the following points with the NOHV.

1 HV skills were not being correctly utilized. The questions they were expected to ask made them feel like 'busybodies'.
2 The prime function of the first HV visit to a family was to establish relationships. Form-filling interfered with this.
3 It was generally found impossible to persuade parents to decide on immunization and sign a form for this at the first visit.
4 Some HVs said that their relationships with GPs had worsened. They were no longer given access to patients' records in the surgeries as GPs were convinced they wanted the information for the computer.
5 Forms were being returned to the HVs for clarification (for example, did 'engineer' mean 'civil engineer' or 'mechanic' or what?).

The NOHV said she understood the problems and would arrange for a meeting with the DNO and the epidemiologist. She went to see the DNO to ask for this and was told 'as a nursing manager' to inform her staff that because they were employees of the AHA they had to co-operate.

The crisis: opposition from the British Medical Association (BMA)

Meanwhile, the DNO had been informed that the BMA had advised its members not to co-operate and to have no dealings with the Blankshire Child Health Care Scheme.

Next day the AHA had an emergency meeting with a BMA representative and with the Medical Defence Union. The main problem was identified as 'written parental consent for immunization'. The AHA's Ethical Committee was told that the presentation of a child for immunization was, in itself, sufficient consent, and so it was unnecessary to obtain written consent also. The BMA then withdrew their objections.

The meeting of health visitors with the epidemiologist

The DNO called the meeting which had been requested by the steward for HVs. The epidemiologist praised the work that the HVs had done so far and explained why each question on the form needed a specific answer. Race relations officers had been consulted about the ethnic questions. Answers to these would be useful in identifying needs for forward planning for education and housing. He said that eventually there would be a reduction in the amount of manual recording required of HVs, but full co-operation must precede any modification to the scheme. It was imperative that the initial stages should be effective in every way.

The HVs left the meeting still unconvinced about the use of the computer and the value of the data they were asked to obtain.

Question

What course of action might have resolved the 1978 impasse? (You may find Chapter 2, Figure 2.1 and Tables 2.4 and 2.5 relevant.)

Epilogue

Four years later all stages were operating and some benefits for children and staff were beginning to accrue.

CULTURE SORT

Introductory remarks

This exercise can be done on your own, or can form the basis for group discussion. The purpose is for you to experiment with the idea of organizational cultures. To help you, thirty-two items have been taken from a questionnaire called *The Business Organization Climate Index* (BOCI). Payne (1991) explains that the term 'climate' has been used by psychologists, whereas 'culture' is used by anthropologists. You will find the thirty-two items after the instructions.

The task

Imagine that you want to find out about the culture where you work, and so you have asked a friend to send you a questionnaire. You have received this, but your friend forgot to send you the key. All you know is that eight items are about a power culture, eight about a role culture, eight about an achievement culture and eight about a support culture. Your task is to group the items as best you can. (Refer to Chapter 1, Sections 4.1–4.4.)

Your friend enclosed a covering letter from the researcher which tells you that the full BOCI contains 160 items which are given to people with the following introduction:

> This questionnaire contains statements which describe the environment in which people work. The statements refer to daily activities, to rules and policies, to typical interests and ways of doing things. Please decide which statements are characteristic of the organization for which you work and which are not. Your answers should tell us what you personally believe the organization is actually like, and NOT what you might personally prefer. Be sure you answer true (T) or false (F) for all questions.

The researcher also tells you that T scores 1 and F scores 0. (For the purpose of the exercise some items have been altered to meet this condition.)

Instructions

You need four lists, headed 'Power', 'Role', 'Achievement', 'Support', each of eight items which you think might describe the culture. If you do not wish to copy out the statements, just the numbers which identify them will suffice. You may find that you want to place more than eight items under one heading, and fewer under another, or that you can think of new items that come closer to your idea of what each culture signifies, but please keep to the instructions. If you are with others, it is best for each person to work out his or her own provisional solution before comparing notes to see what agreement there is amongst those present.

When you have compiled your four separate lists, you are ready, if you wish, to answer the questions (T or F) with regard to an organization you know. Give 1 point for all the Ts so that you build a score from 0 to 8 for each culture.

Does the organization have one culture which scores much higher than the others, or are the scores about equal? Is the answer what you expect?

You can repeat the process for how you would wish the organization to be. Is there a small or large difference between what exists and what you would like?

Thirty-two Business Organization Climate Index statements

1 People will work hard here even if they realize that someone else may get the credit.
2 Everyone here has a strong sense of being a member of a team.
3 Work is well organized and progresses systematically from week to week.
4 Most activities here are planned carefully.
5 Criticism of policies and practices is not encouraged.
6 People here never try to manipulate the activities of others for their own advantage.
7 People here can get so absorbed in their work they often lose all sense of time or personal comfort.
8 When people disagree with a decision they dare not work to get it changed.
9 People get sufficient notice of policy decisions to be able to plan their own work accordingly.
10 People here are likely to accept senior managerial ineptitude without complaint or protest.
11 There are few opportunities in this place for informal conversations with senior personnel.
12 People set high standards of achievement for themselves here.
13 There is so much to do here that people are always busy.
14 If something happens to go wrong, people do not go around seeking whom to blame.
15 The standards set here are challenging to achieve.
16 Work is checked to see if it is done properly and on time.
17 The flow of information downwards is smooth and efficient.
18 Personal rivalries are uncommon here.
19 No one here has a chip on their shoulder.
20 People avoid clashes with senior personnel at all costs.
21 People here follow the maxim, 'Business before pleasure'.
22 Many people hesitate to give support to a project that senior management is opposed to.
23 There seldom seem to be any quarrels here.
24 There is no wasted time here: everything is planned right to the minute.

25 People who get pushed around here are not expected to object.
26 There is a specific place for everything and everyone here.
27 The quality of your work is rated or evaluated frequently.
28 There is a recognized group of leaders who receive special privileges.
29 People here feel they must really work hard because of the important nature of their work.
30 People here are always ready to support each other.
31 People are always very serious and purposeful about their work.
32 Most people seem to enjoy one another's company.

The BOCI scales are not exact equivalents of other measures of the four cultures. The exercise will have served its purpose if it has set you thinking about the answers you might give.

Researchers normally give statistics to enable others to judge whether their work is reliable and valid. If you want to know more about the BOCI, you can find references in the bibliography, Pheysey and Payne (1977) and Payne and Pugh (1976).

A suggested solution is given on page 307.

THE DILEMMA OF AN ADMINISTRATIVE OFFICER

Introductory remarks

This case is about the administration of a college of arts, science and technology in Nigeria. It can be used with Chapters 2 or 3, or 8, since it deals with misunderstanding across levels of a hierarchy. There is interpersonal conflict which is related to an unsuccessful attempt to control the activity of members of a trade union. The relevant part of the college's organization chart is shown in Figure C2.

The case

On 15 April, Mallam S. Mohammed tendered his resignation via his head of department, the Registrar. This was the culmination of a progressive deterioration in the relationship between Mr Mohammed and Mr Malcon, which could be traced to an earlier incident.

More than half the non-academic staff were illiterate and may not have been aware of the fact that (under the Nigerian Labour Act 19) no worker is obliged to join any trade union. The Non-Academic Staff Union (NASU) was able to have 2 per cent of monthly salary

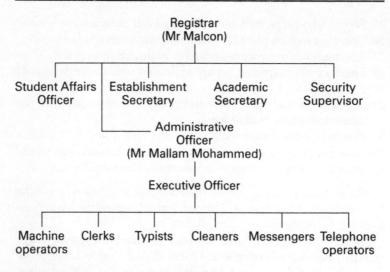

Figure C2 College organization chart

deducted from everyone as union dues because *two of its officers happened to work in the Finance Office*. It should have obtained the consent of workers to this, but it had no established recruiting procedures and no formal provision for opting out. The union simply assumed that it had 100 per cent membership of non-academic staff in the college.

(The Nigerian Federal Government subsidized all trade unions in the country, partly as a means of exercising some control over them and partly to prevent unions from exploiting workers. Unions were encouraged to invest their funds or even to run businesses, so that they could survive without conscripting members to obtain income.)

One day, the Registrar asked the Administrative Officer to issue a staff circular reminding employees of their rights under the Nigerian Labour Act 19. The circular should be signed by Mr Mohammed, acting for the Registrar. When the circular had gone out, Mr Malcon called Mr Mohammed on the intercom and told him to get a list of workers who wanted the 2 per cent deductions from their salaries to be discontinued because they were not interested in being members of a union. The NASU regarded this action as an act of sabotage and promptly called an emergency meeting which threatened a total boycott of work.

At this point, the management invited the NASU to a meeting. The union was represented by its branch Chairman, Secretary and Treasurer. Management was represented by the Registrar and the Establishment Secretary. The union complained that the Administrative Officer was going round and openly suggesting that people should resign from union membership. The Registrar stated that, on the contrary, management was not anti-union. It had acted because there had been a written complaint by some workers that money was automatically being deducted from their wages as a subscription fee when they had not consented to join the union in the first place. However, the union was not satisfied with the management case. Pressure was put on the Registrar who conceded that the Administrative Officer had acted improperly in going round in person to get the list of those persons who did not want to belong to the NASU. The NASU accepted this apology and the status quo ante was restored.

Next morning, the Registrar called another meeting involving himself, the Establishment Secretary and the Administrative Officer. He wanted it put on record that the Administrative Officer had misinterpreted the instructions he had received. He had not been told to go round the college to get a list of those workers who were not interested in trade unionism. This angered Mr Mohammed, who refused to take the blame and even accused Mr Malcon of eating his own words. The Establishment Secretary attempted to mediate, but to no avail. Henceforth the Administrative Officer insisted that all verbal instructions from his superior should be put in writing. The Registrar, for his part, decided to bypass the Administrative Officer and to deal directly with the Executive Officer who was in charge of the main registry office. In this way Mr Mohammed found himself deprived of his functions and he therefore decided to tender his resignation.

Questions

1 How could the provisions of the Nigerian Labour Act 19 have been enforced at this college, given the information provided in this case? Make any further assumptions you wish that are consistent with what is said about the union and the management, and with the organization chart.

2 If you were the Registrar and had received complaints from workers that dues for the NASU were being deducted from their

wages by the finance office without their prior consent, what would you have done?

3 Comment on Mr Malcon's leadership style, and on the fact that he was able successfully to bypass Mr Mohammed once the latter had refused to accept oral instructions.

4 If you had been Mr Mohammed, how would you have dealt with the attempt by your superior to have it put on record that you had misinterpreted the instructions you received? What would have been your short-term and longer-term aims?

5 If you had been the Establishment Secretary, what arguments would you have used in your attempts to mediate between Mr Malcon and Mr Mohammed?

THE DUTY ROSTER

Introductory remarks

This case could equally well be used with Chapter 6 or Chapter 7 since it concerns an attempt by a nursing officer to involve colleagues in changing a familiar system. It is written in the first person. The site is in the UK.

The case

Fairfield Hospital was a large psychiatric hospital which served the needs of what were then two Area Health Authorities. A hundred and fifty beds at the hospital provided the only special facilities for the care of those who were aggressive or suicidal and needed a medium secure environment, or who were mentally abnormal offenders referred from courts, prisons and state security hospitals. There were a further 200 patients in the Rehabilitation Department which had medium- to long-term accommodation. The remaining 500 beds were occupied by the long-stay elderly and psychogeriatric cases. The patients at the hospital therefore were dependent in varying degrees. They required different attitudes and different techniques of care.

The wards were divided into two main blocks, but spread over a wide area. The nineteen wards in one block catered for disturbed patients who required short or long periods in hospital. The remaining eighteen wards were mainly for the elderly and psychogeriatric cases.

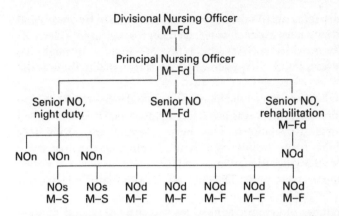

Figure C3 The management structure of the hospital: M–F, Monday to Friday; M–S, Monday to Sunday; d, days from 08.00 to 17.00; s, shift from 07.00 to 14.00 or from 14.00 to 21.00; n, nights from 21.00 to 07.00; NO, Nursing Officer

In these thirty-seven wards, at any one time during the day, there were approximately a hundred nurses on duty, of whom about twenty-five were learners allocated to the hospital. The remaining seventy-five were not all qualified. Some were unqualified nursing assistants who had served a minimal induction period. These had little further training apart from what was given by the staff on the wards where they worked. The ratio of qualified to unqualified staff was 1:3.

Figure C3 shows an organization chart for the hospital's management, that is, persons ranked above the ward staff. It can be seen that all but two of the officers worked from 08.00 to 17.00 hours. The officers who worked from 07.00 to 14.00 hours and 14.00 to 21.00 hours shared responsibilities and duties. They worked alternating shifts which included weekends and bank holidays. The system had been operating for eight years, even though, in practice, it sometimes involved nursing officers working from 08.00 to 21.00 hours if emergencies arose.

I joined the staff in August 1978 as a Nursing Officer. I formed the opinion that insufficient professional assistance was given to ward staff. Because of the high proportion of unqualified staff it was vital that those who were qualified should be properly deployed, especially if some trained nurses were absent through sickness.

The day-to-day needs varied. Extra staff might be wanted in 'secure' areas to provide nurse escorts to other hospitals or to other internal departments. As the hospital was surrounded by woods and fields and two large areas of water, searches for confused, elderly or potentially suicidal patients could become urgent. It might be necessary for a search party to co-ordinate its efforts with those of the police.

Throughout weekends and bank holidays and before 08.00 or after 17.00 hours when there was less cover by doctors, there was only a single nurse duty officer. This person would then have sole responsibility for co-ordinating activities throughout all thirty-seven wards, for arranging redeployment and for providing advice, support, counselling and discipline. The duty officer also had administrative duties.

The number of geriatric admissions was increasing, and so were admissions of seriously disturbed patients. I thought something ought to be done to provide more balanced cover, with at least a second duty officer available in case of emergencies. I sounded out my colleagues informally on a one-to-one basis, on the following proposal:

> There should be two duty officers from 07.00 to 14.00, and a further two from 14.00 to 21.00, but the shifts would be for five consecutive days, not seven, and days off would be taken in rotation. One of each pair would be for the block of eighteen wards, and the other for the block of nineteen wards, but only one person would be designated as duty officer to co-ordinate the system.

I discovered that, if there were increased payments for weekend duties and some flexibility in the way in which off-duty periods were fixed, then five of the seven nursing officers were in favour of the proposed change.

The next stage was to call a meeting at which all seven were present. The two opponents were persuaded, under protest, to co-operate on a trial basis.

The Senior Nursing Officer and Principal Nursing Officer were then approached. They asked that all advantages and disadvantages of the present and proposed systems should be considered, together with any possible alternative systems. Eventually they agreed to give the proposal their support at a forthcoming meeting of Divisional Nursing Officers.

At that meeting I introduced the proposal as a group effort, produced after consultation with more senior officers. The meeting was invited to discuss the proposal, and the Divisional Nursing Officer in particular was asked for comments before the next meeting a fortnight later. The Divisional Nursing Officers at their next meeting decided to go ahead for a trial period, to keep progress reports and to indicate what, if any, problems arose and how they were handled.

The new system made it possible for staff to have two weekends a month off duty. Pay was more attractive because of the increased rates for unsociable hours (after 20.00 hours and holidays and weekends). It did provide the more balanced cover that it set out to do. It provided a model for the medical staff who subsequently followed suit and provided each block with a duty medical officer on a similar basis.

Questions

1 Comment on the way in which the writer went about getting the approval of colleagues for his ideas.
2 How would you describe the writer's own decision-making, and the collective decision-making by the senior nursing management?

INNOVATION AT A TECHNICAL COLLEGE

Introduction

This case concerns a British College of Further Education in the year 1980. At that time there was pressure upon Colleges of Further Education to change their business studies courses. This pressure was exerted by the Business Education Council (BEC). The purpose of BEC, as set out by the Secretary of State, was to plan, administer and keep under review the establishment of a unified national system of non-degree courses for people whose occupations fall within the broad area of business administration. To fulfil this role BEC would devise or approve suitable courses and assess standards of performance. The changes recommended by BEC found favour with employers because the courses were more task oriented than previously. Local Authorities and Regional Advisory Councils welcomed the changes demanded by BEC, but offered the colleges very little help to accommodate them.

The BEC philosophy was for an inter-modular and interdisciplinary approach which required both organizational change towards a matrix structure and staff development. BEC called upon the college in this case to submit other courses for validation, and so it was important to learn from the first attempt. Chapters 3 and 9 are especially relevant.

The case

In September 1980, a member of staff at the college, who will be known as the course co-ordinator (CC), received a verbal instruction from his head of department to produce a submission within thirteen weeks for BEC approval. No other instruction was given and no formal authority was delegated.

The role of CC is poorly defined in terms of authority and responsibility. The role can work within a single department, but it is difficult where several departments are involved. In this case, the material needed for the submission involved three heads of departments, two staff of the same status as the CC, and nine of lower status than the CC, but six of the latter worked in other departments. The organization of the college is shown in Figure C4. There were two faculties, each of three departments. It could be regarded as a classic or full bureaucracy (see Chapter 3, Section 1.4).

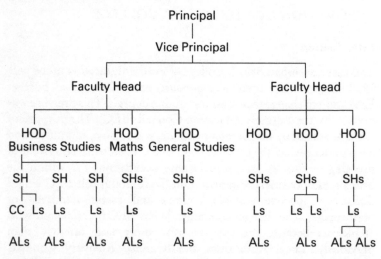

Figure C4 Structure of the college in September 1980: HOD, Head of Department; SH, Section Head (or Senior Lecturer); CC, the Course Co-ordinator with rank of lecturer; L, Lecturer; AL, Assistant Lecturer (a junior member of staff on lower pay scale)

The CC had the task of asking his colleagues to produce various Core modules and other material for the submission. He asked for the material to be ready by week 10.

The request came at a very bad time, as staff in September had just started a new session and were immediately involved in enrolment. The economic climate was such that enrolment was not easy and staff had to work to recruit students. Lectures started immediately after the enrolment period which meant that staff were under stress getting to know their new students. New courses were also begun, which put an extra load on some of the staff involved in providing the CC with material. The additional workload caused some staff to get into a downward spiral. By week 10 very few staff had produced their modules, and those who had done so had sent material that had to be rejected as below the standard that BEC would expect. The situation was not stable. Staff were threatening to apply sanctions such as working to rule and going absent.

One lecturer in particular got behind with his work and things got steadily worse for him. The CC could foresee a problem but was powerless to take any corrective action. By the eleventh week the lecturer had failed to produce the required material. His head of department took him off the work.

The CC reported the situation to his own head of department. The result was that the CC and two other members of staff were given yet more to do.

Throughout the thirteen weeks the CC found it difficult to communicate across departments or to get disciplinary groups to comply with the BEC philosophy which involved an integration of subjects. He himself had attended two seminars on this philosophy and had also carried out research into new teaching methods which encourage students' problem-solving skills.

Staff were informed of BEC recommendations through notices and through briefings at staff meetings, but the CC had no opportunities for presenting to staff the findings of his research. He felt that the goals of lecturers were to teach to traditional methods. The college management, however, was in favour of the new BEC methods and philosophy. But college management gave a head of department the responsibility for producing the first programme. This head, in turn, asked the CC for a submission (which ran to 250 pages). It involved the CC in working an extra thirteen hours every week.

Questions

1 This case has been written from the point of view of the course co-ordinator. How might it appear from the viewpoint of the head of the Department of Business Studies and of the faculty heads?

2 What changes in terms of reorganization and staff development might be needed if further courses were to be prepared for submission to BEC?

3 What means might you recommend to the principal for implementing the suggestions you made in answer to question 2 above?

AN INTEGRATED LOCAL OFFICE

Introductory remarks

Because the British government department formerly called the Department of Health and Social Security (DHSS) is publicly visible, and questions can be asked in Parliament of the Minister in charge, 'working to the rulebook' is regarded as just as essential as it was in the aircraft cockpit (Chapter 7, Section 8.1, 'Disadvantages'). This programmed nature of the work raises questions of job design (compare with the case on job enrichment, next) and of control and public accountability, which are linked with Chapter 2. The questions posed at the end of the case however, are based on the text of Chapter 7.

In 1980, a confidential report by a young civil servant in the DHSS was leaked to the journal *New Society* and formed the basis of an article[1] which was sharply critical of an office which 'was operating a significantly different social security scheme from the model constructed by the policy makers'. The present case was written by someone who worked in such an office some years before the article appeared. It seems things had not changed much in the interim.

The case

Mary was an executive officer (EO) in an office which had about 5,000 cases on its books at any one time. She worked in the Contribution Section (the National Insurance side). Much of the work was dealing with huge direct payment schedules that came from employers, but, in times of less pressure, the section members took

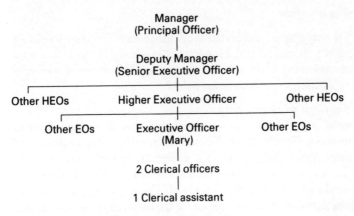

Figure C5 Local office organization chart

their share of the normal run of contribution work, processing queries and dealing with the public on the counter. The organization chart is reproduced in Figure C5.

Usually, each subsection (under an EO) had a laid-down set of duties and tended to have little contact with other sections, even with officers of the same grade in the same office. Social distance was maintained between grades, and drinking tea with a person of lower grade in one's own section was regarded as slightly suspect behaviour. Impersonality ruled, and people seemed to huddle together more for protection than anything else. EOs never approached the deputy manager or manager directly but only through their own Higher Executive Officers (HEO)s. Among peers, few had friends.

The staff were rarely, if ever, consulted about their work, their careers or themselves. People were transferred out of the section and sometimes even out of the office. They had all been through the same impartial selection procedures, they had been accepted and so they were regarded as interchangeable spare parts and treated accordingly. The Principal Officer (PO) was a former pupil of Cheltenham Ladies' College, a queenly lady referred to as 'Auntie'. She had little in common with her staff who were an intellectual proletariat. Any contact she had with clients came as a culture shock. The office was held together by strict discipline, and it is difficult to describe the atmosphere of misery and fear that prevailed.

Norms in the office

All EOs entering an integrated local office have thirteen weeks of training at a special school. However, it is mainly at work that they acquire something of the ethos of the service. The six major precepts in Mary's office were those listed below.

1 Do enough work to get by
   Incentive schemes were negated by the crassness of their operation. Credits were allocated to specific tasks such as new claims, reassessments, callers at reception, interviews and so on. This led to short cuts, forms of rationing and defensive procedures to adjust the workload. There was small chance of being thanked by anyone higher in the hierarchy, and EOs might wait six years for the chance of a promotions board.

2 Never 'drop someone else in it'
   Even if an officer made a mistake that could, perhaps, affect a member of the public adversely, it had to be covered up.

3 Keep out of trouble yourself
   The staff lived in a constant state of fear of breaking either office rules, or 'the Code'. The counter staff in particular were under constant pressure from immediate superiors, and from the public. Superior officers never offered any protection for their juniors.

4 Conform to the rules
   For protection, and from the need to quote rules for benefits in a uniform way, strict compliance with the Code was essential. Inflexibility developed bordering on ritualism.

5 Do not appear different from anyone else
   Most of the clerical and lower executive staff were women and were profoundly unadventurous in lifestyle. (Mary was regarded as some sort of political extremist because she was once seen reading *The Guardian*.)

6 Do not appear unduly sympathetic to claimants
   All new officers were instructed never to tell people what they were entitled to – even on the National Insurance side, where people only get the benefits for which they have paid contributions. Staff were not obliged to identify themselves over the telephone and could, for example, promise to look into a case and then do nothing about it (sometimes because they could not find the file).

The role that was reinforced by the structures, procedures and culture of the office was that of society's policemen, there to pick out the scroungers, investigate false claims and protect the public purse.

There was an alternative role, however – that of social worker, coping with humanity, with people under stress, and offering flexibility and fairness. The outside sociopolitical environment might emphasize this, and so did DHSS policy, but local staff did not. Claimants could, and did, abuse officers, and sometimes even assault them. The managers did not consider they had the right to make any structural or procedural alterations unless authorized to do so by a circular from DHSS headquarters.

Working there was an experience that defeated Mary totally, and she voted with her feet, as did some 20 per cent of EOs every year. Turnover among lower grade staff was even higher. Those who stayed coped by retreatism or ritualism, and by retailing the occasional party piece. There was even an appropriate paragraph in the Code to cope with the railway shunter who came in to ask for 'his' insurance card to be changed to 'her' card! The more outrageous cases of fraud or abuse were gossiped about and contributed to the general attitude.

Note

1 Cf. Moore, P. (1980) 'Counter-culture in a social security office', *New Society*, 10 July, pp. 68–69.

Questions

1 The clerical officers in this case were dealing with the public under conditions where the staff were supposed to keep one eye on welfare needs and the other on the possibility of fraud. Clients tended, however, to be seen as 'the enemy' rather than as the needy. Do you consider this attitude is linked with the cohesiveness of the staff? Give your reasons.

2 Staff were regarded as interchangeable spare parts by their superiors. What affect, if any, would this have on cohesiveness?

3 Can you reconcile the answers you have given to the two questions above, and indicate how the performance and morale of employees is affected by the section's failure to obtain the advantages of either low cohesiveness or high cohesiveness.

4 What would be needed to get staff of this office to adopt norms of patient, pleasant, and painstaking and efficient attention to clients' welfare?

JOB ENRICHMENT IN THE BRITISH NATIONAL HEALTH SERVICE

Introductory remarks

This case is in two parts, and to get the most out of it, you should *not* look at Part II until you have answered the question for Part I.

The accounting section described happened to be in the British National Health Service, but it might just as easily have been in a commercial company and/or in another country. The writer was involved in work which he found boring. Later he returned to the same section as its head.

The case – Part I

Accountancy, like so many other professions, has become extremely specialized. Sub-specialisms have emerged such as financial accountancy, management accountancy, audits and cost-effectiveness work.

In my early days I had worked in a management accountancy section which was part of the Treasurer's Department in a Health Authority. It was responsible, basically, for the preparation of budgets and for the subsequent control of expenditure against these. When I joined the section, it consisted of a section leader (the Chief Management Accountant) and five other people. The duties were roughly as shown in Figure C6.

As number two in the chart, I calculated the cost of wages and salaries. My calculations were passed on to the section leader who did not tell me what became of these figures. My job was repetitive, I had no autonomy and no feedback. I wondered if my dissatisfaction stemmed from being over-trained for the job, but I discovered that my four colleagues felt the same.

A few years later I came back to this section as Chief Management

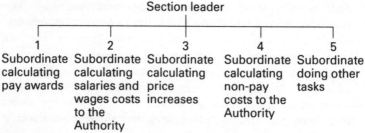

Figure C6 Structure prior to job enrichment

Accountant, the section leader. I found that former colleagues had left through boredom, and that there was a high rate of absenteeism and turnover among the present staff. The Treasurer, my superior, gave me the authority to make any changes I saw fit.

A question on Part I

What would you do to improve matters in this section?

DO NOT CONTINUE READING UNTIL YOU HAVE THOUGHT ABOUT THE QUESTION SET.

The case – Part II

I talked to the staff about my ideas. I explained that my proposals for change did not stem from any dissatisfaction with their existing performance. Instead of dividing the work into separate operations, as shown in Figure C6, I proposed that each member of staff should perform all the operations shown, but in respect of certain budget-holders only. Thus, one subordinate might do all the necessary calculations for nursing budgets and another for medical budgets, for example.

Obviously, this approach relied on considerable delegation and trust, because I was allowing staff to deal personally with client budget-holders, and I was allowing them to produce statements which were ultimately my responsibility. I instituted a system of monthly meetings with my staff which enabled me to receive feedback on any operational problems. There were also some instances where I got involved in the day-to-day work of a member of my staff, but, in the main, they managed their own groups of budget-holders for themselves. Though at first there was some reluctance to adopt this system, staff subsequently reported that they enjoyed the increased responsibility and autonomy, and the system has continued even though I have now been promoted out of the section.

Questions on Part II

1 Comment on what the case writer did.
2 Why do you think that 'at first there was some reluctance to adopt the new system'?

3 How would you calculate the benefits and costs of the change?
4 Do you think there is scope for enriching jobs where you work?

FOUNDING OF THE KABZEYAN CLUB

Introductory remarks

This is an account of how an educated Nigerian woman founded an organization of women to undertake community development work. The case could equally well be used in conjunction with Chapter 7, on groups, or Chapter 8 which deals with leadership.

The case

Politicians in Nigeria make use of community development activities to secure good positions for themselves, both locally in the community and also in government. For example, politicians will start projects from which they perceive that the community will benefit. Later, they use the existence of the project as a lever for extracting further funds to give more help to the area.

Most of these initiatives have been taken by local governments, or by individual men. Ms Kayit was pondering this fact one morning as she ate her breakfast. She said to herself, 'If anybody should come up to me and ask, 'Hannatu, what have you done to help your area?', would I have to reply, 'I have done nothing, because I am a woman'?' She then thought about what women could do, and was surprised at the possibilities.

Here are three examples.

1 Help the orphanage
   A home for orphans was started a long time ago by missionaries who had since left the country. It was currently being run by elderly Christian men.
2 Provide a nursery
   There was a shortage of dedicated teachers at the post-primary and post-secondary schools in the area. The reason was that there were no facilities for the children of such teachers.
3 Build student hostels
   There was an acute shortage of living accommodation for students. If hostels were built, places in them could be let.

These could be lucrative projects which politicians could use to bring more government development to the area.

Beginning the task

She set about contacting women whom she knew very well, in the hope of forming a group. It would be non-religious, non-political and non-tribal. However, any group of people which comes together for any length of time for some common purpose will need some form of organization. In this case, each of the women contacted was assigned an area to educate about community activities that could be undertaken by women. The feedback from this was encouraging, apart from minor incidents arising from petty jealousies among women and men alike. Some potential leaders with power and influence were identified, a meeting was held, and a caretaker committee was set up to run the affairs of the group.

Circulars were sent out calling a public meeting of women. Daughters and wives of the Kaje tribe, and also non-Kaje women, turned up in large numbers. The aims and objectives of the founding group were circulated, and read out, and the name Kabzeyan Club (= 'there is no one to help you') was chosen. National officers were elected, and Ms Kayit was voted into the office of President.

The group runs into difficulties

The new President had mixed feelings when, after the meeting, people started to put forward more ideas for action and encouragement. They set a leadership role for her in terms of functions within the Club, and also in terms of helping the Club to grow. Members assumed that, as leader, she was uniquely responsible for the quality of the Club's performance, for motivating members to participate, for setting the right group goals and for getting jobs done.

Ms Kayit saw that it would be necessary to distinguish between carrying out roles which were relevant to the group's growth and accomplishment, and using the group as a means to personal ends. This distinction became important when one of the ladies who had been nominated as a patron made use of the Club's name to form a religious group. This lady spread strong but ill-founded and hurtful rumours which diverted the attention of most members. First, she interpreted 'club' to mean a place where people drink alcohol, dance and enjoy themselves, and this was quite contrary to what it was. Second, she criticized the non-religious and non-tribal ethos. Finally, she stated that the president, because of her single status, was unfit for office. The patron was a recognition-seeker who would have preferred to have been president rather than patron, as she thought the latter position was of lower status. She therefore drew attention to herself by boasting, by reporting on her personal achievements and by acting in unusual ways. Because of her behaviour two members of the executive committee were forced by their husbands to resign, and some ordinary members withdrew from the club.

Ms Kayit was in a dilemma. At the time she was elected President she was not married, and here was the same group of women, three-quarters of whom had voted for her, who were now complaining. She was stirred into action to defend her role. She picked a few members at random and presented her case as soberly as she could in order to win their confidence. She also pleaded with them that there should be no open clash with the other faction, as this would put the club's objectives in jeopardy. They gave her their promise, and dispersed.

Traditional techniques

In the villages, religious leaders are recognized and accepted, just as people recognize and accept the village headmen. The Club could not make use of the religious leaders, but the traditional chiefs could be approached. The executive met the chiefs, and explained to them the Club's aims and objectives, and sent circulars, through them, to the women within their jurisdiction.

Kabzeyan Club had high hopes that this meeting was going to be successful, but the recognition seeker misinterpreted the reasons for the circulars sent through the chiefs. The local women were wrongly informed that the Club was interested only in the attendance of chiefs and their wives at the meeting. There are no telephones or postal agents in the area, but there is a very powerful means of communication – word of mouth! Every day of the week, Monday to Sunday, is a market day in one or two of the villages, and news gets round this way. About fourteen chiefs were approached but, despite the promises that women made to them, very few turned up. Ms Kayit was discouraged, and retired from the scene for a while.

A constitution

One day Ms Kayit thought of something for the Club to do. The secretary had been asked to resign by her husband, the assistant secretary was not very well educated and the vice-president was about 400 miles away. All the same, she plucked up courage and called a meeting to draft a constitution for the Club which, she was convinced, could be revived. Members came, but they ended up by having a cooking lesson! Most had no idea of how to draft a constitution, and the president was left with no alternative but to do the job herself. At the next meeting members became interested since there was an outline to work from. However, the constitution was a compounding of four different models and so was over complex. It provided for full-time members, part-time members and honorary members. Rumours now circulated that Ms Kayit was organizing a group to take over powers from the men, and so the Club allowed men to come to general meetings to see for themselves that the rumours were false.

Growing membership

Just as Ms Kayit was thinking for the umpteenth time of giving up the role of leader, one of the chiefs contributed to the Club's progress. He had given a piece of land to his women, and had encouraged them in various ways. They sent an invitation to Ms Kayit asking her to visit them to open a branch of the Kabzeyan Club. She went, with most of the executive committee members. Their hosts had also invited neighbouring chiefs. This gave the committee a good forum to outline what they, 'the élite' hoped to learn from the 'illiterates'. One could see from the nods of heads, and from people's faces, how astonished they were that the Club thought it could learn so much from them. The élite is not always the teacher. The reverse can be true, because some traditional knowledge is of value and cannot be taught in the classroom. The President also seized the opportunity to say what a pity it was that the very people who needed the Club were the ones who were throwing the chance away. Within a month of this meeting, four more invitations came for branches to be opened in different villages. The chief concerned was made an honorary member.

By now the members had become active once more. An executive meeting was called and the members prepared the agenda for the next annual general meeting. It was well attended and lasted for over three days, and even then the women wanted more. There were lectures on such subjects as hygiene, community development and home counselling. There was drama and traditional songs were sung, and other entertainments were arranged. There was an encouraging number of donations, showing a change of heart of the menfolk.

Now the Club had funds, it approached the orphanage to offer help, only to find that the rival faction had already been there and offered its services. Not only had it done this, but it had also taken over the Kabzeyan Club's constitution. This provoked another crisis, but Ms Kayit managed to dissuade her friends from taking the other group to court. There was, after all, plenty of work to be done, and so why not welcome rivals so long as they were also undertaking laudable projects. So Kabzeyan Club members turned their attention to obtaining a Home Economics Centre, and became active in most of the five political parties at local level. Just four years after the first annual general meeting the Governor of the State was guest of honour on 'Kabzeyan day'.

Questions

1 What individual differences (Chapter 7, Section 2) contributed to the group's early problems and to their resolution?
2 What stages of the Tuckman cycle (Chapter 7, Section 3) can you identify in this account?
3 Do you think a women's group starting up in your country would face similar problems to this one, in Nigeria? Why, or why not?

MERIVALE ELECTRIC PLC

Introductory remarks

This case centres on the relationship between a superior and a subordinate in a UK company, as illustrated in an appraisal interview. It therefore lends itself readily to role-playing. The reader can imagine alternative ways in which the interview could be handled. The background indicates that the behaviour of participants is affected by their different perspectives and ages. It is recommended for use with Chapter 8, on leadership.

The case

The company designed and manufactured a complete range of electrical equipment for motor vehicles. A recent statement by the Chairman in the company's annual report read as follows:

Setbacks last year arose from a series of unofficial strikes in the motor industry, some of which were prolonged. The early months in the home market were therefore worse than expected. There were, however, notable export achievements. Shipments to Common Market countries were doubled. It promises well for the time when British products can be offered on equal terms to those of European competitors.

Our own factories have been striving to re-establish a satisfactory level of profitability in the face of higher material, wages, and other costs. We have been compelled to adjust our selling price to meet increasing costs but we have undertaken, in response to an appeal from the Confederation of British Industry, to keep our prices stable over the next twelve months.

It is, however, only by an improved product design and new methods of manufacture that significant increases in product costs and prices can be avoided. We have made considerable investment over the years in both men and money to enable us to make progress in these directions.

One of the investments to which the chairman referred was the purchase one year ago of a factory on a development estate some twenty miles from the parent company. This factory, known as East Works, was to be devoted to the manufacture of ignition equipment, using the very latest production techniques.

Because it was on a 'green fields site' the locally recruited labour force would have to be trained, and there was a division of opinion as to how this should be done.

An ex-army officer, Major Bampton, had just been taken on as factory manager, and he believed that training should be given on the job by the supervisors, whom he regarded as similar to sergeants in the army. The difficulty was that the supervisors themselves were newcomers without previous experience of factory work. They had been mining overseers. Major Bampton had full authority from his boss, the Manufacturing Director, to develop production as he saw fit. Fifty workers would be hired in the first three months, and ten times that number would eventually be needed when all ignition

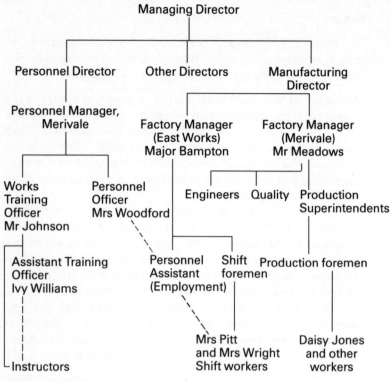

Figure C7 Partial organization chart: ——, line authority; - - - - , functional authority

production would be carried out at East Works. Major Bampton was given a personnel assistant for recruiting (Figure C7).

The Central Personnel Department at Merivale was against the 'sitting next to Nellie' method of training on the job. It was a firm believer in the use of full-time trained instructors. Plenty of capable women were available but, because shift-work was to operate at East Works, applicants were generally not willing to travel to the Works Training Department at Merivale where non-shift hours were in operation. There would therefore be a breach in the long-established practice at Merivale for all new women employees engaged by the Personnel Department to be given a period of 'vestibule'(or pre-factory) training.

The Works Training Department provided a facility where people could learn the skills required before being exposed to full production conditions. In some years as many as 1, 500 trainees passed through. The methods of training were based on research into the nature of manual skills and how they can best be acquired. The scheme was introduced by consultants; training times had been cut from six months (to reach experienced worker speed) to four weeks or less, and quality of output had been improved considerably. The method involved some simulation devices in the early days, but trainees were soon working on real components under the supervision of skilled instructors. The slowness of beginners is usually attributable to their making inaccurate moves (fumbles) which have to be corrected. When precision is understood and practised from the start, and when trainees have immediate feedback, learning can be rapid. Recognition of faults, their causes and consequences, was another important part of the training. The period in the Department was one in which decisions could be taken, based on the test performance and daily work record during training, about job matching for the factory. The department therefore served as an internal placement agency, and as a provider of induction for new employees. Periods at the work bench were interspersed with lectures for trainees about the company, its products, its payment system, its services to employees and so on. This period of familiarization (which included factory visits) led to a reduction in the levels of labour turnover that had been experienced prior to the work of the consultants.

George Johnson (aged 45) was employed as Training Officer in charge of Merivale Electric's Works Training Department, and Ivy Williams (aged 26) was his assistant. Details of the requirements for her position are given in Appendix 1 to the case. George had managed to get Major Bampton to agree that Ivy Williams should study the jobs at East Works with a view to discovering what assistance could be given with the training there. George hoped that vestibule training could ultimately be introduced at East Works, but he realized that, in the early stages, this would not be economic, and he therefore offered the possibility of an instructor on each shift to assist the foreman. Major Bampton had accepted on the understanding that the women so employed would be immediately responsible to his foremen and, through them, to himself. Any future links with the Training Department would be at his discretion.

George's decision to send Ivy to East Works served another purpose. She was now 26 years old, had been with the company four years and had made rapid progress from a graduate traineeship to her present responsibilities. When he himself had been seconded overseas for six months, Ivy had run the department (of eight full-time staff) single-handed, and she had been somewhat restive since his return. Though he had heard generally good reports of her, there had been one unfortunate incident during his absence when she had given way to pressure from a factory manager (who had threatened to 'take people off the streets') and had allowed semi-trained employees to be placed in the main factory. The personnel officer, Mrs Woodford, was naturally annoyed at this breach of policy, and had reported it to Mr Johnson on his return, though he had not raised the matter with Ivy. This would be an opportunity for him to assess for himself how she handled members of the production departments. He therefore arranged that, for four weeks, she should travel daily to East Works in a company van, with certain other headquarters personnel.

Ivy obtained all the method study breakdowns for assembly workstations and decided that there would be no real instructional problems with these. She persuaded the maintenance foreman and the inspector to construct a panel display of assembly faults and a working model of an ignition coil showing what happened if windings short-circuited. The major problem was with the new machines for winding the coils. These were quite unlike any employed at Merivale's main works, and yet Major Bampton was using a main works operator to 'train' the first recruits. Fortunately the operator, Daisy Jones, was herself not prepared to travel indefinitely to East Works.

Ivy reported to George Johnson, just before the expiry of her four weeks, that she had studied the American manufacturer's technical manuals for the winding machines and had discovered that solenoid switches would stop the machines for any of twenty different reasons. Operators had to 'mind' three machines at once, and to join wires which broke, straighten insulating paper which creased, re-tension wires or paper which had become slack and so on. Some stoppages might occur as frequently as twenty times per shift, while others might be as infrequent as once in six months. This meant that some failures would have to be deliberately created if trainees were to experience them during a four-week training period. She was working on an instructor's manual which would suggest a suitable sequence of activity, some of which could take place on a dummy machine. She had also made suggestions to the design engineers about the repositioning of certain switches. She had noticed that down-time was longer than necessary because an operator had to walk round to the back of the machine to restart it. Safety could still be taken care of if the switch was placed at the front. She did, however, need another four weeks if she was to complete a training programme which was fully operational in documentation.

Ivy then made a big mistake. She asked for an interview over lunch with Major Bampton to tell him about her work. The more she enthused about it the more he felt he was being 'lectured'. He telephoned Mrs Woodford to ask her to 'have that woman removed at once'.

On the same Friday, Mrs Woodford telephoned George Johnson, who felt that he had no option other than to recall Ivy to base. He had already commenced an instructor-training programme for two locally hired women, Mrs Wright and Mrs Pitt, who would now have to manage without any assistance on the spot from Ivy. He did not want the humiliation of the Works Training Department to be any more public than need be, and so he decided that he would ring Ivy and make the annual appraisal the pretext for getting her to call at headquarters the following Monday. He would then tell her what had happened.

Mr Johnson completed the 'Merit Rating Form' which is shown as Appendix 2 to the case. The dialogue which took place is given as Appendix 3. Below are some questions for you to consider.

Questions

1 Examine the contents of Appendix 1 and Appendix 2. How would you give a lead to this employee? (Remember that we defined leadership as 'guiding or directing others'.)

2 Behind the relationships of the two principals in this case there is a problem concerning the relationship between line managers and staff (see Chapter 3, Section 1.4). Can you suggest how Ivy might have acted if she was to be successful in getting East Works to accept 'leadership' with respect to training matters from the Works Training Department?

Appendix 1: Job evaluation

Assistant Training Officer (ATO)

(a) *Education and/or experience called for*
Graduate education. It is also part of the conditions of this job that a professional qualification in personnel management be obtained by part-time study in the employee's own time. The ATO has to be capable of administering psychological tests and interviewing employees. Knowledge of all production processes is required.

(b) *Initiative required*
Willingness to take decisions on matters affecting the suitability of trainees for placement in particular jobs, Ability to devise improved methods of work and improved instructional techniques.

(c) *Responsibility to be undertaken*
Responsible for the allocation of new employees to appropriate training, for their safety and for following their progress. Responsible for maintaining high standards of trainee performance on completion of training. Responsible for seeing that the production quotas of the Training Department are met both as to quantity and quality, and that due delivery times are observed.

(d) *Authority over assets, spending and people*
May requisition supplies of consumables, and order minor works to be done to a value of £250 per month.

(e) *Amount of co-operation with others involved*
1 With instructors over the allocation of trainees to their sections.
2 With factory personnel in the investigation of training requirements, the follow-up of ex-trainees and in progressing production work subcontracted to the Training Department.
3 With specialist departments to ensure that tooling, methods, quality etc. are as they should be.
4 With own superior in matters of policy, and in connection with capital expenditure.

(f) *Working conditions/problems/constraints*
The work is varied and interesting, but involves some mental stress as it is not always possible to satisfy competing factory requirements for skill, output, quality and speed. Recruitment is outside the control of the department. The job involves a considerable amount of walking, since most requests from the factory demand on-the-spot investigation.

Appendix 2: Merit rating form

Managers are asked to rate their subordinates according to a five-point scale represented by letters as follows:

A   could not be bettered
B   more than satisfactory
C   adequate
D   barely adequate, needs attention
E   totally inadequate
Name of employee being rated: Miss Ivy Williams
Position: Assistant Training Officer
Rater: Mr George Johnson
Position: Works Training Officer

Merit heading	Rating	Comments
Knowledge of work	B	Grasps technical matters easily
Output of work	A	Tends to overdo it sometimes
Accuracy and reliability	B	Good
Common sense and initiative	C	?
Co-operation and helpfulness	D	Wants to get on well with people but is bad at human relations
Responsibility to Merivale	C	Has been known to criticize company before visitors
Attendance	A	No absence
Supervisory abilities	C	Takes responsibility but is not diplomatic with seniors

Appendix 3: The appraisal interview

Mr Johnson had the documents in Appendix 1 and Appendix 2 on his desk when Ivy Williams came to see him.

Mr J.   Sit down, Ivy. Two things have made me ask you to see me this morning. The first is that East Works do not want you to continue your visits there, and so I cannot grant you the extension of time you asked for last week. The second is that, in view of the way you have mishandled this matter, I am unable to recommend any increase in salary for you for the coming year.

Ivy   (taken aback) Can you tell me why they don't want me there?

Mr J.   It seems that you are extremely poor at human relations.

Ivy   But I got on very well with everyone except Mr Bampton, and nobody likes him. The foremen complain that he is always out to impress the

	directors, and he does this by pinching the foremen's ideas and presenting them as his own.
Mr J.	Ivy, *Major* Bampton's relations with his foremen are no concern of yours, but his relations with the Works Training Department are, and you seem to have spoiled these. What did you do?
Ivy	He got very angry when I was trying to explain company training policy to him last Thursday, but I do not see what he has got against our department. The foremen have welcomed the idea of their own instructors, for they know they can't keep Daisy Jones much longer. Even now, she doesn't work shifts.
Mr J.	Well, I don't know what you said to Major Bampton, but he told Mrs Woodford that you gave him indigestion!
Ivy	He's nearly always got some visitor in his office, and so I thought the easiest way to put him in the picture about what we are doing for him was to do it informally over lunch. There's no canteen yet, and so everyone else takes sandwiches. But he always goes alone to the Kings Arms, and so I asked if I might join him, and he agreed.
Mr J.	You seem to have made a hash of it! And this is not the first time. Mrs Woodford told me you failed to back her up six months ago, while I was away. She tried to save you from having to rush untrained people into the switchgear shop, and when she put Mr Meadows on the phone to you, you gave in to him.
Ivy	From my end of the line it seemed that *she* had capitulated, and that I was being asked to do what they both wanted. Besides, I did tell Mr Meadows that there would be a lot of dissatisfaction all round, and that his labour costs would rise. He just bellowed down the phone that he had to have the women at once. Why didn't Mrs Woodford give a hint that she was on our side? All she said was, 'I've got Mr Meadows here, and he's asking for operators for the switchgear shop. He wants to speak to you.'
Mr J.	Well, naturally, she thought you would tell him you did not have enough trained people, and so he would have to wait.
Ivy	I hated doing it, but he was in the mood to take people straight off the street, and, as I said, Mrs Woodford's remarks made me think she was backing him.
Mr J.	You thought wrong. I'm just using it as another illustration of how bad you are at human relations. Now, what can we do about this East Works business?
Ivy	My biggest worry will be the instructors. They've been here for three weeks, haven't they? How have they got on?
Mr J.	I've had very good reports of them from everyone here, but, of course, they've not had a chance to learn anything about the type of winding done at East Works, though they have practised joining wires on our machines.
Ivy	As I told you, last week, I was just about ready to sit down and write a training manual for them. I could still do this. The method study and production engineers are now working part time at East Works and part time back at headquarters. They'll help me with any queries I may have. This part of the job can still be finished. The Central Quality

Control department approves my ideas for getting the feel for various tensions, and they'll make a bench trainer for this for me. Also, I suggested to the foremen that the new instructors would find it easier to start with assembly work. They've met most of the compressed air tools here. It's only the jigs and fixtures that are different, and they're simple.

Mr J.   What can we do about the winding?

Ivy   East Works are not going to take on any more winders for the next three weeks. I can have the manual ready by then, and go through it with the instructors here.

Mr J.   I suppose I shall have to pay Major Bampton a visit.

Ivy   Do you think he'll let me go back when the manual's ready?

Mr J.   No. I'll send him a copy. If and when he approves it, I'll ask if the instructors can spend one more day over here.

Ivy   I think everyone else will approve it, because they've all contributed something. And I don't really think it was fair to say, as you did, that I'm bad at human relations, when I get on well with everyone except the factory manager.

Mr J.   You may well manage all right with colleagues and juniors, but you seem to have difficulty with more senior people. I find no fault with the work you do. If anything, you drive yourself too much. But people in supervisory positions like yours must be acceptable to superiors, and you do not seem to behave appropriately towards them. You'd better work in your own office from now on, though you can spend time, if you need to, visiting other headquarters departments. Mrs Woodford is going to East Works again today, and she'll tell the people there that you've been recalled for urgent work here. She will bring back with her any belongings you may have left there, if you'll let me have details. I'll visit Major Bampton and the instructors myself later this week. I just hope we can salvage something, that's all. You'd better go now and write out what you want Mrs Woodford to fetch.

Ivy   Very well, Mr Johnson, but, I must say, this has come as a big shock to me, just when everything seemed to be going so well. I was really looking forward to seeing the job through.

Mr Johnson wrote along the bottom of Ivy's merit rating form the date and the following words above his signature:

Saw Miss Williams today and told her that her ability to relate to superiors is so bad that I have been forced to withdraw her from East Works. No merit rise is recommended this year. A sensitivity training programme might enable her to see herself as others see her.

Ivy wondered if she could go on working for Mr Johnson much longer as he never seemed to give her credit for all her hard work, or to see her side of things. One single slip seemed to have blackened her future irretrievably. Well, she would prove that she had a sound training scheme for East Works winders, if it was the last thing she did for Merivale Electric. Then she would look around for a job elsewhere.

POLITICS AND BUSINESS IN MALAYSIA

Introductory remarks

This case is about a real organization, but the events reported took place some time ago and the three main characters have not been given their true names.

There are lessons to be drawn in connection with Chapter 8 on the power and authority of leaders and the reasons for non-compliance by a member of staff in a hierarchical organization. The case can also be used in connection with Chapter 2 on regulative and appreciative control.

The location is Southeast Asia where the primarily rice-growing economy has resulted in small tightly packed social and political cells. The southeast Asian places great value on being taken as a complete person in whatever situation he is in. It is said that he is not as much of an individual as the American because of the network of responsibilities that limit his freedom of choice; neither is he as much of a group-oriented man as the Japanese, perhaps because he has so many groups to which he is emotionally committed that he ends up being free to make his own choice from among his albeit limited range of alternatives.

The case

Sabah State, in East Malaysia, on the Island of Borneo, did not join the Federation of Malaysia until 1963. It was then given a powerful Chief Minister's Department which controlled all the key areas of state. Some of this department's powers were later curbed, but at a time after the events described below.

One of the key areas was investment in industry and commerce. The state-owned agency Permodalan Bumiputra Sabah (PBS) was responsible for handling such investment. It acted as a holding company for twelve subsidiaries whose businesses included stock-broking, property management, insurance, plantations, hotel projects, holiday resorts, motor car dealership, housing development, banking, newspaper and glue manufacture.

Mr K was employed as Information Officer for PBS, and was responsible for handling all publication matters for the holding company and for all its subsidiaries. His job included production of a newsletter, campaigns, promotions and providing information for potential investors, business associates, and the general public.

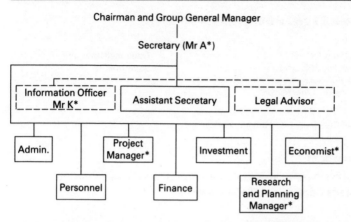

Figure C8 Organization chart of the top management of Permodalan Bumiputra Sabah. * Member of the editorial committee.

The monthly PBS newsletter was considered most attractive, and Mr K was praised by the management for every issue. As the sole organ for PBS its importance was such that, from the early days, the management decided to appoint an editorial committee. Its members were the PBS Secretary, the Research and Planning Manager, the Project Manager, the Economist and the Information Officer (see Figure C8).

Mr K's work involved a lot of travelling to get news and spread information, since there are eleven states in West Malaysia and two in East Malaysia. His base, at Kota Kinabalu, was about a thousand miles from Kuala Lumpur, where the PBS Chairman and and Group General Manager had his office.

One year, in May, Mr K was granted leave to visit his parents who lived some two hundred miles from Kota Kinabalu. It so happened that a general election was pending, and the day after he reached his parents' home his uncle, Mr S, came to see him there to ask for his help. Mr S was going to stand as an opposition candidate for the constituency. Would Mr K do some writing in the local party newsletter and do some canvassing in the village from which Mr K's mother had come and where she still had relatives? It was traditional that younger members of a family should help their elders if asked, and so Mr K did as he was asked during the last five days of his leave. He attended one political meeting, but not as a speaker. There were, however, several issues which he raised in the party newsletter. The government had failed to complete one major road construction to

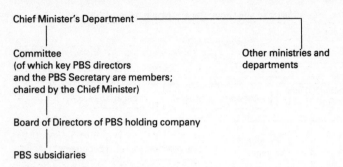

Figure C9 Permodalan Bumiputra Sabah in relation to the Chief Minister's Department, Sabah State

the village, and also it had not kept its previous election promise to provide irrigation.

After two weeks Mr K arrived back at the office. Campaigning was then at its peak. It was a rather one-sided affair as all communication networks in the state were controlled by the ruling party. Newspapers, radio and television all supported it. The opposition parties had no chance to project their views. On his first day back, Mr K heard that a few civil servants had been sacked for their involvement in the campaign against the ruling party.

The link between PBS and the Chief Minister's Department is shown in Figure C9. The Department had overall responsibility for PBS, though the legislation which created state agencies gave PBS some independence in day-to-day management.

The main functions of the committee shown in Figure C9 were to determine the allocation of resources directly obtained from state funds, to make feasibility studies and to guide policy.

Soon after Mr K returned from leave, his superior, Mr A, the PBS Secretary (see Figures C8 and C9) sent for him. Mr A announced that he, himself, would be on leave for two months, and that the Assistant Secretary would take his place during that time. Then he said that the Board of Directors wanted Mr K to go for a week's tour of all the PBS subsidiaries, because only a small proportion of the many projects that were going on were receiving publicity. Air tickets and hotel reservations had already been arranged.

Mr K was somewhat bewildered by this turn of events, but he went on the scheduled visits. On his return he was too busy to think of anything else. The next day, however, he received, from the Acting Secretary, a memorandum from the Chief Minister's Department which required him to write a report on what he did when he went to stay with his parents.

At first he treated it as something of a joke, and did nothing. Three days later, however, a second memo came urging him to respond immediately to the first. He wanted to clarify his position with his superiors, but Mr A was on leave and the Chairman and General Manager was in Australia at the time.

By now polling day was very close. Mr K was under constant observation from the Acting Secretary who was a strong supporter of the ruling party. He was allowed no visitors, and he had to log in a book all his movements outside. Even so, he was not alarmed. He still did nothing about the memo, as he thought that any response would be used against him, and he was hoping that the opposition party would win.

In the event, the opposition lost by about twenty-five seats but, in Mr K's constituency, the opposition won with the biggest majority ever. Some three weeks later most of the government departments were reorganized and reshuffled. Many civil servants who, in the view of the Chief Minister's Department, had been campaigning against it were sacked, and it was difficult to challenge the sackings in the courts.

Another month went by and Mr K, as was his habit, put out the new issue of the PBS newsletter. Copies were distributed free, nation-wide, as part of the campaign to promote PBS businesses. They went to all government departments, to public sectors, private sectors and overseas.

On this occasion, from the many items featured, the national media spotlighted one item:

> PBS to spend sixty-five million Malaysian dollars
> on a condominium and hotel at Likas Bay
> to attract more tourists to Sabah

(Likas Bay is considered to be the most expensive site in the state.)

On the morning this happened, Mr A, who was supposed to be still on leave, came into his office and summoned Mr K. Mr A said that the Chairman and he himself were very angry that the figure of 65 million dollars had been made public. Mr A had been sacked by the Chairman because, as Secretary, he was held responsible. He wanted to know, however, who had actually released the information to the media. Mr K told him that it could have been taken from the PBS newsletter which had just gone out. It was, in fact, quoted as the source.

Mr A could not say much as he was a member of the Committee (see Figure C9), and every committee member was given the draft copy of each issue prior to printing, with sufficient time for checking. Whenever there was a special project Mr K personally took the copy to the member concerned.

That evening the Chairman called a management meeting. It transpired that the Board had not yet reached its final decision on the figure of 65 million dollars.

Perhaps the Chief Minister's Department feared controversy with the Federal Government. How would the latter view spending on this luxurious project when Sabah, at that stage, needed more funds to improve rural villages? Perhaps Mr K was even suspected of inflating the issue to provoke such a reaction?

Whatever the reason, it was two days later that he received another memo from the Chief Minister's Department, giving him a deadline by which to reply to the question raised in the first memo, and threatening that 'appropriate action' would be taken immediately if he failed to respond.

Since Mr A was unavailable, having been sacked, Mr K contacted the Group General Manager in Kuala Lumpur. He was a prominent business man and a political figure at national level. Sabah state needed his expertise badly, and so it could not treat him with impunity. He had already been informed of the memoranda by the Chief Minister's Department. He observed that PBS was not entitled to discharge an officer because of outside activities in which he engaged. The only exception to this would be if the activities contravened the PBS contract of employment, or other regulations. There were insufficient grounds in Mr K's case since, if any disloyalty did exist, it would not be against PBS as such, but against the ruling party. If Mr K were wrongfully dismissed he could take his case to court, and it would be likely to embroil PBS in political controversy.

Mr K decided on a policy of 'wait and see'. The Likas Bay project was no longer considered secret. Work there had already started, and the public had a right to know about it. If the Chief Minister's Department was concerned about the access which Mr K, as the Information Officer, had to special information, the fault lay with their initial appointment of him. It was not an easy matter for them to find a replacement for him from this state.

No direct action occurred. Mr K was moved into a less private office, however, and deprived of his access to a direct dial telephone. His salary increment and confirmation of employment service were witheld. The strain of working under such conditions led him to resign.

Questions

In answering the questions below you may make any assumptions you wish provided they are consistent with the information given in the case.

1 Comment on the positions occupied by the Chairman and General Manager and by the Secretary, in terms of their power, and give examples of ways in which, in your opinion, they each acted, or failed to act, as leaders. You should bear in mind that relations with the media are often critical for organizations with a high political profile.
2 Discuss Mr K's non-compliance with the memoranda he received from the Chief Minister's Department. From the information we have, was his behaviour likely to have helped or hindered his retention of the post of Information Officer?

QUICK CONTAINERS: AN EXERCISE IN DECISION-MAKING

Introductory remarks

There are a number of ways in which this exercise can be undertaken, depending on the number of persons available to take part. If the reader is working as a lone individual, then the instructions marked A and B should be followed. If there are two or more persons, then instructions marked A and C should be used.

The exercise – Part A

Your company, Quick Containers, makes containers to customer specification. (Assume the company is registered as privately owned, and you may put any letters, such as 'Ltd' appropriate to your country's usage after the name.) Your plant at present consists of a single cutter. (A pair of scissors will simulate this machine.) The cutter is currently being used to complete an outstanding order. It will be available in time to commence your next order. You have obtained a contract from a government-owned freight carrier to produce as many containers as your present, or augmented (see below), production facilities will allow in a specified period (see below).

Spend up to fifteen minutes' actual time making your plans in the light of the information provided below. Once your plans are complete, assume that manufacture commences, that two minutes of actual time is equivalent to one month of company time and that the production period takes twelve minutes of actual time, or six simulated months, for Quick Containers. Your contract expires at the end of six months, and no more 'production' will be permitted.

Figure C10 represents a blueprint and customer instructions for making the containers from sheets of raw material. (Old newspapers can be used, but you will need to make a template first by tracing the diagram onto a sheet of plain paper.)

If you follow the instructions above the drawing in Figure C10, you should have a square lidless box. There should be

- a flat bottom to the box, both inside and outside;
- a cross (x) on the inside at the bottom (formed by the four points);
- corners which are perpendicular to the base, with neat right-angled joins;
- no slits in the exterior of the base or sides of the box except at the corners.

The above four points are the quality standards to aim for if you want repeat business.

You have enough material in stock to make one container. Any additional material must be purchased. There are discounts on bulk purchase as shown in Table C1. The currency (X) is not stated, but it is that of your own country – pound sterling, dollar, kwatcha, rouble, yuan or whatever. Payment to you from the customer is 2,000 X per container completed for delivery during the period allowed.

You may purchase all the material you think you will need in advance so as to qualify for the discount on larger purchases, in which case you may risk not recovering the full price of the material from the number of containers you complete for sale. You may be more cautious, and order a smaller quantity. In this case, you may reorder material after three months (six actual minutes) of production. Your second order will not be added to the first for purposes of discount. You may hire extra cutters at a cost of 2,000 X per cutter per quarter.

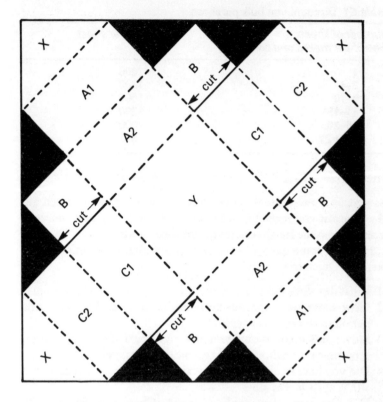

Figure C10 Customer specification for container, and instructions for
making up.
Cut along solid lines. The shaded parts are waste. Fold X triangles
backward. Fold A1 rectangles onto A2 rectangles. Crease along the
broken line between the A2 rectangles and the Y square by folding
A2s towards Y, to form two sides with the broken lines between the
A1s and the A2s along the top edge. Crease along the broken lines
between the C1 rectangles and the Y square by folding C1s towards
Y. Fold small B squares towards A2s to make corners. Bring C1s up
on the outside of the Bs. Fold C2 rectangles down over the inside of
the Bs, so that the broken lines between the C2s and the C1s now
form the top edges of the other two sides of the box. Press all the X
triangles flat against the inside of the Y square

Table C1 Discounts on bulk purchase

Number of sheets (one sheet makes one container)	cost in X per sheet
1	2000
2–4	1800
5–10	1500
11–15	1200
16–20	1000
over 21	800

The exercise – Part B (for one-person businesses)

As you are a one-person business you will want to pay yourself out of any profit you make between your costs of production and your receipts from the freight carrier for finished goods.

Here are some questions to ask yourself after completion of the exercise 'Quick containers'.

1 What decisions did you make?
2 How close were the business results of your manufacturing period to those you expected?
3 How many marks would you now give yourself out of 10 for (a) economic rationality and (b) technical rationality?
4 Did you have to use the implicit favourite or intuitive methods at all? Why? Or why not?
5 Did Gresham's law apply to you? (Chapter 6, Section 2.2, 'Routine programmes').

The exercise – Part C (for two or more persons)

The same 'rules' can apply if there are two people but now there is an additional problem, namely how to share the work, and the profit or loss. For larger numbers there can be a production workshop, and it will be necessary to agree on payments to the workers. What job design principles were used? (See Chapter 4, Sections 2.1–2.4.) Extra questions can be asked about the decision-making of the organization. Was it collaborative, competitive or hierarchical, for instance?

In a class, an additional complication has been introduced. When numbers rise above six, a government inspector can be introduced to insist on quality standards and to determine which containers shall be paid for and which shall be reworked or scrapped. This introduces an element of conflict into the situation.

Records can be designed to routinize the accounting and a supplier's representative can be created with whom fresh bargaining over terms can be introduced.

A further modification has been used by the author for inter-group decision-making. This has assumed that another company buys up Quick Containers. The brief for the purchasers, Amalgamated Manufacturing, is as follows.

The firm you have just purchased, Quick Containers, is about to embark on a new manufacturing contract which demands redesigning the jobs of its production workers. It has been agreed that you may send a team from your own management to act as consultants to the manager(s) of your new subsidiary. Your task, for the first fifteen minutes (actual time) is to study Part A above and then to determine how you can most effectively act as consultants. Will you divide amongst yourselves different aspects – purchasing policy, job design, overall strategy, production efficiency, profitability etc. – or will you operate as a committee? Once production has commenced, you may visit Quick Containers at any time, but you have agreed that, for the first quarter (six minutes actual time) you will simply observe, and not intervene in any way. After this period you may ask to meet those in charge on an individual or group basis, question members of the workforce, or do anything else that you consider necessary in the best interests of Amalgamated Manufacturing.

These added complications can lead to role playing, and to discussion about inter-group and intra-group relations, leadership, conflict and other topics.

The author has found, for example, that some consultants consider themselves to be supernumeraries; other consultants exercise a highly authoritarian leadership style which, in one case, provoked an 'industrial dispute' with total cessation of production. As a minimum, the same questions can be discussed as in Part B above.

REBELLIOUS ROBOTS

Introductory remarks

This case is one of job enrichment in reverse – that is, job impoverishment. It was originally written for students at the School of Business and Industrial Studies at the University of Zambia. It concerns the growth of a firm from an owner–manager with six workers to a much larger concern; and a change in product from craft-work on special jobs to customer specification, to mass production of standardized output on semi-automatic machines. It involves a change from a 'cell' structure to a centralized one. (See Chapter 3).

Time and motion study, or work study, is used in many organizations to determine what the simplest ways of going about tasks are and how long each movement, and each positioning of components, should take. A stop-watch may be used, and the time study engineer has to estimate whether the worker he is watching is using average effort or is working faster or slower than average. He adds allowances for rest pauses, and issues a 'standard time' for producing a given quantity of output. Pieces produced in excess of the stated quantity for a standard hour are paid extra by the piece. (There are variants on this 'payments by results' scheme, but the underlying principle is the same. Chapter 4 refers to the origins of 'piecework' in the writings of F.W. Taylor.)

A special feature of this case study is that the names of the four managers are indicative of their membership of the same tribe. Most countries, by custom, have reserved certain kinds of jobs for particular groups in the population, whether it be on the basis of tribe, caste, sex, age, social class or skin colour. Chapter 4 was concerned with the design of jobs, rather than with who should do the jobs. Chapter 5 had a suggestion that simple jobs might suit people with low growth needs, and complex jobs might suit people with high growth needs. If the 'best' jobs are reserved for a favoured few, however, and the majority of workers are 'alienated', the issue of job design is placed in a broader context. The craft workers who have become 'rebellious robots' in this case study have been able to do something about their dissatisfaction. What can, and should, Sipula do, and why?

The case

Daniel Sipula is the owner of the Sipula Engineering Company Ltd (SIPENCO), a light engineering company which assembles electrical and electronic components for the motor industry.

The founder, Sipula, has a Bachelor's degree in engineering and a Master's degree in production management (specializing in operations research). After three years as production manager in the

Zambian branch of a multinational engineering organization, he decided to set up on his own account, and formed the company in 1970.

At first SIPENCO consisted of one small workshop with six employees. Sipula's office was in a partitioned area at one end of the workshop.

Business grew very slowly at first, as Sipula sought to establish his company and gain the confidence of potential customers. By 1973 it had only been necessary for him to take on two more workers, bringing the total to eight.

The reputation of SIPENCO was growing, however. It was regarded as a firm which put a high value on customer service. It kept to promised delivery dates, produced goods of high quality and was always ready to help out on 'specials' (individual pieces of work designed to meet the highly specific needs of particular customers).

One reason SIPENCO was able to enhance its reputation through breaking into the specials market was that it employed fully trained, highly skilled, craftsmen. Each of them was on friendly and relatively informal terms with Sipula himself, in the intimacy of the small workshop.

When a request for a special came in, Sipula would select the worker he considered most suitable and discuss with him personally the requirements and specifications of the customer. That worker would then be responsible for the whole of the order. Sipula always saw to it that his men were well rewarded for their efforts and, as a consequence, he had excellent labour relations, and the men frequently worked overtime in order to meet deadlines.

Sipula's hard work in establishing his firm's good reputation began to pay dividends, and orders rose, in 1974 by 45 per cent and in 1975 by 39 per cent. These increases led to more workers being taken on and by 1975 the total employed was fourteen.

By this time the original workshop was inadequate. Sipula sought new premises, thinking not only of his present level of production but also of increasing orders in the future. He was lucky in finding a factory close by his old workshop and once the purchase was completed SIPENCO moved into its new premises. This was in March 1976.

The new factory had two production areas and a large store. There was sufficient space for fifty production workers, and the offices were in a separate wing of the building.

There was a limited, though lucrative, 'specials' market, and a relative shortage of highly skilled workers. Sipula realized, therefore, that SIPENCO would have to crack the market for standard products if its growth was to be maintained. In order to do this he bought some second-hand semi-automatic machines and employed five machine operators to produce standard components on a mass production basis.

To his surprise, Sipula discovered that this standard line was more profitable than his original special products – so much so that by June 1977 he had employed another ten operators and begun purchasing new equipment. By March 1977 it had become apparent that he needed help in managing the company. He therefore took on John Banda (BBA, University of Zambia) as marketing manager, Ken Mkandawire, a professional engineer, as production manager, and Alex Phiri (BAc, University of Zambia) as financial manager.

After a detailed examination of the company's finances, Alex Phiri reported at a management meeting in October 1977, that the price of specials would have to be raised by 37 per cent to make them as profitable as standard products. At the same meeting, John Banda reported that, whereas the specials market was stagnant and might even decline, the market for standard components was buoyant, and he felt that if output in this area could be increased there was even a chance of breaking into the export market.

So it was decided that, from the beginning of the financial year 1978–9, specials would be gradually phased out, and those people now engaged in their production would be redeployed in the standards section.

By March 1981 all but three of the fourteen men who had worked on special products were engaged in producing standard components, and Sipula had engaged an additional twelve machine operators, giving a total workforce of forty-one.

John Banda prepared some market forecasts, and on the basis of these it was estimated that SIPENCO would outgrow its present premises by the end of 1982. However, Ken Mkandawire made the point that the capacity of the present plant could be substantially increased if the workshops were reorganized on a production line basis, with work flowing in a more organized and efficient manner from one production process to the next.

It was also suggested, on the basis of figures prepared by Alex Phiri, that the workers who had formerly worked on special products were not as efficient at producing the standard items as their less skilled counterparts, and that it may therefore be desirable to undertake some time and motion study exercises and to introduce a standardized (piecework) payment system. These suggestions were considered by Mkandawire and in April 1982 they were adopted.

In the six months from April to September 1982, six of the former special products workers left (including five of the original six). Three of the leavers went to jobs in smaller companies which actually paid less money than they had been getting at SIPENCO, and none of the three other leavers went to a significantly better job. In addition to this, five more recent employees left for other jobs, and Sipula quickly discovered that it was not as easy to replace them as he had expected on the basis of his past recruiting experience.

In July 1982 a worker set up a trade union branch at SIPENCO, and, by the end of August that year 70 per cent of the production workers had joined. Lateness and absenteeism rose significantly, as a result of which Mkandawire imposed a clocking-on system for production workers.

In October 1982 a large rush order from an important customer came in. Ten years earlier, when such orders were received, Sipula had no difficulty in getting the men to work overtime, for which he paid them 'cash in hand'. Now he found it hard to attract anyone to work overtime, and when the subject of overtime was brought to the union's attention, they demanded 'time and a half' for all overtime worked, 'double time' after 19.00 hours and on Saturdays, and two and a half times the normal rate for Sunday work.

SIPENCO eventually got the order out only one week late, but lack of co-operation on the part of the workforce and high overtime rates, meant that on a contract of K850,000, the company only made K7,250 pre-tax profit.

Following this, Sipula wondered whether it would ever again be worth his while to accept rush orders, and he wondered also why success had brought with it so many problems.

What do you think?

RIVERS STATE

Introductory remarks

This is an example of how a power distance culture in a nation can affect individuals and organizations within that nation. It is written in the first person by a Nigerian journalist. However, the *Guardian* newspaper in the UK published, on 24 October 1982, an account of similar incidents in Kenya, Zambia, Uganda and Tanzania. Under the heading 'All the news that governments see fit to print', the article stated that government authorities in the countries mentioned

> are beating back into position journalists and newspapers who overstep the official line. Where harassment and the threat of Government acquisition have not cowed journalists and newspapers, sackings, bans, and even imprisonment have been resorted to.

Chapter 1 of the present book refers to how 'order' goals become important when civil disorder occurs. It should be remembered that Nigeria had experienced civil war from 1967 to 1970 when Biafrans had attempted to set up an independent state. Chapter 8 refers to the sources of power that leaders have in handling disturbances, and what reasons people may have for not following their leaders. Freedom of the press and civil liberties are issues in 'Rivers State'. These things are valued in some cultures and devalued in others.

Questions to consider

What economic, ideological and order goals can you identify in this case? Whose goals are they? Do 'order goals' justify the suppression of news? If so, when?

The case

The Rivers State Newspaper Corporation of Nigeria is a state-owned organization responsible for printing and publishing the Nigerian Tide group of newspapers.

I was employed as a news reporter, responsible with four other colleagues, for covering news in the Port Harcourt district.

The organization chart shows the News Editor as my immediate superior. Above him was the Editor-in-Chief.

State Newspaper Corporation
Editor-in-Chief
News Editor (and other editors)
Reporters

On 22 October 1976, my boss received a telex message from the Bendel State Newspaper Corporation, printers and publishers of the

Observer group of newspapers, complaining that one of their reporters, stationed in Port Harcourt, had been detained and tortured in a military camp on the orders of the Rivers State Military Governor. The reporter's crime was that he reported, and the *Observer* published, a critical news item about the Military Governor's birthday party, which was estimated to have cost £50,000 at a crucial period when the State was claiming to be bankrupt.

I was immediately detailed by my boss to investigate the incident and to make a newsworthy report, based on the facts, for publication in our paper. From contacts with some civil servants in the State Treasury and Cabinet Office and with some junior ranking military personnel, I concluded that the *Observer* reporter had been tortured and detained for publishing true allegations. My editor published my findings as a front-page news item, under the heading 'The Press is Laid to Rest'.

The Military Governor of Rivers State ordered the immediate detention of our Editor-in-Chief, the News Editor and all other editors, and of all other persons directly concerned with the publication of this news. My boss, under cross-examination at the military camp, mentioned that I was responsible for the facts published in the paper. I defended myself by claiming that I acted as directed by my boss, to whom I was accountable, and so he was responsible.

While we were in detention, cut off from the world outside, many sympathizers, from the Nigerian newspaper industry and elsewhere, made representations to the National Executive Military Council in Lagos (the Federal level) to order our release. These representations had no effect. It was possible for the Federal Military Government to override the actions of a State Military Governor, but nothing was done in this case. The inaction was seen as a calculated attempt to suppress press freedom, not only in Rivers State but throughout the country.

The workers of the Rivers State and Bendel State Newspaper Corporations were angry, and they embarked on strike action in sympathy with our detention. The Nigerian Union of Journalists (NUJ) (a strong pressure group) applied to the Rivers State Chief Magistrate's Court for a writ of Habeas Corpus. (The resort to the court was seen as our last chance for release, as the Nigerian judiciary was, and is, free from government interference, whether the government be civil or military.)

The court ordered our release, whereupon we were immediately dismissed from our posts. The job of a state-owned newspaper is 'to support the government'. But even if the newspaper group had not been owned by the state it would have been treated as we were for publishing such an item. Our dismissal was therefore a threat to others.

The NUJ therefore joined forces with the weaker trade unions in the industry and sued the Rivers State Government (on whose behalf the Military Governor had acted) for unlawful detention and unlawful dismissal of members of the NUJ.

The legal case rested chiefly on points of law, as there were different interpretations of the military decrees governing unlawful detention and unlawful dismissal. The issue therefore became a test case in the struggle for press freedom in Nigeria.

The state judges ordered our reinstatement in our jobs, and ordered that £40,000 should be paid by the Rivers State Government to the national press. The court strongly criticized those in power for trying to stifle press freedom.

After the incident was over, those of us directly involved were invited to the Military Governor's office for 'friendly discussions' about the roles of the military administration and the press in Rivers State. In my opinion, this was an attempt to undo the effects of the court judgement. However, I was conscious of my own position and I refused to make any comment which might lead to another incident. My Editor-in-Chief remarked that there were valid arguments for curbing the freedom of the press under special circumstances (when the country was at war, or when the disclosure of certain information is seen to threaten the security of the country). During peacetime, however, the press should be seen as a carrier of modern civilization, an educator, raising awareness.

After this, I still worked in fear, and my experience and attitude influenced my colleagues. I resigned in 1977. In 1980 a civilian regime took over from the military. Freedom of the press was formally guaranteed in a document handed by the politicians to the NUJ. This document required journalists to make 'constructive criticisms' of government policy or personnel where necessary without 'bias'. However, the document did not define 'constructive criticism' or 'bias'.

ROLE ANALYSIS EXERCISE

Introductory remarks

Chapter 2, Section 5.3, explained that a 'role set' is those persons who have dealings with someone in 'the focal role'. This is an opportunity for you to put yourself in the focal role and to consider how you relate to your 'role senders' and whether you want to change anything about your role. You may also find it useful to glance at Chapter 9, Section 4.3, 'Mentor and understudy', and 4.4, 'Role consultation'.

It may be helpful to use a large sheet of paper, and to place a circle in the centre to represent yourself. Then put other circles for people you have to see frequently and/or people who are important to you. You may confine the people to those connected with your job or include members of your family, as you wish. These we call your 'role set'.

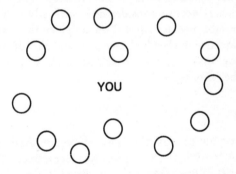

The exercise

Consider each person in turn. You may need to head a sheet of paper with a name, starting with your own, and then write down, below the name, your answers to the following questions.

Consider your own ideas about your role.
What is important to you?
What would you be willing to drop?
What would you like to take on?

Now consider the other names.
What expectations do you think that this person is likely to have of you?
Is it always clear what this member expects?

Does this member sometimes want contradictory things?

Consider the role set as a whole (including yourself.)
Do the things some members want sometimes contradict what other members want? (Include your own expectations of yourself).

Is there anything you now want to do, as a result of having answered the questions above?
If so, make out an action list.

A SOCIAL SERVICES DEPARTMENT

Introductory remarks

This is an exercise, rather than a case. A quotation from Argenti in Chapter 3 (Section 1.4) argued that there has been a great growth in the numbers of advisory staff who cannot be adequately accommodated in the pyramid form of bureaucracy. The object of this exercise is to help you to consider how such advisors can best be linked with established activities. You are given the opportunity to take the perspective of the chief executive and also of the advisor in question. You may want to read Chapters 3, 4 and 9 before attempting the exercise.

The exercise

Imagine that you occupy the post of Senior Assistant, Mental Handicap (SA MH), in the Social Services Department of an English Local Authority. Your post has the following duties:

1 to keep under review the services for the mentally handicapped in the whole territory covered by the Local Authority (LA);
2 to provide management with information and advice to aid policy formation;
3 to represent the Social Services Department (SSD) on matters affecting the mentally handicapped;
4 to collate and co-ordinate the SSD response to the needs of the mentally handicapped for 'joint care planning' (with the Health Authority, which is not part of the LA but of the National Health Service);
5 to stimulate, guide, co-ordinate and develop work with the mentally handicapped in the SSD;

Table C2 Staff of the Social Services Department (excluding the 'operating level' units)

D	Director (the top post)
DD	Deputy Director

Three Assistant Director (AD) Posts

AD A	Administration
AD C	Care
AD F	Fieldwork

Seven Principal Officer (PO) Posts

PO A	Adult Care
PO C	Child Care
PO H	Home Helps
PO PT	Personnel and Training
PO RPD	Research, Planning and Development
PO T	Technical Services Unit
PO V	Voluntary Services Liaison Unit

Eight Principal Assistant (PA) Posts

PA A	Adults
PA C	Children
PA DCA	Day Care, Adults
PA DCC	Day Care, Children
PA Ho	Housing
PA P	Planning
PA RCA	Residential Care, Adults
PA RCC	Residential Care, Children

Seven Senior Assistant (SA) Posts

SA A	Adoption and Fostering
SA B	Blind
SA I	Intermediate Treatment (for children in trouble)
SA MH	Mental Handicap YOU
SA MI	Mental Illness
SA PI	Placements
SA R	Rehabilitation

Four District Manager Posts (Care side)

DM E	East
DM N	North
DM S	South
DM W	West

Four Group Leader Posts (Fieldwork side)

GL E	East
GL N	North
GL S	South
GL W	West

6 to take initiatives and play a major role in the development of new projects;
7 to liaise with and assist voluntary organizations in the development of services (the SSD has a 'Voluntary Services Liaison' section);
8 to provide professional and other guidance to all SSD staff;
9 to assist the Placements Unit by advising on individual priorities for placement of clients, as required.

The titles used in the SSD are shown in Table C2. It may be helpful for you to know that *mental handicap*, your concern, refers to a *permanent* mental impairment (for example from accidental damage in a road traffic injury, from brain damage at birth or from genetic subnormality). *Mental illness*, on the other hand, can in many cases be cured, whether it be of an acute or a chronic nature. It may also vary in severity over time.

The District Managers shown have several care units in their districts. Care units are places to which clients come. They are staffed by a variety of workers, including residential care staff and ancillary workers. Someone is in charge of each unit.

Each Group Leader (on the fieldwork side) has a Principal Hospital Social Worker (PHSW) reporting to him and three Area Managers (AMs). Below them are the fieldworkers, social workers who go to visit the clients.

Remember, too, that, although they do not appear on the list, you work a lot with people from voluntary organizations and with others outside the SSD.

Your task for the exercise

Draw an organization chart using the information provided. Try to imagine who is likely to report to whom on the basis of type of work being done. Although the posts in your list are in status groupings, it is possible for someone to report directly to a superior two or more ranks higher if this appears to be justified in terms of the information needed, decisions to be taken or internal or external relations. Persons whose jobs begin with the same status initial will tend to have similar pay, however. You should show lines of authority and any reciprocal or co-ordinating links. You may distinguish between weak or informal links and strong formal links if you wish by using broken or solid lines. The post of SA MI, has similar responsibilities to yours, but for mental illness. The figures in Chapter 3 may suggest how to lay out your chart. You can use the initials instead of full titles.

Leave your own position (SA MH) until last. Now review each of the duties in the specification for your post and decide where you would like to be located in the structure. What advantages or difficulties do you think you may have as a result of the location you have chosen?

Now try to imagine that you are the DSS. If he had been the person who had to decide where the SA MH should fit in, do you think he would have made the same choice that you have done? Why, or why not?

THE STUDENT LOANS BOARD

Introductory remarks

This case is similar to the 'Case of mismanagement' and the 'Integrated local office' in that it was supplied by someone who was a junior official in a civil service department. It raises questions about the goals of maintaining internal order while working in conditions that are externally politically sensitive. The first person account is retained. From the description, the organization was a classic bureaucracy operating at a time when the country was under military rule. The case can be used in conjunction with Chapters 2, 3 and 9 to illustrate the delicate balance between appreciative and regulative control and the difficulties in using a hierarchy to monitor conflictual work of this kind.

The case

The Student Loans Board administers loan and bursary awards to students in institutions of higher learning at home and abroad. I was responsible for directing the processing of a multitude of application forms, and for the manning of the secretariat. I had to ensure that all officers in my registry adhered to the criteria set out by the Board for the registering, scoring and compiling of applications. I devised random checks to guard against nepotism and other irregularities. The hierarchy of the department is shown in Figure C11.

One of the criteria we had to work to was that the final published list of awards should 'reflect the federal character of the nation'. A quota system had therefore to be used to reflect tribal groupings. However, this meant that candidates from some groups, who had

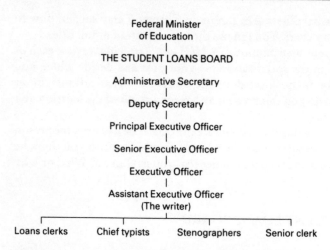

Federal Minister
of Education
|
THE STUDENT LOANS BOARD
|
Administrative Secretary
|
Deputy Secretary
|
Principal Executive Officer
|
Senior Executive Officer
|
Executive Officer
|
Assistant Executive Officer
(The writer)

Loans clerks   Chief typists   Stenographers   Senior clerk

Figure C11 **Student Loans Board organization chart**

otherwise achieved better qualifications, would have to be turned
down on tribal grounds. Often, when I had a conflict over where to
draw the line between official criteria and 'catering for minority
interests', I would simply put up a memorandum and pass the file
upstairs to my immediate superior. As soon as the file got to his tray
he would endorse the relevant paragraph for the next officer. This led
to a continuum of buck-passing. The routing of files to other
departments was also a sign of organizational ill-health.

Each time we published a loans list it triggered a spate of queries,
criticisms and adverse newspaper comment. Representatives of the
universities, student unions and other oganizations protested. I had
to take the brunt of this, although I was under no statutory obligation
to reply to enquiries. It was bad public relations not to do so,
however. The Official Secrets Act debarred me from disclosing the
Board's criteria. If applicants got to know our check list they could
falsify the information they submitted to help their case. Interested
parties could also misrepresent the policies of the Board. Within the
service one was required by the Civil Service General Orders to be an
obedient servant. There was not much room for constructive
criticism even though policies seemed to some of us to be unwise.
There was a criterion, for example, to favour courses that were
deemed to be relevant to the manpower needs of the country. Some
of the specialisms sounded bizarre. They did not coincide with
subjects that were esteemed, yet we could not query them.

One afternoon, towards closing time, I had a very unpleasant experience. A beefy, swashbuckling, middle-aged man literally crashed into the office and demanded attention. His overbearing manner did not suggest an indigent student. He wanted to know why his son, studying in Bulgaria, had missed out on the most recent award. I told him that his son's name was not on the list as it was assumed that students in Iron Curtain countries were being sponsored by the host countries. (However, the Board did not explicitly notify students that grants would not be made for this reason. They were still encouraged to apply.) The father then became very angry and demanded to see his son's file. This was tantamount to asking a physician to disclose a medical history to a plain clothes detective. It was not something a civil servant could contemplate. I refused. It turned out that he was a well-known socialite in that part of the country, and so he tried to pull rank. When I did not respond he stormed off to the Deputy Secretary.

After granting him an audience, the Deputy Secretary summoned me over the intercom, bypassing all intermediate levels. This was almost unprecedented. I was dressed down in the presence of the socialite for 'misquoting' and 'misinterpreting' official policy. The father demanded that I be subjected to some more drastic disciplinary action for departing from official guidelines. I was puzzled as to how the Deputy Secretary could allow himself to be overawed by such a man. However, he instructed me to draw up a 'supplementary list' immediately on which the man's son was to be included. I consented, provided the instruction was put in writing and sent through the normal channels. At this stage the Deputy Secretary was obviously piqued by my reply, and I withdrew before the situation became any more explosive.

Next day I received an official 'Query' which, among other things, asked me to explain why I should not be disciplined for disobeying the lawful commands of a superior officer. This high-handed action was just what my colleagues were waiting for to display an unsolicited show of solidarity. What started as a two-man episode was conflated into class warfare. My immediate superior, the Executive Officer, told me not to acknowledge the Query or defend myself as the Deputy Secretary had short-circuited the traditional channels of communication. It took the personal intervention of the Administrative Secretary to resolve the crisis. Having risen from the ranks himself, he knew how to wheedle himself out of tricky situations. The bad feeling between executive officers and administrative officers remained, however. Pressure was exerted through the Association of Executive Officers to discourage any form of social mixing with those above. (Executive Officers regard Administrators as upstarts who reap profits where they have not sown. Administrators regard Executives as 'dead wood' who have outlived their usefulness.)

Questions

1 What conflicts are evident in this case?
2 To what do you attribute them?
3 If the bureaucracy of the Student Loans Board were redesigned in the direction of more flexibility, would its performance be likely to improve, worsen or stay the same? Give your reasons.
4 What recommendations would you make?

THEATRE PROBLEMS

Introductory remarks

This case is in four parts. To get the most out of it you should *not* look at Part II until you have answered the questions for Part I. Likewise, please attempt the questions for Part II *before* you look at Part III, and those for Part III before you read Part IV.

The problems arise at a hospital. The chapter for which the case is recommended is Chapter 2, because there is an attempt to control what is happening. Chapters 5–9 inclusive are also relevant.

The case – Part I: Some problems

On taking up an appointment in an acute general hospital, the new Nursing Officer (NO) for theatres found herself with the problem of controlling four theatre suites on three separate sites. Although each had a small nucleus of permanent trained staff, these had experience only in their own particular speciality. The general level of staffing was low, and there was a high turnover. This was also true of superintendants. There had been six in eight years. Sometimes an operating list had had to be cancelled if key staff were ill.

Student and pupil nurses allocated to the theatre spent their whole time in one theatre and were never given the opportunity to see other surgery or to find out what the other theatres were like. Very few trainees came back to theatre work after they had completed their training. They were never asked and rarely volunteered. Recruits for the theatres came in response to advertisements, and were mainly theatre staff from other hospitals.

The hospital as a whole was short of trained nurses. Many trainees left as soon as they were qualified. The age range of theatre staff was 21 to 30 years. They were pleasant, but lacked confidence, and did not feel competent enough to help out elsewhere in case of emergency. One thoracic surgeon had moved his list to a different theatre in the hope that this would help, but the theatre staff there simply took time off (which was due to them in lieu of overtime for which they had received no pay).

Cross-infection rates were 14 per cent, compared with a national average of 10 per cent. The turnover of patients was also lower than desirable. Instrumentation in all theatres was limited, and recent research had shown that the techniques used, although not incorrect, could be improved upon. Prepared trays make checking easier, for example. The central sterilizing department was ready to co-operate in the event of instrumentation changes or procedural changes being made in the theatres.

The hospital had its own school of nursing whose co-operation would be needed if training programmes were to be changed or extended. The medical staff were well aware of the problems and were prepared to support changes if they led to improvements. The Divisional Nursing Officer (the NO's superior) was also ready to give support, and allowed the NO a free hand. It was expected that the hospital would expand in the not too distant future, when more theatres and wards would be built.

Some questions on Part I

1 Which people would it be advisable for her to consult at this stage?
2 What objectives might the NO formulate with their assistance?

DO NOT CONTINUE READING UNTIL AFTER YOU HAVE CONSIDERED THESE QUESTIONS.

The case – Part II: Objectives

The NO formed the following objectives:

1 to retain existing staff;
2 to recruit more staff;
3 to introduce the 'tray' system into the theatres;
4 to streamline existing instrument sets to save duplication of excess instruments, thereby saving money for expenditure on essential equipment;
5 to improve in-service nurse training and initial nurse training;
6 to improve the organization of the theatre complex by making staff available to work in any theatre;
7 through the above, to provide a better standard of service.

Question on Part II

What actions would be needed, and by whom, to achieve these objectives?

DO NOT CONTINUE READING UNTIL AFTER YOU HAVE CONSIDERED THIS QUESTION.

The case – Part III: Consultations

The NO consulted the school of nursing to ask if some senior student or pupil nurses could be allocated to the theatres. Pre-allocation induction was also arranged to reduce the anxiety felt by many trainees about theatre work.

She also consulted the permanent staff in the theatres:

1 to get their help in drawing up and implementing suitable training for students and pupils so that all types of surgery would be covered;
2 to get their co-operation in obtaining further training for themselves through rotation, reassuring them that no one would be moved against their will, but that they could have priority in gaining experience of a new speciality:
3 to issue them with a recording system to indicate knowledge acquired and experience obtained, and to reassure each nurse that she would not be asked to take charge of any theatre except by mutual agreement when she had the experience, competence and confidence to do so;

4 to issue them with duplicated lecture notes so that a common standard of teaching was obtained;

5 to get their agreement to changing to the tray system by allowing them to decide initially what the contents of the tray should be, and by allowing supplementary single-instrument packs.

The NO also consulted the surgeons to get their agreement to the trial usage of trays and on the contents of the trays. She asked them to contact her if there were any problems (as she wished to protect the permanent staff).

Question on Part III

What results might you anticipate from the actions just described?

The case – Part IV: Results

1 Staff turnover was reduced but not eliminated. Most new staff were women aged about 21 years, and some left later for family reasons.

2 The programme for student and pupil nurses was successfully implemented. All aspects of theatre work were covered (for example, no one left the theatre without having 'scrubbed' for an operation).

3 The nursing school reported that students and pupils were subsequently less anxious about being allocated to a theatre, and that they enjoyed the allocation once there.

4 No further advertising for staff was necessary as sufficient numbers of applicants for training came forward without advertising.

5 Permanent staff rotated as part of their in-service training and were only allocated to one theatre after completing the scheme. (Those already in a theatre asked for their own repertoires to be completed when they realized that juniors would otherwise have an advantage.)

6 No operations had to be cancelled for lack of staff.

7 Permanent staff took a pride in teaching their speciality (aided by the packaged notes), though some were better at teaching than others.

8 Staff were initially against the 'tray' system, as they feared that the streamlining might mean that instruments were insufficient. Day

staff left the trays for the night staff, and night staff left the trays for the day staff. The new sets contained fewer instruments than the old sets, though the excluded instruments were available as sterile units. However, to ease the introduction of the trays, the NO suggested that the old large set be sterilized and remain in the autoclave while the new set was laid out and used. Once the staff became confident that the new set was more than adequate for its purpose, much easier to check and use, and that it saved time and work, they began voluntarily to make up smaller sets from the old large ones.

9 The surgeons co-operated.
10 Basic sets for each theatre were done first, and more specialized sets followed. Progress was at the rate it took staff to become familiar with each tray and ready to undertake a fresh one. The central sterilizing department provided a sterilizing process only in the first instance but later processed the trays themselves, offering a complete washing, resetting and sterilizing service.
11 Cross-infection rates were reduced from 14 per cent to 4 per cent.
12 The turnover of patients in two mixed-surgery theatres increased by 25 per cent in the first year.

Question

To what do you attribute the successes outlined above?

TROUBLE IN THE REGISTRY

Introduction

The case which follows can be used for discussion purposes or it can be turned into a scenario for role-playing by a group of students as investigators and three or four main protagonists. The 'presenting problem' appears to be a relatively simple one, but there is inter-ethnic suspicion and a mishandled reorganization which suggests that some of the techniques used in organizational development (see Chapter 9) may be appropriate.

The case

The students of the Faculty of Medicine had assembled in groups in front of the Trenchard Hall for their MBBS examination in biochemistry. The Dean of the Faculty, Professor Tokema, wearing a worried look, walked to the noticeboard, affixed a notice to the board, and went away in the direction of the examinations office. The notice stated that the examination scheduled for that morning had been postponed indefinitely owing to a 'technical hitch', and that a new date for the examination would be announced in due course. Rather disappointed, the students dispersed in various directions, proposing to themselves what the technical hitch could be. Before long rumour had it that the questions prepared for that morning had been leaked. The next day the *Daily Times*, a national newspaper, carried this version of the story in an article headed 'Exam leakage in University Teaching Hospital'. The packet of missing papers was never found. Responsibility for their custody lay with the Examinations Division of the Registry, a division which had been carved out of what was formerly the Academic Office. An investigating committee was set up to look into the matter of the missing papers and to make appropriate recommendations.

The Investigating Committee

The chairman was the Dean of the Faculty of Political Science. Members of the committee were from academic and administrative departments not in any way connected with the case. The committee found that the unfortunate incident could be traced back to the reorganization of the Academic Office within the registry.

Reorganization of the Registry

The Registry had previously consisted of five sections (see Figure C12). These were each headed by Administrative Officers (AOs). All of these were accountable to the Academic Secretary, Mr Kahn, who reported to the Registrar or, if the Registrar was absent, to the Assistant Registrar. Because of the growth in size of the university and its planned further expansion, it became necessary to restructure the administration. The Academic Office was retitled the Affairs of Senate and Students Office (ASSO) and a taller hierarchy was introduced. (Figure C13). Mr Kahn was made Deputy Registrar (DR) in charge of the Examinations Division. His immediate superior was a new Senior Deputy Registrar, Mr Esho, former Secretary of the Establishments Office, which was not part of the Registry.

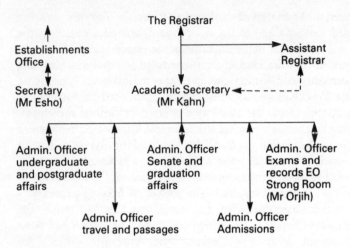

Figure C12 **The Registry before reorganization: AO, Administrative Officer; arrows indicate the prescribed information channels**

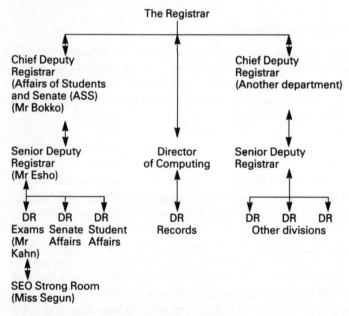

Figure C13 **The Registry after reorganization: DR, Deputy Registrar; arrows indicate the prescribed information channels**

Written regulations available to the committee

The regulations indicated the following

1 Examination questions set by academic staff are sent to the DR, Examinations Division (who then was Mr Kahn).
2 The DR is responsible for sending all papers for printing to the Maximum Security Printing and Minting Corporation (MSPMC).
3 When proofs are received from the MSPMC the DR is responsible for inviting members of staff to proof-read them and make the necessary corrections.
4 The DR returns corrected proofs to the MSPMC.
5 The DR is responsible for collecting printed papers, when ready, from the MSPMC, and for secure storage of the papers until required.
6 The DR is responsible for the delivery of the papers to the examination rooms.

Events leading up to the loss of the papers

The examination was scheduled for the 21 May. Mr Kahn was ill during May and unable to report for duty until the 21st. On 19 May Mr Esho sent Miss Segun, who looked after the Strong Room, to the MSPMC which was 120 miles away from the university. She had a number of papers to collect and signed for them all before she left the MSPMC. She claimed that she placed all the packets in the strong room immediately upon her return. She could not be held accountable for them as Mr Kahn was in the habit of visiting the Strong Room. Mr Kahn claimed that he was not accountable since he was on sick leave when the papers were brought. Mr Esho said he was not interested in the representations made by either party.

The parties involved

Mr Kahn had served the university for eight years and had an MSc. degree in Public Administration. He was a member of the Ibo tribe and he made no secret of his resentment that his former peer, Mr Esho, a Yoruba, should have been imposed on him as his superior. He bypassed Mr Esho and dealt with another Ibo, the Chief Deputy Registrar for the ASSO.

Mr Esho had no university degree, but he did have a chain of certificates and diplomas in administration and he had served the university for twelve years. His last post was outside the Registry in the Establishments Office. On taking up his new post he requested that Mr Kahn's former secretary be assigned to him as his personal secretary. In exchange he sent Miss Segun, another Yoruba, to be secretary to Mr Kahn. The latter believed that this was a sinister move and refused to accept her in that position, and so she was made a Senior Executive Officer by Mr Esho and put in charge of the Strong Room. The former custodian, an Ibo Executive Officer, was moved to another part of the office to make room for her. He protested but to no effect.

The findings of the Investigating Committee

The Investigating Committee found that Mr Kahn had a record without blemish and there was no cause to suspect him of sabotage, although he had a key to the strong room. Miss Segun also had a good record as a confidential Secretary. She had worked at the university for eight years. There was no way of holding her directly responsible for the loss since 'arrangements for control of the Strong Room appeared diffuse'. However, it recommended that Miss Segun should revert to her 'proper job' of confidential secretary.

TROUBLE IN THE REGISTRY: ROLE-PLAY VERSION

The Investigating Committee

An *ad hoc* Investigating Committee has been set up to find out why the biochemistry question papers were missing on the day of the examination, and to make appropriate recommendations. The chairman will be Professor Kayit, who is Dean of the Faculty of Political Science. Members of the committee are from academic and adminstrative departments which are not in any way connected with the case.

Persons who may be called before the committee (or interviewed by one of the members of the committee) are the following:

1 Professor Tokema, Dean of the Faculty of Medicine
2 The Registrar, Mr Ansah, a Yoruba
3 The Chief Deputy Registrar, Affairs of Senate and Students Office (ASSO), Mr Bokko, an Ibo
4 Senior Deputy Registrar, ASSO, Mr Esho, a Yoruba

5 Deputy Registrar in charge of Examinations Division, Mr Kahn, an Ibo
6 Senior Executive Officer in charge of the Strong Room where examination papers are kept, Miss Segun, a Yoruba
7 Executive Officer previously in charge of the Strong Room, Mr Orjih, an Ibo
8 Biochemistry teacher, Mr Malam

Briefing for Mr Bokko

You are the Chief Deputy Registrar (CDR), Affairs of Senate and Students. Before the reorganization in 1979, you were Assistant Registrar. A taller hierarchy was introduced in order to cope with the planned expansion programme, though work has not yet built up to full capacity.

Your superior, the Registrar, is very concerned with future plans, and especially with the growth of computing, so he expects you and the other CDR to deputize for him in many of the operating committees of which he is a member.

Your former colleague, Mr Kahn, who used to report direct to you when the Registrar was away, has refused to change this habit of personal contact now that there is a new intervening level. You have allowed this contact to continue, as you, personally, believe that the appointment of Mr Esho was somewhat premature. Only when the total numbers of students and staff reach the targets will the Senior Deputy Registrar posts be needed, but you well understand why the Registrar built up his department. He is a Yoruba and an ambitious man, and, when he suggested that it would be appropriate to strengthen the Registry with 'outside' experience, such as that which Mr Esho, another Yoruba, would bring you did not protest. You do, however, feel some sympathy for Mr Kahn, who is a man of integrity with a good record. He also belongs to the same (Ibo) tribe as yourself. Until now the bypassing of Mr Esho has caused no trouble, and you are aware that Mr Esho can bypass you if he so wishes.

Mr Esho has responsibilities for student affairs and senate affairs, as well as for examinations, and so he has tended to leave Mr Kahn alone except for the initial drafting of Miss Segun into the Examinations Section. Mr Kahn protested about that, and about the special post found for her at Mr Orjih's expense, but you acquiesced in these moves because you could need help from the Establishments Office on other matters, and Mr Esho had assured you that the Strong

Room job was wrongly graded and Mr Orjih was unsuited for promotion to a higher grade. You had seen Miss Segun's good secretarial record. She had been with the university as long as Mr Kahn, and you thought he was a little unreasonable not to have accepted her.

You have just received an official report from Mr Kahn on the missing examination papter, in which he alleges the following.

1 Miss Segun has on several occasions been missing from her post during office hours.
2 He has issued queries asking her to explain her absences, and she has ignored these.
3 He returned from two days' sick leave at 9.00 a.m. on Wednesday 21st May, and went with Miss Segun to the Strong Room to pick up the day's examination papers.
4 Papers for the biochemistry examination were missing.
5 He issued Miss Segun with a written Query asking her to state within twelve hours, in writing, why she should not be disciplined, since it was she who collected the papers from the printers on Monday 19th May.
6 Miss Segun has not replied, but, instead, in the presence of Mr Orjih and Professor Tokema who were with Mr Kahn in the Strong Room, deposited the Query on the table and made rude remarks about Mr Kahn.

This is all you know about the affair.

Briefing for Mr Ansah

As Registrar of a rapidly expanding university, you believe in the practice of delegation. You have heard that there has been the loss of an examination paper from the Examinations Division. The head of that division, Mr Kahn, is a man of integrity, and you feel sure that there would have been no deliberate leakage. If the committee sends for you, however, you will first need to confer with the Chief Deputy Registrar, Mr Bokko, or you will ask the committee to interview him instead.

Briefing for Mr Malam

You are extremely annoyed that the Examinations Division has been so careless as to lose the papers you set. You saw the proofs on Monday 28th April in Mr Kahn's office. There were two corrections required. You understood that the papers would go back to the printers the following day.

The next thing you hear is that, on the morning of the examination itself, Wednesday 21st May, the papers are missing. You were outside Trenchard Hall at 9.55 a.m., just before the exam was due to begin, when you saw your Dean affix a notice to the noticeboard saying that the examination had been postponed indefinitely. Since the papers have not been found, and there are rumours of leaks (though you have not met anyone who has seen the questions), you will have to set another paper. Your Faculty has not yet fixed the date for the postponed examination, but Professor Tokema has asked you to prepare another paper without delay.

Briefing for Mr Esho

Just under one year ago you held the position of Establishments Secretary but when you heard that there would be two Senior Deputy Registrar (SDR) positions in the reorganized Registry you applied for, and got, one of them.

One of your three immediate subordinates, Mr Kahn, formerly held a position equivalent to your own, and had hoped to be promoted to SDR. You have worked for the university for twelve years, and have several certificates and diplomas in adminstration. These are more relevant than the Master's degree which Mr Kahn believed would secure him promotion. Nevertheless, he is unwilling to assist you in any way.

Since you had no experience of Registry work you thought it would be important that you should have a long-serving personal secretary who could brief you on any matters that you should know. You accordingly arranged that the most suitable person, who happened to have worked for Mr Kahn, should be transferred to work for you. In her place you offered Mr Kahn a Miss Segun, who had impeccable references as a Deputy Registrar's secretary. He quite unreasonably refused to accept her, alleging that you were planting Miss Segun, who is of the same tribe as yourself, for 'sinister' purposes.

As some recompense to Miss Segun for this humiliating refusal of Mr Kahn's, you arranged for her to be in charge of the Strong Room, where examination papers were held, and you granted her the rank of Senior Executive Officer, in view of the responsibility attached to this post. (From your previous position as Establishments Secretary, you are familiar with the grading of posts.) The person who was formerly in charge of the Strong Room, a Mr Orjih, was, and is, on the grade below, that is, Executive Officer, and this is about right for a person with his background. You moved him to a more suitable position. He objected, but you told him that complaints should be channelled through his immediate superior. You heard nothing further.

On 19 May you learned that Mr Kahn was away with gastro-enteritis. Since examinations were due to be held on 21 May, you directed Miss Segun to go to the printers to collect the papers. The printers, The Maximum Security Printing and Minting Corporation, (MSPMC) are 120 miles away.

On 21 May, you learned from Professor Tokema that the biochemistry examination papers were missing. Miss Segun is a trustworthy person, and her evidence that she signed for the papers has been corroborated by MSPMC. She saw you late on the afternoon of 21 May and told you that Mr Kahn had recalled Mr Orjih to help him and Professor Tokema in their search, and that he had served a Query on Miss Segun. She claims that he often uses a duplicate key to go to the Strong Room himself, and believes that this is the latest in his attempts to discredit her.

You believe that you did all you could to ensure the papers were available, and that the responsibility now rests firmly with Mr Kahn.

Briefing for Mr Kahn

You have been in the service of the university for eight years. Before the reorganization in 1979 you were the Academic Secretary, responsible for five Administrative Officers in the Registry.

Two extra levels have now been interposed between you and your former boss, and a Yoruba from the former Establishments Office, who held a post of the same grade that you did, has now become your superior. His name is Mr Esho, and he is less well qualified than you, since you hold an MSc degree in public adminstration and he has nothing higher than a diploma. He also has no experience of Registry work, even though his service is slightly longer than yours.

You are a man of principle, and you have always performed your duties to the best of your ability.

You feel strongly that Ibos are being discriminated against. Another example is that Mr Orjih, the Ibo who used to look after the Strong Room where examination papers are kept, was moved out of his job by Mr Esho. The reason was that Miss Segun, a Yoruba girl who is a protégé of Mr Esho, did not have a job. Mr Esho stole your own secretary, and then tried to foist Miss Segun on you. You refused to take her as your personal secretary. How could you tell what she might pass on to Mr Esho? You asked for her to be transferred out of the Examinations Division altogether, but instead Mr Orjih was moved and Miss Segun was given his job, and at a higher grading. A Senior Executive Officer salary was made personal to her. Mr Orjih protested, but what could you do? He protested also to Mr Esho, who had the nerve to refer him back to you. It was Esho who refused to remove Miss Segun.

You suspect that Mr Esho's interference is a form of spying. You decided, therefore, that you would have to supervise Miss Segun rather closely, and so you have a key to the Strong Room. You have sometimes found her missing from her workplace when she ought to be there. You have served Queries on her for this but she has not replied.

The last straw was when, after two days' sick leave, you came back to work on the morning of Wednesday 21st May to find there were no papers for the biochemistry examination. Such a thing was unknown in all the years that you had been Academic Secretary before the reorganization.

On Mr Esho's instructions, Miss Segun had been to fetch the papers for this and other examinations from the Maximum Security Printing and Minting Corporation 120 miles away. You checked with the printers that they had her signature for the papers, so she must have been careless with them on the way back, or perhaps she left the Strong Room unattended and unlocked for some period between the 19th and the 21st May.

This time her noncommital attitude to her work has created a scandal of major proportions. The press has got hold of it. You therefore issued a Query asking her to explain, in writing, within twelve hours, why disciplinary action should not be taken against her.

On Wednesday afternoon you were in the Strong Room, with Professor Tokema and Mr Orjih, searching for the missing paper, when Miss Segun came in and, in front of these witnesses, deposited your Query on the table, referred contemptuously to the previous Queries, and walked out. Her rudeness is quite insufferable.

You do not recognize Mr Esho as your superior, and, in any case, he is responsible for this mess. You have therefore sent a memo to Mr Bokko telling him what has happened. He is an Ibo, like yourself, but this may reduce his ability to put your case.

Briefing for Mr Orjih

You are extremely annoyed that the Examinations Division was ever 'taken from you'. You know that you would never have allowed papers to be lost. Miss Segun ought never to have been put in charge. She was a secretary, and she should have continued to be one. You have heard that she has even been awarded the salary of a Senior Executive Officer whereas you are only paid as an Executive Officer. They put you into the general office to make room for her, and although you did not lose pay you felt you had lost status and responsibility through no fault of your own. They said it was all part of the reorganization, and when you complained to Mr Esho for moving Miss Segun into your job, Mr Esho said that he had sent Miss Segun to work for Mr Kahn, as his secretary. He told you that you should complain to Mr Kahn. You did so, but Mr Kahn said that he had asked for Miss Segun to be moved out of the Examinations Division, but that his request had been refused. He was not prepared to have any further dealings with Mr Esho. So you are stuck with work you do not like.

You were pleased when Mr Kahn asked you to help him and Professor Tokema to look for the missing paper. You had set up a really good system. The paper was not where it should have been. Indeed, it was not in the Strong Room at all. You reckon Miss Segun either dropped the packet somewhere on the way on Monday 19th May, in which case she had failed in her duty to check every item into the record book, or she left the Strong Room unlocked so that someone could get in.

Briefing for Miss Segun

You have been in the service of the university for eight years. Until the reorganization in 1979 you were a confidential secretary. Your former boss is now a Deputy Registrar in one of the other divisions of the Registry. He had been very pleased with your work. He thought you should be allowed to be a secretary to a Senior Deputy Registrar (SDR), and he suggested this to Mr Esho who needed a secretary. However, the girl who had been working for Mr Kahn was given the job of SDR's secretary, and Mr Esho posted you to work for Mr Kahn.

This did not suit Mr Kahn. You think that Mr Kahn had wanted the SDR job himself, and so he tended to object to anything Mr Esho suggested.

You like Mr Esho. He is of the same tribe as yourself. Mr Kahn wanted to push you out of the Examinations Division altogether, but Mr Esho found you this job in charge of the Strong Room, and gave you a personal salary at Senior Executive Officer level, which is more than the last person, Mr Orjih, got.

There have been difficulties, however. Once you had got to know the layout, and the routines, there was really no need for you to sit around near the Strong Room all day. You liked to take lunch with some of your former friends, and sometimes overstayed the lunch hour. What was there to come back to? It was only in the months when papers were coming in or going out that there was plenty to do. Mr Kahn had once or twice served Queries on you to show why you were absent without permission during working hours. You had not replied. He could not do anything, since Mr Esho would take your part.

The worst aspect of the job was the way Mr Kahn kept snooping on you. He had a duplicate key to the Strong Room, and he would go there at unscheduled times to see that everything was as it should be. Until 21st May, it was!

You reckon that this suspiciousness of his will be his undoing. He has just had the nerve to serve you another Query asking you to explain why disciplinary action should not be taken against you for the biochemistry papers. You collected them with the other papers on Monday 19th May. Mr Kahn normally went to the Maximum Security Printing and Minting Corporation (MSPMC), the printers, himself. He was ill, so he says, on Monday 19th and Tuesday 20th May, so Mr Esho trusted you to go. The MSPMC made you sign a document listing all the papers they gave you. It was 120 miles you had to go. You travelled by train, and when you got back you put all the packets in the Strong Room.

On the morning of Wednesday 21st Mr Kahn went with you to the Strong Room, and the biochemistry papers were not there. You cannot be held responsible for their disappearance since he also has a key. He could have been in himself, and left the door unlocked, on Tuesday night, the 20th May. After all, he was well enough to come in before you did on the 21st May, so why not after hours on the 20th? He has never liked you, but then he is an Ibo, and Mr Orjih, your predecessor, is also an Ibo. You were quite prepared to be Mr Kahn's secretary, but he would not have that.

This time, you were really angry with him for trying to pin something on you. The Query was the last straw! You gave him a piece of your mind when you found him in the Strong Room with Professor Tokema and Mr Orjih on Wednesday afternoon.

Briefing for Professor Tokema

You are extremely annoyed that the Examinations Division has been so careless as to lose the papers for biochemistry. This reflects very badly on the university. Your own Faculty will collect some of the odium.

The first you knew about it was at 9.15 a.m. on the day of the examination, the 21st May. You received a telephone call from Mr Kahn. You got your secretary to type a notice to inform students that the examination was being postponed. You posted this notice on the board outside Trenchard Hall, at 09.55, just five minutes before the MBBS students were due to be admitted to the Hall. You then went straight to the Examinations Office and spent some time questioning Mr Kahn. You knew him from the time when he was Academic Secretary, and had believed him to be a man of integrity.

You learnt that he had been on sick leave on the Monday and Tuesday and had only just returned. The Senior Executive Officer in charge of the Strong Room, Miss Segun, had fetched the papers on 19 May from the printers and had put them in the Strong Room. You telephoned Mr Esho on 21 May to inform him of what had happened, and of your displeasure. He claimed that the Deputy Registrar, Mr Kahn, had been running the division alone, and that your dealings should therefore be with him.

Later in the day, when you were in the Strong Room helping Mr Kahn to look for the papers, Miss Segun came in and put down a piece of paper on the table. This was, apparently, a Query which had been served on her by Mr Kahn. She made a few rude remarks to him and left.

You think the Registry has got much too big since the 1979 reorganization, and that the centralization of the administration of examinations need not include centralization of typing, printing and storing papers. Each Faculty has its own safe, and you think that the secretaries to the Deans of Faculties could provide a collection and storage point for each Faculty.

You have no idea what happened in this case except that the papers were signed for by Miss Segun when she called at the printers on 19 May. It is rather ridiculous to travel 120 miles for 'security' and then not be able to produce the papers when required. You do not think there is any need to use the Maximum Security Printing and Minting Corporation.

You welcome the fact that the matter is being investigated, and will certainly put forward your views. You are to have a meeting on 30 May in your own Faculty to decide on the timing of the deferred examination. There is no hard evidence that anyone has seen a copy of the missing paper, in spite of the rumours, and you have said so when journalists telephoned your office.

Questions

1 Comment on the possible advantages and disadvantages of the reorganization, ignoring, for this purpose, the actual individuals who were appointed to the new posts created.
2 Comment on the behaviour of Mr Kahn and Mr Esho after the reorganization.
3 What can be done to guard against ethnic hostility at work?
4 What OD techniques might have been used?

THE VANISHING STAPLERS

Introductory remarks

This case is about a problem which developed in the stores and supplies department at a university teaching hospital in a developing country. The problems of organizing and running an efficient service are touched on. It is possible to define the problem narrowly as that of catching a thief, or much more broadly as one of creating the type of culture which discourages theft.

The hospital

The hospital was established in 1971 and started to operate with 325 beds in 1972. At the time of opening, the first phase of the building programme had been completed. It included

Catering Department	Pathology Department
Laundry	Pharmacy
Medical Records Department	Theatres (six)
Outpatients Department	Wards (ten)

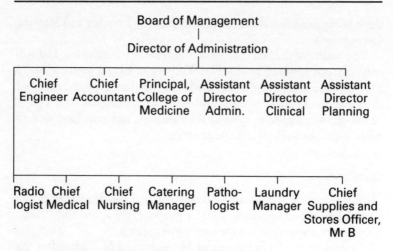

Figure C14 Simplified hospital organization chart

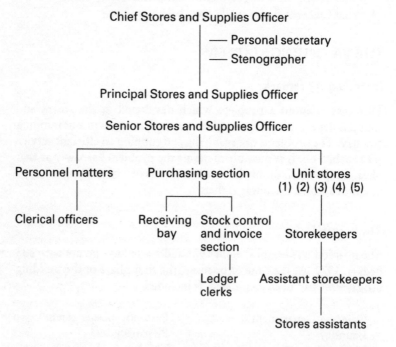

Figure C15 Organization chart of the Stores and Supplies Department

Other departments, which were housed in temporary prefabricated structures in the hospital grounds, included

Engineering Department   Physiotherapy Department
Finance and Audit Department   Stores and Supplies
                                                           Department

The new institution was able to begin to function with these departments and locations. A Board of Management was appointed whose ten members included university professors and representatives of the general public. The chief executive of the hospital, the Director of Administration, was secretary to the Board. (See Figure C14).

The Stores and Supplies Department

The Stores and Supplies Department was opened in January 1973. Prior to that, departmental heads stored the few stock items they had bought in the space that was available in their own departments. As the work of the hospital got off to a slow start, there were not many items requiring storage.

The Chief Stores and Supplies Officer, Mr A (Figure C15) was an expatriate. In 1973 he was busy recruiting junior staff and equipping the wards and other departments with their requirements. Little time could be found to institute stores procedures. The Assistant Chief Stores and Supplies Officer, Mr B, commenced work on 5 September 1973. He was a national of the country but had had post-qualification experience with hospitals in the UK – at Liverpool, and at the teaching hospital attached to Southampton University.

In April 1974, Mr A, who had then been fifteen months in his post, returned to Britain on leave. From there he wrote to say that, owing to ill-health, he would not be returning. The news was a shock to Mr B, who had expected to understudy Mr A for at least two years. Instead, Mr B found himself promoted to Acting Chief Stores and Supplies Officer and Head of Department. He was immediately confronted with the task of organizing the department on sound principles. This was a rare opportunity for a young man and he set to work to draw up a development plan which he submitted to the Board of Management for approval. His requests were speedily granted. He had proposed the following.

1 A purpose-built Stores and Supplies Department: his sketch was worked on by the architect and approval to build was given. By January 1976 the building was complete.

2 An organization chart and job descriptions and specifications should be provided for every post in the department.

3 A manual of procedures was compiled for use within the department, and a handbook giving guidance to all users was also prepared.

4 Three more officer posts were filled.

5 Staff training was instituted: junior staff were trained on the job, intermediate staff had an orientation course, and the new Assistant Stores and Supplies Officer was sent to London for a twelve-week course on stores management.

6 Various printed forms were designed and approved.

7 The Stores and Supplies Department instituted a system of monthly ward rounds and visits to all users to solicit feedback on the effectiveness of the department.

8 There was a receiving bay for all deliveries from suppliers. Here quality, quantity and price were checked before goods were sent to any of the unit stores. (There were such stores for bedding and linen; cleaning materials and hardware; dressings; medical requirements; printed forms and stationery.)

Mr B was responsible to the Director of Administration for the day-to-day running of the department, whose aims he saw as being: to provide the right quality items at the right time, at the right price, from the right source, in the right quantity. Personal relationships had to be developed with the heads of all user departments. Correct maximum, minimum and reorder levels had to be established for every unit store. The Internal Audit Department carried out random checks on stock items. There was also an elaborate stocktaking each March when the financial year ended. Lesser checks were made each month.

A loss from the stationery stores

By January 1976 the Department had moved into its permanent quarters. At the March 1976 stocktaking there were some discrepancies in the books but, after rechecking had taken place, all figures were reconciled. Human error, inaccuracy or carelessness can lead to temporary discrepancies, but deliberate falsification of figures (as happens with theft or pilferage) is a criminal offence and persons can be prosecuted. First, however, there has to be some evidence to support any allegations.

In April 1976 the stationery stores were unable to account for ninety staplers. The storekeeper, X, had only served three months in this unit store. Prior to that he had had an induction course followed by a three-month period of on-the-job training with another storekeeper. Now the Stores Officer in charge of the Stationery Stores asked Mr B to have X transferred to another stores unit. The missing staplers were worth the equivalent of £720. X was *suspected* of stealing them but there was no proof that he had done so.

Mr B had not been in favour of hiring X, as he considered him to be 'rather a rough type'. However, recruitment of staff was centralized at this hospital. It was the responsibility of the Establishment Department, though it was the practice, when selection interviews were held, for the head of the department whose vacancy was being filled to be present. Mr B had therefore been one of the panel. His fellow members were in favour of X and Mr B had dropped his own objections when told that X was first cousin to one of the Assistant Directors at the hospital. Now, in April 1976, he wondered what he should do.

Question

What would you do if you were Mr B? Would you have granted the request of the Stores Officer in charge of the Stationery Stores? Give your reasons. You may state any assumptions you are making about the probable investigatory procedures at this hospital, and the authority that Mr B is likely to have. You need to consider the possible consequences of different actions on your own department and its personnel.

DO NOT READ THE FURTHER INFORMATION UNTIL YOU HAVE CONSIDERED THE QUESTIONS ABOVE.

Further information

Instead of transferring X from the stationery stores, Mr B moved another stores assistant, N, into the area. N was a member of a small religious sect which set a high value on telling the truth. He was asked to inform the officer in charge of anything suspicious. After a time he reported that X regularly disappeared during breaks. He was seen to go to the parking lot. X came to work on a motor scooter which had a locked tool box on the pannier. The security officer on the exit was asked to check the contents of this box when X left the premises. X refused to open the box, but the security man forced open the lock and found a stapler inside.

Question

How does this information affect the suggestions you made in answer to the previous question?

SUGGESTED SOLUTION FOR THE 'CULTURE SORT' EXERCISE

Power	Role	Achievement	Support
5	3	1	2
8	4	7	6
10	9	12	14
11	16	13	18
20	17	15	19
22	24	21	33
25	26	29	30
28	27	31	32

Bibliography

Abbeglen, J.C. (1958) *The Japanese Factory: Aspects of Its Social Organization*, Glencoe, IL: Free Press.

Adair, J. (1973) *Action-Centred Leadership*, New York: McGraw-Hill.

Adams, J. (1965) 'Inequity in social exchange' in Berkowitz, L. (ed.) *Advances in Experimental Social Psychology*, vol. 2, New York: Academic Press.

Alderfer, C.P. (1974) 'Change processes in organizations', in Dunette, M.D. (ed.) *Handbook of Industrial and Organizational Psychology*, Chicago, IL: Rand McNally.

—— (1977) 'Organizational development', *Annual Review of Psychology* 28: 197–223.

Algie, J. (1983) 'Budget priority system', *Health and Social Service Journal* 3 November: 1320–1.

Algie, J., Mallen, G. and Foster, W. (1983) 'Financial decisions by priority scaling', *Journal of Management Studies* 20 (2): 233–60.

Allen, D. and Hughes, J.A. (1983) *Management for Health Service Administrators*, London: Pitman.

Allison, G.T. (1971) *Essence of Decision: Explaining the Cuban Missile Crisis*, Boston, MA: Little, Brown.

—— (1981) 'Model III: governmental politics', in Zey-Ferrell, M. and Aiken, M. (eds) *Complex Organizations: Critical Perspectives*, Glenview, IL: Scott Foresman, ch. 7, 137–55.

Anisuzzaman, M. and Abdel-Malek, A. (1984) *'Culture and Thought'*, *Transformation of the World Series* (ed. A. Abdel-Malek), vol. 3, London: Macmillan.

Argenti, J. (1968) 'The pyramid, the ladder and the matrix', *Management Decision* 2 (3): reprinted in Folkertsma, B. (ed.) *Handbook for Managers*, London: Kluwer Harrap, 1972.

—— (1976) *Corporate Collapse: the Causes and Symptoms*, New York: McGraw-Hill.

Argyris, C. (1957) *Personality and Organization*, New York: Harper & Row.

—— (1964) *Integrating the Individual and the Organization*, New York: Wiley.

Argyris, C. and Schon, D.A. (1976) *Theory in Practice: Increasing Personal Effectiveness*, San Francisco, CA: Jossey Bass.

Aristotle, (1955) *Ethics*, translated by Thompson, J.A.K., London: Penguin.

Ashby, W.R. (1981) *An Introduction to Cybernetics*, 3rd edn, New York: Harper & Row.

Assaglioni, R. (1980) *Psychosynthesis: a Manual of Principles and Techniques*, 2nd edn, Wellingborough: Turnstone Books.

Astley, W.G. and Van De Ven, A.H. (1983) 'Central perspectives and debates in organization theory', *Administrative Science Quarterly* (June) 28 245–73.

Ayittey, G. (1990) 'Guns, idiots, screams', *New Internationalist* 208 (June) 8–9.

Bales, R.F. (1950) *Interaction Process Analysis*, Reading, MA: Addison Wesley.

—— (1953) 'The equilibrium problems in small groups', in Parsons, T., Bales, R.F. and Shils, E.A. (eds) *Working Papers in the Theory of Action*, New York: Free Press; reproduced in Argyle, M., *Encounters*, Harmondsworth: Penguin, 1973.

Ballou, R.O. (ed.) (1939) *The Bible of the World*, London: Kegan Paul.

Balogun, M.J. (1983) *Public Administration in Nigeria: a Developmental Approach*, London: Macmillan.

Barker, R.G. and Gump, P.V. (1964) *Big School, Small School: High School Size and Student Behavior*, Stanford, CA: Stanford University Press.

Barnes, L.B. (1981) 'Managing the paradox of organizational trust, *Harvard Business Review* 59 (March/April): 107–16.

Bartlett, C.A., Doz, Y. and Hedlund, G. (1989) *Managing the Global Firm*, London: Routledge.

Baumgartel, H. (1979) 'Using employee questionnaire results for improving organizations', in French, W.L. and Hellriegel, D. (eds) *Personnel Management and Organization Development: Fields in Transition*, Boston, MA: Houghton Mifflin, ch. 32.

Baumgartner. T., Burns, T. and De Ville, P. (1979) 'Work, politics, and social structuring under capitalism: impact and limitations of industrial democracy reforms under capitalist relations of production and social reproduction', in Burns, T., Karlsson, L. and Rus, V. (eds) *Work and Power: the Liberation of Work and the Control of Political Power*, London: Sage.

Bennis, W.G. (1959) 'Leadership theory and administrative behavior: the problem of authority', *Administrative Science Quarterly* (4) 6: 259–301.

Bennis, W.G., Benne, K.D. and Chin, R. (eds) (1977) *The Planning of Change*, 2nd, New York: Holt, Rinehart & Winston.

Benson, K. (1977) 'Organizations: a dialectical view, '*Administrative Science Quarterly* 22 (1): 1–21.

Berelson, B. and Steiner, G. (1964) *Human Behavior: An Inventory of Scientific Findings*, New York: Harcourt Brace.

Berne, E. (1966) *The Structure and Dynamics of Organizations and Groups*, New York: Grove Press.

—— (1967) *Games People Play: the Psychology of Human Relationships*, London: Penguin.

Beyer, J.M. (1981) 'Ideologies, values, and decision-making', in Nystrom, P.C. and Starbuck, W.H. (eds) *Handbook of Organizational Design*, Oxford: Oxford University Press, 166–97.

Beynon, H. (1973) *Working for Ford*, Wakefield: E.P. Publishing (reprinted 1975).

Biddle, B.J. (1979) *Role Theory: Expectations, Identities and Behavior*, New York: Academic Press.

Binsted, D. (1980) 'The design of learning events for management', *Management Education and Development* 11 (2, 3): 81–94, 174–89.

Bion, W.R. (1948) 'Experiences in groups', *Human Relations* 1: 314–20, 487–96.

Blake, R. and Mouton, J.S. (1964a) *The Managerial Grid*, 2nd edn, Houston, TX: Gulf.

—— (1964b) 'Breakthrough in organizational development', *Harvard Business Review* 42 (November/December): 133–8.

Blake, R., Shepherd, H.A. and Mouton, J.S. (1964) *Managing Intergroup Conflict in Industry*, Houston, TX: Gulf.

Blau, P.M. and Schoenherr, R.A. (1971) *The Structure of Organizations*, New York: Basic Books.

Blood, M.R. and Hulin, C.L. (1967) Alienation, environmental characteristics and worker response', *Journal of Applied Psychology* 51 (3): 284–90.

Bloor, M. (1986) 'Who'll make the tea?', *New Society* 75 (1205): 185–6.

Blunt, P. (1983) *Organizational Theory and Behaviour: an African Perspective*, London: Longman.

Bocock, R.J. (1971) 'The Ismailis in Tanzania: a Weberian analysis', *British Journal of Sociology* 22 (4): 365–80.

Boddy, D. and Buchan, D. (1985) 'New technology with a human face', *Personnel Management* 17 (4): 28–31.

Bohm, D. (1980) *Wholeness and the Implicate Order*, London: Routledge and Kegan Paul.

Borgatta, E.F., Bales, A. and Couch, S. (1954) 'Some findings relevant to the great man theory of leadership', *American Sociological Review* 19: 755–9.

Bowers, D.G., Franklin, J.L. and Percorella, P.A. (1975) 'Matching problems, precursors and interventions in OD: a systematic approach', *Journal of Applied Behavioral Science* 11: 391–409.

Bowey, A. and Connolly, R. '(1975) 'Application of the concept of working in groups', *Management Decision* 13 (3): 181–92.

Brager, G. and Holloway, S. (1978) *Changing Human Service Organizations: Politics and Practice*, New York: Free Press.

Braybrooke, D. and Lindblom, C.E. (1970) *A Strategy of Decision*, New York: Free Press.

Brewer, R. (1978) 'Personnel's role in participation', *Personnel Management* 10 (September): 23–9, 45.

Brimmer, A.F. (1955) 'The setting of entrepreneurship in India', *Quarterly Journal of Economics* 69: 560f.

Brooke, M.Z. and Remmers, H.L. (1978) *The Strategy of Multinational Enterprise*, 2nd edn, London: Pitman.

Brown, L.D. (1983) *Managing Conflict at Organizational Interfaces*, Reading, MA: Addison Wesley.

Brown, R.G.S. (1970) *The Administrative Process in Britain*, New York: Methuen.

Brown, R.G.S. and Steel, D.R. (1979) *The Administrative Process in Britain*, 2nd edn, London: Methuen.

Brownsberger, W.N. (1983) 'Development and governmental corruption – materialism and political fragmentation in Nigeria', *Journal of Modern African Studies* 21 (2): 215–33.

Bryman, A. (1984) 'Leadership and corporate culture: harmony and disharmony', *Personnel Review* 13 (2): 19–24.

Buchanan, D.A. and Huczynski, A.A. (1985) *Organizational Behaviour: an Introductory Text*, Hemel Hempstead: Prentice-Hall International.

Buckley, W. (1981) 'Society as a complex adaptive system', in Open Systems Group (eds) *Systems Behaviour*, 3rd edn, London: Harper & Row for the Open University.

Burns, J.M. (1978) *Leadership*, New York: Harper & Row.

Burns, T. (1955) 'The reference of conduct in small groups: cliques and cabals in occupational mileux', *Sociology* 8: 467–85.

Burns, T. and Stalker, G.M. (1966) *The Management of Innovation*, London: Tavistock Institute of Human Relations.

Burns, T., Karlson, L. and Rus, V. (1979) *Work and Power: the Liberation of Work and the Control of Political Power*, London: Sage.

Burns, T., Baumgartner, T. and de Ville, P. (1984) *Man, Decisions, Society*, New York: Gordon & Breach.

Burrage, M. (1969) 'Culture and British economic growth', *British Journal of Sociology* 20 (2): 117–33.

Business Roundtable, (1988) *Corporate Ethics: A Prime Business Asset: A Report on Policy and Practice in Company Conduct*, New York: The Business Roundtable.

Buzzard, R.B. (1973) 'A practical look at industrial stress', *Occupational Psychology* 47: 56–61.

Cammann, C. and Nadler, D.A. (1976) 'Fit your control systems to your managerial style', *Harvard Business Review* 54 (1): 65–72.

Campbell, D.N., Fleming, R.L. and Grote, R.C. (1985) 'Special Report: discipline without punishment at last, *Harvard Business Review* 85 (4): 162–76.

Campbell, J.P., Dunnette, M.D., Lawler, E.E. and Weick, K.E. (1970) *Managerial Behavior, Performance and Effectiveness*, New York: McGraw–Hill.

Carby, K. and Thakur, T. (1976) *Transactional Analysis at Work*, IPM Information Report 23, London: Institute of Personnel Management.

Castles, F.G., Murray, D.T. and Potter, D.C. (eds) (1971) *Decisions, Organizations and Society*, London: Penguin.

Chambers, C. (1990) 'Changing culture', *Personnel Management* 22 (3): 69.

Chandler, A. (1962) *Strategy and Structure*, Cambridge, MA: MIT Press.

Checkland, P.B. (1981) 'Towards a systems-based methodology for real-world problem solving', in Open Systems Group (eds) *Systems Behaviour*, 3rd edn, London: Harper & Row for the Open University, ch. 19, 288–314.

Child, J. (1984) *Organization: a Guide to Problems and Practice*, 2nd edn, New York: Harper & Row.

Child, J. and Ellis, A. (1973) 'Predictors of variation in managerial roles', *Human Relations* 26 (2):227–50.

Clegg, S. (1983) 'Organizational democracy, power and participation', in Crouch, C. and Heller, F. (eds) *International Year Book of Organizational Democracy*, vol. 1, New York: Wiley.

Cohen, J.M. and Cohen M.J. (eds) (1960) *The Penguin Dictionary of Quotations*, London: Penguin, 155 (Empedocles).

Cohen, M.D., March, J.G. and Olsen, J.P. (1972) 'A garbage can model of organizational choice', *Administrative Science Quarterly* 17 (1): 1–25.

Collignon, R. and Cray, D. (1981) 'New organizational perspectives: critiques and critical organizations' in Zey-Ferrell, M. and Aiken, M. (eds) *Complex Organizations: Critical Perspectives*, Glenview, IL: Scott, Foresman.

Constas, H. (1958) 'Max Weber's two conceptions of bureaucracy', *American Journal of Sociology* 63: 400–9.

Conyers, D. (1983) 'Decentralization: the latest fashion in development administration', *Public Administration and Development* 3: 97–109.

Cope, D.E. (1982) *Organizational Development and Action Research in Hospitals*, Aldershot: Gower.

Corwin, R.G. (1961a) 'The professional employee: a study of conflict in nursing roles', *American Journal of Sociology* 66: 604–15.

—— (1961b) 'Role conception and career aspiration: a study of identity in nursing', *Sociological Quarterly* 60 (2): 69–86.

Coser, L. (1956) *The Functions of Social Conflict*, Glencoe, IL: Free Press.

Cox, M. and Cox, C. (1980) 'Ten years of transactional analysis', in Beck, J. and Cox, C. (eds) *Advances in Management Education*, New York: Wiley.

Cross, M. (1991) 'Monitoring multiskilling: the way to guarantee long-term change', *Personnel Management* 23 (3): 44–9.

Crouch, C. and Heller, F. (1983) *International Yearbook of Organizational Democracy*, New York: Wiley.

Crozier, M. (1964) *The Bureaucratic Phenomenon*, Chicago, IL: University of Chicago.

Cumming, S.L.L. and Elsami, A.M. (1970) 'The impact of role diversity, job level, and organizational size on managerial satisfaction', *Administrative Science Quarterly* 15 (1): 1–10.

Dalton, M. (1959) *Men Who Manage*, New York: Wiley.

Daniel, W.W. (1970) *Beyond the Wage-Work Bargain*, London: P.E.P.

—— (1972) 'What interests a worker?', *New Society*, 23 March: 495.

Davis, L.E. and Taylor, J.C. (eds) (1972) *The Design of Jobs*, London: Penguin.

Davis, S.M. (1971) *Comparative Management: Organizational and Cultural Perspectives*, Englewood Cliffs, NJ: Prentice Hall.

—— (1984) *Managing Corporate Culture*, Cambridge, MA: Ballinger.

Deal, T. and Kennedy, A. (1988) *Corporate Cultures*, London: Penguin.

Dearlove, J. (1973) *The Politics of Policy in Local Government*,Cambridge: Cambridge University Press.

De Bono, E. (1971) *Lateral Thinking for Management* New York: McGraw Hill (reprinted, London: Penguin, 1982).

De Charms, R., Carpenter, V. and Kuperman, A, (1965) 'The 'origin-pawn' variable in person perception', *Sociometry* 28: 241–58; reprinted in Smith, P.B. (ed) *Group Processes*, London: Penguin, 1970.

Deeks, J. (1976) *The Small Firm Owner-Manager*, New York: Praeger.

Denhardt, R.B. (1981) 'Toward a critical theory of public organization', *Public Administration Review* 43 (November/December): 628–36.

Denton, F.H. and Phillips, W, (1968) 'Some patterns in the history of violence', *Journal of Conflict Resolution* 12: 182–95; reprinted in Smith, C.G. (ed.) (1972) *Conflict Resolution: Contributions of the Behavioral Sciences*, Notre Dame, IN: University of Notre Dame Press.

Derr, C.B. (1972) 'Conflict resolution in organizations', *Public Administration Review* 35 (5): 495–501.

Deutsch, M. (1969) 'Conflicts: productive and destructive', *Journal of Social Issues* 25 (1): 7–41.

—— (1972) 'Conflict and its resolution', in Smith, C.G. (ed.) *Conflict Resolution: Contributions of the Behavioral Sciences*, Notre Dame, IN: University of Notre Dame Press.

Diederich, P. (1942) 'How to run away from an educational problem', *Progressive Education* 19 (8); cited in Thelen, H.A. *Dynamics of Groups at Work*, Chicago, IL: University of Chicago Press, 1954, 212–13.

Douglas, T. (1978) *Basic Group Work*, London: Tavistock Institute of Human Relations.

Dresang, D.L. (1974) 'Ethnic politics, representative bureaucracy and development administration: the Zambian case', *American Political Science Review* 68 (December): 1605–18.

Dunkerley, D. (1980) 'Technological change and work: upgrading or deskilling? ', in Boreham, P. and Dow, G. (eds) *Work and Inequality*, vol. 1, London: Macmillan.

Dunning, J.H. (1985) 'Multinational enterprise and industrial restructuring in the U.K.', *Lloyds Bank Review* 158: 1–19.

Dunsire, A. (1973) *Administration, the Word and the Science*, Oxford: Martin Robertson.

Dyar, D.A. and Giles J. (1974) *Improving Skills in Working with People*, London: Training Services Agency, HMSO.

Eccles, A. (1981) *Under New Management*, London: Pan.

Edmonstone, J. (1982) 'Human service organizations: implications for management and organizational development', *Management Education and Development* 13 (3): 163–73.

Edwards, R.C. (1979) 'The social relations of production at the point of production', in *Contested Terrain: The Transformation of the Workplace in America*, New York: Basic Books.

—— (1981) 'The social relations of production at the point of production', in Zey-Ferrell, M. and Aiken, M. (eds) *Complex Organizations: Critical Perspectives*, Glenview, IL: ch. 8, 156–82.

Ejiougu, A.M. (1983) 'Participative management in a developing economy – poison or placebo', *Journal of Applied Behavioral Science* 19 (3): 239–47.

Elias, N. and Dunning, E. (1966) 'Dynamics of group sports with special reference to football', *British Journal of Sociology* 17 (4): 388–401.

Ellerman, D.P. (1983) 'The employment relation, property rights and organizational democracy', in Crough, C. and Heller, F.A. (eds) *International Yearbook of Organizational Democracy*, New York: Wiley.

Elms, A.C. (1976) *Attitudes*, Milton Keynes: Open University Press, Social Psychology course, 1976.

Enayat, H. (1982) *Modern Islamic Political Thought*, London: Macmillan.

Etzioni, A. (1961) *A Comparative Analysis of Complex Organizations*, New York: Free Press.

—— (1974) *Political Unification: a Comparative Study of Leaders and Forces*, New York: Krieger.

Eysenck, H.J. (1973) *Uses and Abuses of Psychology*, London: Penguin.

Ferguson, J. (1988) *Not Them But Us: In Praise of The United Nations*, East Wittering: Gooday Publishers.

Ferrari, S. (1979) 'Transactional analysis in developing countries', *Journal of European Industrial Training* 3 (4): 12–15.

Festinger, L.A. (1954) 'A theory of social comparison processes', *Human Relations* 7: 117–40.

Fiedler, F.E. (1967) *A Theory of Leadership Effectiveness*, New York: McGraw-Hill.

Firth, R. (1964) *Essays on Social Organization and Values*, London: Athlone Press.

Fishbein, M. and Ajzen, I. (1975) *Belief, Attitude, Intention and Behavior: an Introduction to Theory and Research*, Reading, MA: Addison Wesley.

Flamholtz, E.G. and Das, T.K. (1985) 'Toward an integrative framework of organizational control', *Accounting, Organizations and Society* 10 (1): 35–50.

Fleishman, E.A. and Harris, F. (1962) 'Patterns of leadership behavior related to employee grievances and turnover', *Personnel Psychology* 15: 43–56.

Fligstein, N. (1985) 'The spread of the multi-divisional form among large firms, 1919–1979', *American Sociological Review* 50: 377–91.

Fouraker, L.E. and Stopford, J.M. (1968) 'Organizational structure and multinational strategy', *Administrative Science Quarterly*, 13 June: 47–64.

Fowler, A, (1985) 'Getting in on organization restructuring', *Personnel Management* 17 (2): 24–7.

Fox, A. (1974) *Beyond Contract: Work, Power, and Trust Relations*, London: Faber & Faber.

Franko, L.G. (1977) *The European Multinationals: a Renewed Challenge to American and British big business*, New York: Harper & Row.

French, J.R.P. and Raven, B, (1968) 'The bases of social power', in Cartwright, D. and Zander, A. (eds) *Group Dynamics*, 3rd edn, New York: Harper & Row: 259–69.

French, W.L. and Hellriegel, D. (eds) (1971) *Personnel Management and Organization Development: Fields in Transition*, Boston, MA: Houghton Mifflin.

Friedland, W.H. (1964) 'For a sociological concept of charisma', *Social Forces* 43 (1): 18–26.

Frost, P.J., Moore, L.F., Reis Louis, M.R., Lundberg, C.C. and Martin, J. (eds) (1985) *Organizational Culture*, Beverly Hills, CA: Sage.

Fry, G. (1985) *The Changing Civil Service*, London: Allen & Unwin.

Gadalla, I.E. and Cooper, R. (1978) 'Towards an epistemology of management', *Social Science Information* 17 (3): 349–83.

Gaer, J. (1963) *What the Great Religions Believe*, New York: Signet.

Galbraith, J.R. (ed.) (1971) *Matrix Organizations: Organization Design and High Technology*, Cambridge, MA: MIT Press.

Georgiou, P, (1973) 'The goal paradigm and notes towards a counter paradigm', *Administrative Science Quarterly* 18 (3): 291–310.

Gergen, K.J. (1969) *The Concept of Self*, New York: Holt Rinehart & Winston.

Getsels, J.W. and Guba, E.G. (1954) 'Role, role conflict and effectiveness: an empirical study', *American Sociological Review* 19: 164–75.

Gibbs, G.I. (1974) 'Scientific concepts and gaming', *Programmed Learning and Educational Technology* 11 (1): 32–8.

Gittings, J. (1989) *China Changes Face: the Road from Revolution 1949–1989*, Oxford: Oxford University Press.

Gleick, J. (1987) *Chaos: Making a New Science*, London: Sphere Books.

Glen, T.H. and James, C.F. (1980) 'Difficulties in implementing management science techniques in a Third World setting', *Interfaces* 10 (1): 39–44.

Glueck, W.F. (1974) 'Decision-making: organizational choice, *Personnel Psychology* 27 (Spring): 77–93.

—— (1977) *Management*, Hinsdale, IL: Dryden.

Goffman, E. (1961) *Encounters: Two Studies in the Sociology of Interaction*, Indianapolis, IN: Bobbs Merrill.

—— (1975) *Frame Analysis: an Essay on the Organization of Experience*, London: Penguin.

Goldsmith, W. and Clutterbuck, D. (1984) *The Winning Streak*, New York: Weidenfeld & Nicolson.

Golembiewski, R.T. (1962) *The Small Group: an Analysis of Research Concepts and Operations*, Chicago IL: University to Chicago Press.

Gordon, G.G. and Cummins, W. (1979) *Managing Management Climate*, Lexington, MA: Lexington Books.

Gordon, W.J.J. (1961) *Synectics: The Development of Creative Capacity*, New York: Harper & Row.

Gore, W.J. (1964) *Administrative Decision-Making: a Heuristic Model*, New York: Wiley.

Greiner, L.E. (1972) 'Evolution and revolution as organizations grow', *Harvard Business Review* 50 (4): 37–46.

Guest, D. (1984) 'What's new in motivation?', *Personnel Management* 16 (May): 20–3.

Guest, D. and Williams, R. (1973) 'How home affects work', *New Society*, 18 January: 114–17.

Guth, W. and Taguiri, R. (1965) 'Personal values and corporate strategy', *Harvard Business Review* 43 (September/October): 123–32.

Habermas, J. (1968) *Knowledge and Human Interest*, trans. by Shapiro, J., Boston, MA: Beacon Press.

—— (1970) *Toward a Rational Society*, trans. by Shapiro, J., Boston, MA: Beacon Press.

Hall, J. and Fletcher, B. (1984) 'Coping with personal problems at work', *Personnel Management* 16 (2): 30–3.

Handy, C.B. (1978) *The Gods of Management*, London: Penguin.

—— (1984) 'The organizational revolution and how to harness it', *Personnel Management* 16 (7):20–3.

—— (1985) *Understanding Organizations*, 3rd edn, London: Penguin.

Hannan, M. and Freeman, J. (1977) 'The population ecology of organizations', *American Journal of Sociology* 92: 929–64.

—— 'Structural inertia and organizational change', *American Sociological Review* 49: 149–64.

Harris, T.A. (1973) *I'm OK, You're OK*, London: Pan.

Harrison, E.F. (1975) *The Managerial Decision-Making Process*, Boston, MA: Houghton Mifflin.

Harrison, J.R. and March, J.G. (1984) 'Decision-making and post decision surprises', *Administrative Science Quarterly* 29 (1): 26–41.

Harrison, R. (1972a) 'Understanding your organization's character', *Harvard Business Review* 50 (23): 119–28.

—— (1972b) 'When power conflicts trigger team spirit', *European Business* 33 (Spring) 57–65.

—— (1983) 'Strategies for a new age', *Human Resource Management* 22 (3): 209–35.

—— (1987a) 'Harnessing personal energy: how companies can inspire employees', *Organizational Dynamics* 16 (2): 5–20.

—— (1987b) *Organization Culture and Quality of Service: a Strategy for Releasing Love in the Workplace*, London: Association for Management Education and Development (reprinted 1990).

Hartwig, R. (1978) 'Rationality and the problems of administrative theory', *Public Administration* 56: 159–79.

Hayes, C., Anderson, A. and Fonda, N. (1984) 'International competition and the role of competence', *Personnel Management* 16 (9): 36–8.

Hegel, G.W.F. (1821) *Grundlinien der Philosophie des Rechts*, trans by Dyde, S.W. (1896) as *The Philosophy of Right*; reprinted Oxford: Clarendon, 1942.

Heidenheimer, A.J. (1970) *Political Corruption: Readings in Comparative Analysis*, New York: Holt, Rinehart & Winston.

Heller, F.A. and Wilpert, B. (1981) *Competence and Power in Managerial Decision Making: a Study of Senior Levels of Organization in Eight Countries*, Chichester: Wiley.

Hemphill, J.K. (1959) 'Job descriptions for executives', *Harvard Business Review* 37: 55–67.

—— (1960) 'Dimensions of Executive Positions. Ohio Studies in personnel', *Research Monographs* 98, Ohio: Ohio State University, Bureau of Business Research.

Herzberg, F. (1968) *Work and the Nature of Man*, London: Staples Press.

Hill, S. (1974) 'Norms, groups, and power: the sociology of workplace industrial relations', *British Journal of Industrial Relations* (2): 213–35.

Hill, S. and Thurley, K. (1974) 'Sociology and industrial relations', *British Journal of Industrial Relations* 12: 147–70.

Hilton, G. (1972) 'Causal inference analysis: a seductive process', *Administrative Science Quarterly* 17: 44–54.

Hirota, K. (1953) *Japanese Journal of Psychology* 24: 105–13.

Hoffman, W.M. and Moore, J.M. (1988) *Business Ethics. Readings and Cases in Corporate Morality*, New York: McGraw-Hill.

Hofstede, G. (1980a) *Culture's Consequences*, Beverly Hills, CA: Sage.

—— (1980b) 'Motivation, leadership, and organizational development: do American theories apply abroad?', *Organizational Dynamics* 9 (1): 42–62.

Hofstede, G. and Bond, M.H. (1988) 'The Confucius connection: from cultural roots to economic growth', *Organizational Dynamics* 16: (Spring) 5–21.

Hofstede, G. and Kassem, M.S. (1976) *European Contributions to Organization Theory*, Amsterdam: Van Gorcum.

Holbrook, D. (1985) 'Can collective bargaining ever change? the ICI experience', *Personnel Management* 17 (1): 22–5.

Hollander, E.P. (1964) *Leaders, Groups, and Influence*, Oxford: Oxford University Press.

Horne, J.H. and Lupton, T. (1965) 'The work activities of 'middle' managers', *Journal of Management Studies* 1:14–33.

Horvat, B. (1983) 'The organizational theory of workers' management', in Crouch, C. and Heller, F. (eds) *International Yearbook of Organizational Democracy*, New York: Wiley, ch. 14.

Horvath, D., McMillan, C.J., Azumi, K. and Hickson, D.J. (1981) 'The cultural context of organizational control: an international comparison', in Hickson, D.J. and McMillan, C.J. (eds) *Organization and Nation: The Aston Programme iv*, Farnborough: Gower.

House, R.J. (1971) 'A path goal theory of leader effectiveness', *Administrative Science Quarterly* 16 (3): 321–38.

Huber, G.P., Ullman, J. and Leifer, R. (1979) 'Optimum organization design: an analytic-adoptive approach', *Academy of Management Review* 4: 567–78.

Humble, J.W. (1967) *Management by Objectives*, London: Industrial Education and Research Foundation.

Hunt, J.G., Hosking, D.-M., Schriesheim, C. and Stewart, R. (eds) (1984) *Leaders and Managers: International Perspectives on Managerial Behaviour and Leadership*, Elmsford, NY: Pergamon Press.

Hutchinson, C. (1977) 'Systematic analysis of trends and pressures – a training workshop design', *Journal of European Industrial Training* 1 (2): 17–19.

Jaeger, A.M. (1986) 'Organizational development and national culture: where's the fit?', *Academy of Management Review* 11 (1): 178–90.

Janis, I. (1972) *Victims of Group Think: a Psychological Study of Foreign Policy Decisions and Fiascoes*, Boston, MA: Houghton Mifflin.

Janis, I. and Katz, D. (1959) 'The reduction of intergroup hostility: research problems and hypotheses', *Journal of Conflict Resolution* 3: 85–100.

Janis, I.L. and Mann, L. (1968) 'A conflict theory approach to attitude change in decision-making', in Greenwald, A., Brock, T. and Omstrom, T.M. (eds) *Psychological Foundations of Attitudes*, New York: Academic Press.

Jaques, E. (1976) *A General Theory of Bureaucracy*, London: Heinemann.

Jay, A. (1975) *Corporation Man*, London: Pelican.

Johannisson, B. (1984) 'A cultural perspective on small business – local business climate', *International Small Business Journal* 2 (2): 32–41.

Jung, C. (1953) *Collected Works*, London: Routledge.

Kahn, R.L., Wolfe, D.M., Quinn, R.D., Snoek, D.J. and Rosenthal, R.A. (1964) *Organizational Stress: Studies in Role Conflict and Ambiguity*, New York: Wiley.

Kakar, S. (1971) 'Authority patterns and subordinate behavior in Indian organizations, *Administrative Science Quarterly* 16: 299f.

Karpik, L. (1978) *Organization and Environment: Theory, Issues and Reality*, Beverly Hills, CA: Sage.

Kast, F. and Rosenzweig, J. (1981) 'The modern view: a systems approach', in Open Systems Group (eds) *Systems Behaviour*, 3rd edn, New York: Harper & Row, ch.3, 44–55.

Katz, D and Kahn, R.L. (1966) *The Social Psychology of Organizations*, New York: Wiley.

Kaufman, A. (1968) *The Science of Decision-Making*, London: Weidenfeld & Nicolson.

Kelman, H.C. (1958) 'Compliance, identification, and internalization: three processes of attitude change', *Journal of Conflict Resolution* 2: 51–60.

Kemp, N., Clegg, C. and Wall, T. (1980) 'Job redesign-content, process, and outcomes', *EmployeeRelations* 2 (5): 5–14.

Kennard, D. (1983) *An Introduction to Therapeutic Communities*, London: Routledge & Kegan Paul.

Keys, J.B. and Miller, T.R. (1984) 'The Japanese management theory jungle, *Academy of Management Review* 9(2): 342–53.

Kiely, J. (1981) 'Managers' job satisfaction across time', *West Midlands Regional Management Centre Review* 1 (1): 4–12.

Kiersey, D. and Bates, M. (1978) *Please Understand Me*, 3rd edn, Buffalo, NY: Prometheus Nemisis Press.

King, A., Yeo-Chi (1977) 'A voluntarist model of organization: the Maoist version and its critique', *British Journal of Sociology* 28 (3): 363–74.

Kirzner, I.M. (1973) *Competition and Entrepreneurship*, Chicago, IL: University of Chicago Press.

Kline, R.R. (1985) 'The beginnings of modern management: Alexander and Darius', *Journal of Systems Management* 36 (9): 22–6.

Knight, K. (ed.) (1977) *Matrix Management* London: Gower.

Knowles, M. (1978) *The Adult Learner: A Neglected Species*, 2nd edn, Houston, TX: Gulf.

Kolb, D.A., Rubin, I. and McIntyre, J.M. (1974) *Organizational Psychology: an Experiential Approach*, Englewood Cliffs, NJ: Prentice Hall.

Kotter, J.P. (1982) *The General Managers*, New York: Free Press.

Kraemer, H. (1975) 'The philosophical foundation of management rediscovered', *Management International Review* 15 (213): 47–54.

Kuhn, T.S. (1962) *The Structure of Scientific Revolutions*, Chicago, IL: University of Chicago Press.

Lake, D.G., Miles, M.B. and Earle, R.B. (eds) (1973) *Measuring Human Behavior*, Teachers College Press, Columbia University.

Laljee, M., Stevens, R. and Williams, M. (1976) 'Social interaction', in *Social Psychology*, Milton Keynes: Open University Press, Block 12.

Lammers, C.J. and Hickson, D.J. (eds) (1979) *Organizations Alike and Unlike: International and Inter-institutional Studies in the Sociology of Organizations*, London: Routledge & Kegan Paul.

Lawlor, E.E. (1968) 'Motivation and the design of jobs', in Lawlor, E.E. and Porter, L.W. (eds) *Managerial Attitudes and Performance*, Homewood, IL: Irwin.

Lawlor, E.E. and Porter, L.W. (1968) *Managerial Attitudes and Performance*, Homewood, IL: Irwin.

Lawrence, P. (1984) *Management in Action*, London: Routledge & Kegan Paul.

Lawrence, P.R. and Lorsch, J.W. (1967) *Organization and Environment*, Boston, MA:, Harvard University Press.

Lee, S.M. and Schwendiman, G. (1982) *Japanese Management: Cultural and Environmental Considerations*, New York: Praeger.

Leeds, R. (1969) 'The absorption of protest: a working paper', in Bennis, W.G., Benne, K.D. and Chin, R. (eds) *The Planning of Change*, 2nd edn, New York: Holt, Rinehart & Wilson, ch. 5.1.

Lessem, R. (1984) 'Getting into self-employment', *Management Education and Development* 15 (1): 29–54.

Levinson, H, With J. Molinari and A. Spohn, (1972) *Organizational Diagnosis*, reissued 1977, Cambridge, MA.

Lieberson, S. and O'Connor, J.F. (1972) 'Leadership and organizational performance: a study of large corporations', *American Sociological Review* 37: 117–30.

Likert, R. (1967) *The Human Organisation*, New York: McGraw-Hill.

Lilienfeld, R. (1975) 'Systems theory as an ideology', *Social Research* 42 (Winter): 637–60.

Lindsay, C. and Dempsey, B. (1983) 'Ten painfully learned lessons about working in China', *Journal of Applied Behavioral Science* 19 (3): 265–76.

Lippitt, R. and White, K. (1958) 'An experimental study of leadership and group life', in Macoby, E.E., Newcomb, T.M. and Hartley, E.L. (eds) *Readings in Social Psychology*, New York: Holt, Rinehart, & Winston.

Lockett, M. (1983) 'Organizational democracy and politics in China', in Crouch, C. and Heller, F. (eds) *International Yearbook of Organizational Democracy*, vol. 1, New York: Wiley, ch. 28.

Lorsch, J.W. and Lawrence, P.R. (1970) *Studies in Organization Design*, Ontario: Irwin-Dorsey.

Lorsch, J.W. and Morse, J. (1974) *Organizations and their Members*, New York: Harper & Row.

Lupton, T. and Gowler, D. (1972) 'Wage payment systems', *Personnel Management* 11: 26–8.

MacIntyre, A. (1981) *After Virtue*, London: Duckworth.

Mack, R.W. and Snyder, R.C. (1972) 'The analysis of social conflict: toward an overview and synthesis', in Smith, C.G. (ed.) *Conflict Resolution: Contributions of the Behavioral Sciences*, Notre Dame, IN: University of Notre Dame Press, 3–35.

Macrae, N. (1976) 'Entrepreneurial revolution, a survey', *The Economist*, 25 December: 41–65.

Mair. L. (1962) *Primitive Government*, Harmondsworth: Penguin.

Mansfield, R. and Payne, R.L. (1977) 'Correlates of variance in perceptions of organizational climate', in Pugh, D.S. and Payne, R.L. (eds) *Organizational Behaviour in its Context*, The Aston Programme, vol. III, Birmingham: Saxon House, ch.9.

Mant, A. (1976) 'How to analyse management', *Management Today* October: 62–5, 130, 132.

March, J.G. (1988) *Decisions and Organizations*, Oxford: Blackwell.

Marcuse, H. (1970) *One Dimensional Man*, London: Sphere Books.

Margerison, C. (1980) 'How chief executives succeed', *Journal of European Industrial Training* 4 (5): 1–32.

Markovic, M. (1974) *From Affluence to Praxis*, Ann Arbor, MI: University of Michigan Press.

Marlow, H. (1975) *Managing Change: a Strategy for our Time*, London: Institute of Personnel Management.

—— (1984) *Success: Individual, Corporate and National, Profile for the Eighties and Beyond*, London: Institute of Personnel Management.

Marx, K. (1961) *Economic and Philosophical Manuscripts of 1844*, Moscow: Foreign Languages Publishing House; reproduced in Burns, T. (ed.) *Industrial Man*, London: Penguin.

—— (1975) *Early Writings*, Harmondsworth: Penguin.

—— (1976) *Capital*, Harmondsworth: Penguin.

Maslow, A.H. (1965) *Eupsychian Management*, Homewood, IL: Dorsey Press.

Maslow, A.H. and Murphy, G. (eds) (1969) *Motivation and Personality*, New York: Harper & Row.

Masuch, M. (1985) 'Vicous circles in organizations', *Administrative Science Quarterly* 30 (1): 14–31.

Maturana, H. and Varela, F. (1980) *Autopoiesis and Cognition: The Realization of the Living*, London: Reidel.

McCall, G.J. and Simmons, J.L. (1966) *Identities and Interactions*, New York: Free Press.

McCall, M.W. and Lombardo, M.M. (1983) 'What makes a top executive?', *Psychology Today*, February.

McCarthy, M. (1990) 'Ancient wisdom: new science – towards a philosophy of change', *Management Education and Development* 21 (1): 22–9.

McClelland, D.C. (1962) *The Achieving Society*, New York: Van Nostrand.

—— (1965) 'Achievement motivation can be developed', *Harvard Business Review* 43 (November/December): 6–16, 20–4, 178.

—— (1975) *Power: The Inner Experience*, New York: Irvington.

McGregor, D. (1960) *The Human Side of Enterprise*, New York: McGraw-Hill.

McGuire, W.J. (1969) 'The nature of attitudes and attitude change', in Lindzey, G. and Aronson, E. (eds) *Handbook of Social Psychology*, 2nd edn, vol. 3, New York: Addison Wesley.

McKenna, E, (1978) 'Do too many nodding heads produce poor decisions?', *Accountancy*, November: 48–51.

Meade, G.H. (1934) *Mind, Self and Society*, Chicago, IL: University of Chicago Press.

Meade, R. (1967) 'An experimental study of leadership in India', *Journal of Social Psychology* 72: 35–43.

Michels, R. (1966) *Political Parties*, trans. by Eden and Cedar Paul, New York: Free Press.

Miles, R.E. and Snow, C.C. (1978) *Organizational Strategy, Structure, and Process*, New York: McGraw-Hill.

Milgram, S. (1974) *Obedience to Authority: an Experimental View*, London: Tavistock Institute of Human Relations.

Miller, E.J. (1975) 'Socio-technical systems in weaving, 1953–1970: a follow-up study' *Human Relations* 28 (4): 349–86.

Miller, E.J. and Rice, A.K. (1967) *Systems of Organization*, London: Tavistock Institute of Human Relations.

Milne, R.W. (1970) 'Mechanistic and organic models of public administration in developing countries', *Administrative Science Quarterly* 15: 57–67.

Milton, D., Milton, N. and Schurmann, F. (1974) *People's China*, Harmondsworth: Penguin Books.

Mintzberg, H. (1973) *The Nature of Managerial Work*, New York: Harper & Row.

Mirvis, P. and Berg, D.N. (1977) *Failures in Organizational Development and Change*, New York: Wiley.

Mitroff, I.I. (1974) *The Subjective Side of Science: A Philosophical Inquiry into the Psychology of the Apollo Moon Scientists*, Amsterdam: Elsevier.

—— (1983) 'Archetypal social systems analysis: on the Deeper Structure of Human Systems', *Academy of Management Review* 8 (3): 387–97.

Mitroff, I.I. and Emshoff, J.R. (1979) 'On strategic assumption making: a dialectical approach to policy and planning', *Academy of Management Review* 4 (1): 1–12.

Mitroff, I.I. and Mason, R.O. (1982) 'Business policy and metaphysics: some philosophical considerations', *Academy of Management Review* 7 (3): 361–71.

Mitten, D.G. and Mitten, B.L. (1980) *Managerial Clout*, Englewood Cliffs, NJ: Prentice Hall.

Morgan, G. (1986) *Images of Organizations*. Beverly Hills, CA: Sage.

Moris, J. (1981) 'The transferability of Western management concepts: a Fourth World perspective', *Development Digest* 19 (1): 56–65.

Morris, B. (1971) 'Reflections on role analysis', *British Journal of Sociology* 22 (4) 395–409,

Morris, C. (1956) *Paths of Life*, New York: Brazillier.

Mumford, E. and Ward, T. (1966) 'Computer technologists: dilemmas of a new role', *Journal of Management Studies* 3(3): 244–55.

Myers, C.A. (1959) 'Management in India', in Harbison, F. and Myers, C.A. (eds) *Management in the Industrial World*, New York: McGraw-Hill.

Myers, I.B. and McCaulley, M. (1985) *Manual: a Guide to the Development and Use of the Myers Briggs Type Indicator*, CA: Consulting Psychologists Press.

Nagel, E. (1956) 'A formalization of functionalism', in Nagel, E. (ed.) *Logic without Metaphysics*, Glencoe, IL: Free Press.

Needham, P. (1982) 'The myth of the self-regulated work group', *Personnel Management* 14 (8): 29–31.

Negandhi, A.R. (1974) 'Cross cultural management studies: too many conclusions, not enough conceptualization', *Management International Review* 14 (6): 59–67.

Nelson, E.G. and Machin, J.J. (1976) 'Management control: systems thinking applied to the development of a framework for empirical studies', *Journal of Management Studies* 13: 274–87.

von Neumann, J. and Morgenstern, O. (1944) *Theory of Games and Economic Behavior*, Princeton: NJ: Princeton University Press.

Nevis, E.C. (1983) 'Using an American perspective in understanding another culture: toward a hierarchy of needs for the People's Republic of China', *Journal of Applied Behavioral Science* 19 (3): 249–64.

Nisbett, R. and Ross, L. (1980) *Human Inference: Strategies and Shortcomings of Social Judgement*, Englewood Cliffs, NJ: Prentice Hall.

Nystrom, P.C. and Starbuck, W.H. (eds) (1981) *Handbook of Organizational Design*, Oxford: Oxford University Press.

Olsen, M.E. (1968) *The Process of Social Organization*, New York: Holt, Rinehart & Winston.

Onyemelukwe, C.C. (1973) *Men and Management in Contemporary Africa*, London: Longman.

Organisaion of African Unity (1980) *What Kind of Africa by the Year 2000?*, Final Report of the Monrovia Symposium, Addis Ababa.

Osborn, A. (1981) *Applied Imagination*, New York: Scribner.

Ouchi W.G. (1978) 'Hierarchies, clans, and organizational development', *Organizational Dynamics* 7: 24–44.

—— (1981) *Theory Z*, Reading, MA: Addison Wesley.

Parsons, T. (1951) *The Social System*, New York: Free Press.

Parsons, T., Bales, R.F. and Shils, E.A. (eds) (1953) *Working Papers in the Theory of Action*, New York: Free Press.

Pascale, R.T. (1978) 'Zen and the art of management', *Harvard Business Review* 56 (2): 153–62.

Patterson, C. and Stevenson, D. (1986) 'Why the factory of the future is the challenge of today', *Personnel Management* 18 (3): 46–50.

Pay Board (1973) *Anomalies Arising out of the Pay Standstill*, Advisory *Report 1*, London: HMSO.

—— (1974) *Relativities*, Advisory Report 2, Cmnd 5535, London: HMSO.

Payne, R. (1991) 'Taking stock of corporate culture', *Personnel Management*, 23 (7): 26–9.

Payne R. and Pugh, D.S. (1976) 'Organizational structure and climate', in Dunnette, M.D. (ed.) *The Handbook of Organizational Psychology*, Chicago, IL: Rand McNally.

Perrow, C. (1979) *Complex Organizations: A Critical Essay*, 2nd edn, Glenview, IL: Scott, Foresman.

Peters, T.J. (1978) 'Patterns, and settings, an optimistic case for getting things done', *Organizational Dynamics*, Spring; reproduced in Robey, D. and Altman, S. (eds) (1982) *Organization Development: Progress and Perspectives*, London: Macmillan: 232 –48.

Peters, T.J. and Waterman, R.H. (1982) *In Search of Excellence*, New York: Harper & Row.

Pettigrew, A.M. (1973) *The Politics of Organizational Decision Making*, Tavistock Institute of Human Relations, London.

—— (1975) 'Strategic aspects of the management of specialist activity', *Personnel Review* 4 (1): 5–13.

—— (1979) 'On studying organizational cultures', *Administrative Science Quarterly* 24 (December): 570–81.

Pfeffer, J. (1981) *Power in Organizations*, London: Pitman.

Pheysey, D.C. (1977) 'Managers' occupational histories, organizational environments, and climates for management development', *Journal of Management Studies* 14 (1): 58–79.

Pheysey, D.C. and Payne, R.L. (1977) 'The Business Organizational Climate Index', in Pugh D.S. and Payne, R. (eds) *Organizational Behaviour in its Context*, Farnborough, Hants: Saxon House.

Pocock, P. (1989) 'Is business ethics a contradiction in terms?', *Personnel Management* 21 (11): 60–63.

Pollitt, C. (1984) *Manipulating the Machine: Changing the Pattern of Ministerial Departments, 1960–1983*, London: Allen & Unwin.

Pondy, L.R. (1967) 'Organizational conflict: concepts and models', *Administrative Science Quarterly* 12 (2): 296–320.

Porter, E.H. and Maloney S.E. (1977) *Strength Deployment Inventory: Manual of Administration and Interpretation*, Pacific Palisades, Personal Strengths Assessment Service.

Porter, L.W., Lawler, E.E. and Hackman, J.R. (1975) *Behavior in Organizations*, New York: McGraw-Hill.

Prasad G.K. (1974) *Bureaucracy in India: A Sociological Study*, New York: Very.

Progoff, I. (1956) *The Death and Rebirth of Psychology: an Integrative Evaluation of Freud, Adler, Jung, and Rank, and the Impact of Their Insights on Modern Man*, New York: McGraw-Hill.

Psathas, G. (1973) *Phenomenological Sociology: Issues and Applications*, New York: Wiley.

Pugh, D.S. and Hinings, C.R. (1976) *Organizational Structure: Extensions and Replications*, The Aston Programme, vol. II, Farnborough, Hants: Saxon House.

Pugh, D.S. and Payne, R.L. (1977) *Organizational Behaviour in its Context*, Farnborough, Hants: Saxon House.

Pugh, D.S., Hickson, D.J., Hinings, R. and Turner, C. (1968) 'Dimensions of organization structure', *Administrative Science Quarterly* 13: 65–105.

Pugh, D.S., Hickson, D.J. and Hinings, C.R. (1969) 'An empirical taxonomy of work organization structures', *Administrative Science Quarterly* 14: 115–26.

Pugh, D.S., Hickson, D.J. and Hinings, R. (1971) *Writers on Organizations*, 2nd edn, London: Penguin.

Purcell, J. (1986) 'Employee relations autonomy within a corporate culture', *Personnel Management* 18 (2): 38–40.

Quinn, R.E. (1984) 'Applying the competing values approach to leadership: toward an integrative framework', in Hunt, J.G., Hosking, D.-M., Schriesheim, C. and Stewart, R. (eds) *Leaders and Managers: International Perspectives on Managerial Behaviour and Leadership*, Elmsford, NY: Pergamon.

Quinn, R.E. and Cameron, K. (1983) 'Organizational life cycles and shifting criteria of effectiveness: some preliminary evidence', *Management Science* 29 (1): 33–51.

Quinn R.E. and McGrath, M. (1985) 'The transformation of organizational cultures: a competing values perspective', in Frost, P.J., Moore, L.F., Louis, M.R., Lundberg, C.C. and Martin, J. (eds) *Organizational Culture*, New York: Praeger.

Raybould, J. (1985) 'Ten years of decentralization', *Personnel Management* 17 (6): 40–43.

Reddin, W. (1970) *Managerial Effectiveness*, New York: McGraw-Hill.
—— (1985) *The Best of Bill Reddin*, Trowbridge: Institute of Personnel Management.
Redding, G. (1980) 'Management education for orientals', in Garratt, B. and Stopford, J. (eds) *Breaking Down Barriers*, Aldershot: Gower.
Reif, W. and Monczka, R. (1974) 'Job design, a contingency approach to implementation', *Personnel* 51 (May–June): 18–28.
Rezazadeh, R. (1961) 'The concept of centralization', *Revista International de Sociologia* 27 (11): 425–30.
Rice, A.K. (1958) *Productivity and Social Organisation: the Ahmedabad Experiment*, London: Tavistock Institute of Public Relations.
Ritchie, A.D. (1923) *Scientific Method*, London: Kegan Paul.
Roberts, K. and Boyacigiller, N. (1984) 'Cross national organizational research: the grasp of the blind men', in Staw, B. and Cummings, L. (eds) *Research in Organizational Behavior* 6: 423–75.
Robey, D. and Altman, S. (eds) (1982) *Organization Development: Progress and Perspectives*, London: Macmillan.
Robson, M. (1984) *Quality Circles: a Practical Guide*, Aldershot: Gower.
Roethlisberger, F.J. (1958) *Man in Organization, Essays of F.J. Roethlisberger*, Cambridge, MA: Harvard University Press.
Roethlisberger, F.J., Dickson, W.J. and Wright, H.A. (1939) *Management and the Worker*, Cambridge, MA: Harvard University Press.
Ronen, S. and Shenkar, O. (1985) 'Clustering countries on attitudinal dimensions', *Academy of Management Review* 10 (3): 435–54.
Rose, M. (1978) *Industrial Behaviour: Theoretical Development since Taylor*, London: Penguin.
Rosen, H. (1961) 'Managerial role interaction: a study of three managerial levels', *Journal of Applied Psychology* 45: 30–4.
Rowbottom, R.W. (1973) *Hospital Organization, a Progress Report on the Brunel Health Services Project*, London: Heinemann.
Rowbottom, R.W. and Bromley, G. (1980) *Organizing Social Service Departments: Further Studies*, Brunel: Brunel Social Services Unit.
Rowe, A.J. and Boulgarides, J.D. (1983) 'Decision style – a perspective', *Leadership and Organisation Development Journal* 4 (4): 3–10.
Roy, D. (1960) 'Banana time: job satisfaction and information interaction', *Human Organization* 18: 156–68, 205–22.
Royal Institute of Public Administration (1985) *Politics, Ethics, and Public Service*.
Sales, S.M. (1969) 'Organizational role as a risk factor in coronary disease', *Administrative Science Quarterly* 14 (3): 325–36.
Sanderson. D. (1938) 'Group description', *Social Forces* 16 (3): 309–19.
Sanderson, M. (1979) *Successful Problem Management*, New York: Wiley.
Saward, L.C. (1976) *Strategies for Improving Problem Solving*, PhD thesis, University of Aston in Birmingham.
Sayles, L. (1958) *The Behavior of Industrial Work Groups: Prediction and Control*, New York: Wiley.
Schattschneider, E.E. (1960) *The Semisovereign People*, New York: Holt Rinehart & Winston.

Schaupp, D.L. (1978) *A Cross Cultural Study of a Multinational Company: Attitudinal Responses to Participative Management*, New York: Praeger.

Schein, E. (1970) *Organizational Psychology*, 2nd edn, Englewood Cliffs, NJ: Prentice Hall.

—— (1984) 'Coming to a new awareness of organizational culture', *Sloan Management Review* 26 (Winter): 3–16.

Schein, E.H. (1968) 'Organizational socialization and the profession of management', *Industrial Management Review* 9 (2): 1–16.

Schumacher, E.F. (1973) *Small is Beautiful*, London: Blond & Briggs.

Schutz, A. (1967) *The Phenomenology of the Social World*, London: Heinemann.

—— (1970) *On Phenomenology and Social Relations*, ed. by H.R. Wagner, Chicago, IL: University of Chicago Press.

Seashore, S.E. (1964) 'Field experiments with formal organizations', *Human Organization* 23 (2): 164–70.

Seddon, J.W. (1985a) 'The development of Nigerian organizations', *Nigerian Management Review* 1 (2).

—— (1985b) 'Issues in practice: the education and development of overseas managers', *Management Education and Development* 16 (1): 5–13.

—— (1988) 'Assumptions, culture and performance appraisal', *Management Education and Development* 6 (3): 47–54.

Shaw, M.E. (1964) 'Communication networks', in Berkowitz, L. (ed.) *Advances in Experimental Social Psychology*, vol. 1, New York: Academic Press, 111–28.

—— (1971) *Group Dynamics*, New York: McGraw-Hill.

Shaw, T.M. and Aluko, A. (eds) (1984) *Africa Projected: From Recession to Renaissance by the Year 2000?*, London: Macmillan.

Sheane, D. (1979) 'When and how to intervene in conflict', *Personnel Management*, November.

Silverman, D. (1970) *The Theory of Organizations*, New York: Basic Books.

Simon, H.A. (1960) *The New Science of Management Decision*, New York: Harper & Row.

Skinner, B.F. (1973) *Beyond Freedom and Dignity*, London: Penguin.

Skinner, G.W. and Winckler, E.A. (1980) 'Compliance succession in rural communist China: a cyclical theory', in Etzioni, A. and Lehman, E.W. (eds) *A Sociological Reader on Complex Organizations*, 3rd Edn, New York: Holt, Rinehart & Winston.

Slater, P.E. (1970) 'Role differentiation in small groups', in Smith, P.B. (ed.) *Group Processes*, London: Penguin, ch. 12, 223–44.

Smith, B.C. (1985) *Decentralization: The Territorial Dimension of the State*, London: Allen & Unwin.

Smith, G. (1974) 'A taxonomy of interpersonal skills', *Industrial and Commercial Training* 6 (9): 404–10.

—— (1978) 'Case studies in organization development: an organization-wide approach to Industrial Relations Training in the Health Service', in Thakur, M., Bristow, J. and Carby, K. (eds) *Personnel in Change: Organization Development through the Personnel Function*, London: Institute of Personnel Management.

Smith, I.G. (1983) *The Management of Remuneration: Paying for Effectiveness*, London: Institute of Personnel Management.

Soelberg, P. (1967) 'Unprogrammed decision-making: job choice', *Industrial Management Review* Spring (8): 19–29.

Southgate, J. and Randall, R. *Creative and Pathological Processes in the Self-Managing Work Group*, unpublished conference paper, North London Polytechnic.

Stanworth, J. and Stanworth, C. (1989) 'Home truths about teleworking', *Personnel Management* 21 (11): 48–52.

Steele, F. in Mirvis P. and Berg, D.N. (eds) (1977) *Failures in Organization Development and Change*, New York: Wiley.

Stewart, R. (1967) *Managers and their Jobs*, London: Pan.

—— (1974) *The Reality of Management*, London: Heinemann.

Stewart, V. (1983) *Change. The Challenge for Management*, New York: McGraw-Hill.

Stopford, J.M. and Wells, L.T. (1972) *Managing Multinational Enterprise*, London: Longman.

Strauss, A. (1978) *Negotiations: Varieties, Contexts, Processes and Social Order*, San Francisco, CA: Jossey-Bass.

Streuning, E. and Guttentag, M. (eds) (1975) *Handbook of Evaluation Research*, Beverly Hills, CA: Sage.

Tannenbaum, A.S. and Cooke, R.A. (1979) 'Organizational control: a review of studies employing the control graph method', in Lammers, C.J. and Hickson, D.J. (eds) *Organizations Alike and Unlike*, London: Routledge & Kegan Paul.

Tannenbaum, R. and Schmidt, W.H. (1958) 'How to choose a leadership pattern', *Harvard Business Review* 36 (2): 95–101 revised May/June 1973: 162–80.

Taylor, F.W. (1911) 'Principles of scientific management', reprinted 1947 in Taylor, F.W. *Scientific Management*, New York: Harper & Row.

Teiwes, C. (1984) *Leadership, Legitimacy, and Conflict in China: from a Charismatic Mao to the Politics of Succession* London: Macmillan.

Thelen, H.A. (1954) *Dynamics of Groups at Work*, Chicago, IL: University of Chicago Press.

Thompson, J.D. (1967) *Organizations in Action*, New York: McGraw-Hill.

Thorpe, R. and Moscarola, J. (1991) 'Detecting your research strategy', *Management Education and Development* 22 (2): 127–33.

Torbiorn, I. (1985) 'Managerial roles in cross-cultural settings', *International Studies of Management and Organization* 15 (1): 52–74.

Touraine, A. (1965) *Sociologie de l'Action*, Paris: Editions du Seuil.

—— (1971) *The Post-Industrial Society* trans. by L. Mayhew, New York: Random House.

Tripartite Steering Group on Job Satisfaction (1975) *Making Work More Satisfying*, London: HMSO.

Trist, E.L. and Bamforth, K.W. (1951) 'Some social and psychological consequences of the Longwall method of coal getting', *Human Relations* 4: 3–38.

Trull, S.G. (1966) 'Some factors involved in determining total decision success', *Management Science* 12 (February): B270–80.

Tuckman, B.W. (1964) 'Personality structure, group composition, and group functioning', *Sociometry* 27.

—— (1965) 'Developmental sequence in small groups', *Psychological Bulletin* 27: 384–99; reprinted in Smith, P.B. (ed.) *Group Processes*, Harmondsworth: Penguin, 1970, ch. 17, 322–51.

Tung, R.L. (1982) *Chinese Industrial Society After Mao*, Lexington, MA: Lexington Books.

Ursell, G. (1983) 'The views of British managers and shop stewards on industrial democracy', in Crouch, C. and Heller, F. (eds) *International Year Book of Organizational Democracy*, vol. 1, New York: Wiley.

Van de Ven, A.H. and Joyce, W.E. (eds) (1981) *Perspectives on Organization Design and Behavior*, New York: Wiley.

Van Rest, D. (1982) 'Systems assessment of improved technology for the coffee industry of Puerto Rico', in Luck, G.M. and Walsham, G. (eds) *Selected Readings in Operational Research for Developing Countries*, Oxford: Operational Research Society.

Various authors (1984) 'Indian studies on organizational effectiveness', *International Studies of Management and Organization* 14 (2–3).

Vesper, K.H. (1990) *New Venture Strategies*, 2nd edn, Englewood Cliffs, NJ: Prentice Hall.

Vickers, G. (1965) *The Art of Judgement: a Study of Policy Making*, London: Chapman & Hall.

—— 'Institutional and personal roles', *Human Relations* 24 (5): 433–47.

—— (1973) *Making Institutions Work*, London: Associated Business Programmes.

—— (1981) 'Some implications of systems thinking', in Open Systems Group (eds) *Systems Behaviour*, 3rd edn, London: Harper & Row.

Vroom, V.H. (1964) *Work and Motivation*, New York: Wiley.

Walker, C.R. and Guest, R.H. (1952) *The Man on The Assembly Line*, Cambridge, MA: Harvard University Press.

Wall, T. (1984) 'What's new in job design', *Personnel Management* 16 (4): 27–9.

Walton, R.E. and McKersie, R.B. (1965) *A Behavioral Theory of Labor Negotiations*, New York: McGraw-Hill.

Ward, R. and Jenkins, R. (1984) *Ethnic Communities in Business*, Cambridge: Cambridge University Press.

Warren, R. (1974) *Truth, Love, and Social Change, and Other Essays on Community Change*, Chicago, IL: Rand McNally.

Weber, M. (1947) *The Theory of Social and Economic Organization*, New York: Free Press.

—— (1968) *Economy and Society*, vols I–III, New York: Bedminster Press.

Werbner, P. (1985) 'How immigrants can make it in Britain', *New Society* 73 (1186): 411–13.

Whitley, R. (1977) 'Organizational control and the problem of order', *Social Science Information* 16 (2): 169–89.

Whitmore, D. (1979) *Management Science: Quantitative Techniques and their Application*, London: Hodder and Stoughton.

Williams, A., Dobson, P. and Walters, M. (1989) *Changing Culture: New Organizational Approaches*, London: Institute of Personnel Management..

Wilson, E.K. (1985) 'What counts in the death or transformation of an

Organization?', *Social Forces* 64 (2): 259–80.

Wittfogel, K. (1957) *Oriental Despotism*, New Haven, CT: Yale University Press.

Wojdowski, P. (1978) 'Games bureaucrats play', *Transactional Analysis Journal* 8 (1): 56–9.

Wolfgang, M.E. (ed.) (1984) 'China in transition', *Annals of the American Academy of Political and Social Science* 476 (November): 11–170.

Wong, C.A. (translator) *Confucian Analects: The Great Learning; The Doctrine of the Mean; the Works of Mencius*, cited in Ballou, R.O. (ed.) (1939) *The Bible of the World*, London: Kegan Paul.

Woodcock, M. and Francis, D. (1989) *Clarifying Organizational Values*, Aldershot: Gower.

Wootton, B. (1950) *Testament for Social Science*, London: Allen & Unwin.

Wright, P. (1981) 'Organizational behaviour in Islamic firms', *Management International Review* 21 (2): 86–94.

Wuthnow, R. *et al.* (1984) *Cultural Analysis*, London: Routledge & Kegan Paul.

Zald, M.N. (1970) *Organizational Change: the Political Economy of the YMCA*, Chicago, IL: University of Chicago Press.

—— (1981) 'Political economy: a framework for comparative analysis', in Zey-Ferrell, M. and Aiken, M. (eds) *Complex Organizations: Critical Perspectives*, Glencoe, IL: Scott Foresman.

Zand, D.E. (1972) 'Trust and managerial problem solving', *Administrative Science Quarterly* 17: 229–39.

Zey-Ferrell, M. and Aiken, M. (1981) *Complex Organizations: Critical Perspectives*, Glencoe, IL: Scott Foresman.

Name index

Keys, J.B. 116, 119
Kiely, J. 91
Kiersey, D. 121, 140, 193
King, A. Yeo-Chi 18
Kolb, D.A. 121, 140
Kraemer, H. 6
Kuhn, T.S. 212

Lake, D.G. 212
Lammers, C.J. 49, 53–4
Lau Tzu 156
Lawlor, E.E. 91, 99
Lawrence, P. 152
Lawrence, P.R. 56, 64, 174
Lehman, E.W. 21
Leibnitz, G. 211
Levinson, H. 189
Lieberson, S. 158, 162
Likert, R. 154–5
Lilienfeld, R. 212
Lindblom, C.E. 109, 118
Lippitt, R. 154–6, 196
Locke, J. 211
Lockett, M. 48
Lombardo, M.M. 151
Lorsch, J.W. 56, 64, 174
Lupton, T. 152

Machin, J.J. 29, 41
Mair, L. 115
Maloney, S.E. 121
Mansfield, R. 199
Mant, A. 36, 41, 183
March, J.G. 108, 118, 119
Margerison, C. 151
Marlow, H. 60–61, 149, 154, 156,
   169, 171, 181, 189
Marx, K. 205
Maslow, A.H. 93–4, 99
Maturana, H. 204
Mau Zedong (Mau Tsetung) 11–18
McCall, M.W. 151
McClelland, D.C. 93, 99
McGrath, M. 46, 62, 114, 156
McGregor, D. 88, 99
McIntyre, J.M. 140
McKenna, E. 127, 140
McKersie, R.B. 195
Meade, G.H. 212

Meade, R. 162
Miles, M.B. 212
Miles, R.E. 44–5, 59
Milgram, S. 158–9, 161, 196
Miller, E.J. 76, 136
Miller, T.R. 116, 119
Milton, D. 115
Mintzberg, H. 151, 162, 180
Mirvis, P. 189
Mitroff, I.I. 109, 119, 193, 197, 199,
   201, 211, 212
Monczka, R. 81
Molinari, J. 189
Moore, J.M. 212
Morgan, G. 21, 204
Morganstern, O. 195
Moris, J. 148, 162
Moscarola, J. 193
Mouton, J.S. 154–5, 189
Murphy, G. 99
Murray, D. 118
Myers, I.B. 121

Nadler, D.A. 30–32, 41
Needham, P. 81
Nelson, E.G. 29
Nevis, E.C. 94, 99
Nystrom P.C. 65, 119

O'Connor, J.F. 158–62
Olsen, M.E. 119
Onyemelukwe, C.C. 65
Osborn, A. 107
Ouchi, W.G. 116

Parsons, T. 194
Pascale, R.T. 41, 149
Patterson, C. 60
Payne, R.L. 166, 199
Peters, T.J. 38, 39, 41, 151, 182
Pettigrew, A.M. 146, 162, 182
Pfeffer, J. 111
Pocock, P. 212
Porter, E.H. 121
Porter, L.W. 84–5, 99
Potter, D.C. 118
Prasad, G.K. 65
Psathas, G. 200
Pugh, D.S. 21, 46, 55, 57, 198

Subject index